D0820657

The Clock of the Years

The Clock of the Years

An anthology of writings on
Gerald and Joy Finzi
marking twenty-five years of
the Finzi Friends Newsletter

Compiled and edited by Rolf Jordan
Foreword by Paul Spicer

Best wishes
Rolf Jordan

chosen
press

Chosen Press
Lichfield
2007

First published in Great Britain in 2007 by
Chosen Press, Lichfield, Staffordshire

www.chosenpress.co.uk
books@chosenpress.co.uk

A CIP catalogue record for this book is available
from the British Library

ISBN 978 0 9556373 0 8

This book is printed on acid-free paper

Typeset by Rolf Jordan in Linotype Janson

rolf@chosenpress.co.uk

Printed by Cromwell Press, Trowbridge, Wiltshire, Great Britain

Contents

III: A kind of fostering

IV: Wife and mother, artist and organiser

V: The poems of Joy Finzi

X: The concentrated eye

XI: Making music

XII: Composer's gallery

Acknowledgements

I would like to thank all the respective contributors to this anthology not only for their kind permissions, but also for their careful checking and updating of their texts.

I am grateful to Hugh Cobbe for supplying the images of Howard Ferguson and for granting permission to reproduce material from the Ferguson estate. Richard Shirley Smith bravely agreed to send valuable artwork via the Post Office. Anthony Boden also allowed me to borrow several cherished cards from Joy Finzi in the same way. Robert Gower kindly supplied a remarkably complete set of Friends' minutes that has proved invaluable in providing missing dates and clarifying many matters.

Jo Leighton sent copies of the hitherto-unseen letters from Gerald Finzi, and the photograph of her husband Kenneth. Stephen Barlow, Alistair Hinton, Father Anselm Kramer and Robert Scott all provided help in tracking down the executors of the estate of Alan Ridout. I would like to express gratitude to Mrs Joan Webster (for Donald Webster), Renée Morris Young (for Percy Young) and Edward Thomas (for Myfanwy Thomas) for granting permission to reproduce their relative's words. The Finzi family, Elsie Galbraith, Ann Warner-Casson and the family of Brendan Kerney for images in the plate section.

Thanks are also due to Kiffer Finzi, Rob Barnett (British Music Society), Ralph Blackbourn (Allied Artists Agency), Margi Blunden and James Gill (at PFD) for sorting out so many problems so promptly.

Jim Page and Pamela Blevins (who also loaned Joy's *Twelve Months of a Year*) completed my set of set of newsletters (and provided much encouragement) without which the initial compilation of this anthology would have been impossible. Several members of the Friends' committee supplied a valuable pair of eyes during the creation of the book: Jennie McGregor-Smith (who also loaned copies of English Music Festivals and the Joy Tribute), Martin Lee-Browne and the late Denny Lyster.

Paul Spicer, Philip Lancaster (who additionally set all the musical examples) and Lucia Jordan all provided invaluable technical assistance during the assembly of the finished book. If I have inadvertently missed anyone off, sincere apologies: so many people have been involved in the making of this anthology that it must be inevitable.

In addition:

William Hedley, Editor of *The RVW Society Journal* for permission to reprint Simona Pakenham's piece.

Charles Janz and the Kerney family for the phograph by Brendan Kerney.

The poems by Edmund Blunden are reproduced by permission of PFD (www.pfd.co.uk) on behalf of the Estate of Claire Blunden.

The Trustees of the Ivor Gurney Estate for permission to reproduce 'As Guardian of Genius' from the Gurney Archive.

Extracts from the following works by Gerald Finzi are reproduced by permission of Boosey &Hawkes Music Publishers Ltd:
'At Middle-Field Gate in February'; 'I said to Love' (*I Said to Love*, (1958)); *For St Cecilia* (1948); 'I look into my glass' (*Till Earth Outwears*, 1958); 'In the mind's eye' (*Before and After Summer* (1949)); 'O mistress mine' (*Let Us Garlands Bring* (1942)); 'Proud songsters'; 'Waiting both' (*Earth and Air and Rain* (1936)); 'Shortening days' (*A Young Man's Exhortation* (1933))
© Copyright by Boosey & Co Ltd.
Clarinet Concerto © Copyright 1951 by Hawkes & Son (London) Ltd.

'To M. M. S.' by Ivor Gurney reproduced from *Severn & Somme and War's Embers* edited by R. K. R. Thornton (Manchester,1987) by permission of Carcanet Press Limited.

Extract from the Violin Concerto by William Walton
© Copyright 1941 by Oxford University Press.

'Ode on the rejection of St Cecilia (Arioso)' by George Barker from *The Collected Poems of George Barker* edited by Robert Frazer (London, 1987) by permission of Faber & Faber.

Nigel Finzi for the writings of Joy Finzi.

The Finzi Trust for the writings of Gerald Finzi.

Finally, the biggest debt of gratitude of all is to the past and present Editors of the *Finzi Friends Newsletter*—Diana McVeagh, (especially) Ann Warner-Casson, Chris and John Harris, and Philip Lancaster. Without their collective enthusiasm and vision, this book could not have existed.

Illustrations

Wood engravings on pages 90, 92, 94, 97, 100, 102 and 220 are by Richard Shirley Smith. They were made in 1961 and first published in 1967 in *A Point of Departure* by Joy Finzi. The wood engraving on page 102 is also by Richard Shirley Smith and appeared on Joy Finzi's New Year cards.

Drawings of Ashmansworth on pages 16, 152 and 266 are by Rolf Jordan.

Plate section:

Gerald Finzi in 1926 (Finzi family).
Joy Finzi in 1938 (Finzi family).
Church Farm, 1938 (Finzi family).
Joy and Kiffer, 1938 (Finzi family).
Nigel Finzi, 1941(Finzi family).
'Finzi's two boys', 1940s (estate of Herbert Howells).
Gerald Finzi with Ursula Howells, 1925 (estate of Herbert Howells).
Ralph Vaughan Williams, 1940s (private collection).
Gerald, Nigel and Joy Finzi, Ralph Vaughan Williams and Ursula Wood, 1948 (private collection).
Vaughan Williams and Finzi, 1949 (private collection).
Finzi and Rubbra families, 1948 (private collection).
Ticket for the first performance of the Clarinet Concerto, 1949 (private collection).
Finzi with Frederick Thurston, 1949 (private collection).

Foreword

In 1979 Robert Gower (now Chairman of the Finzi Trust) and I went to see Joy Finzi for the first time. We had tea with her in her lovely woodsmoke-smelling house, Bushey Leaze, and we talked. Robert and I were avid English music people-collectors and we went round talking to various relatives, housekeepers (in the case of John Ireland) or graves (!).

As we talked to Joy that happy afternoon, we realised that 1981 would be the twenty-fifth anniversary of Gerald Finzi's death. We resolved to do two things: organise a Festival around this theme, and run a composition competition. Being Director of Music at Ellesmere College in Shropshire at the time, a school with ideal public facilities, I ran the Festival and Robert organised the competition. Little did we then think how all this would affect our subsequent lives. With our fellow conspirator, Andrew Burn, introduced to us by Joy, we became trustees soon after the Festival.

Slowly but surely the Finzi machine, which had been active since the formation of the Finzi Trust in 1969, gained momentum. Now, in 2007, Finzi is almost a household name. The centenary year in 2001 saw record numbers of performances and broadcasts. CD recordings are rolling off the presses monthly as more and more people want to commit their interpretations of his music to posterity. Boosey & Hawkes (his principal publisher) work very closely with the Trust to promote Finzi's music as widely as possible, and the new official website is a mine of information to gladden any Finzi lover's heart and mind.

The Finzi Friends, as you will read in these pages, began twenty-five years ago, soon after that first Finzi Festival at Ellesmere College. Like the work of the Finzi Trust itself, the Friends organisation has grown and developed to the point where, in 2001, it decided to become a completely separate organisation with its own charitable status. As its Chairman, I wanted to bring on board a group of interested and proactive young people to balance the older, more experienced ones who were already in place. I wanted to try and ensure that the next generation was dipping its toes in the same water from which Robert, Andrew and I had so benefited back in the 80s. This has been a great success, and we hope that this connection with young musicians and others will go on being a feature which marks this organisation out from so many others.

The committee has worked to be a complementary force to that of the Trust, organising various events each year which focus on some element of Finzi's music, often broadening the brief to feature music and musicians who had connections with him. Of all the events we promote, the most popular is the regular Ashmansworth day. Inevitably, Finzi lovers enjoy the opportunity of being able to spend some hours in and around the house which the Finzis built and in which they lived.

The spirit of the twenty-fifth anniversary Finzi Festival has been recreated in the triennial Weekends of English Song, held in Ludlow. 2007 has seen the third of these wonderful musical experiences organised by the Friends, headed by Jim Page, and directed artistically by our President, Iain Burnside.

The *Finzi Friends Newsletter* has been a feature of the organisation from its start. It rapidly grew to become a journal which is a collectors' item. It became the format as we now know it in 1984 when the *Newsletter* was edited and compiled by Ann Warner-Casson. When she relinquished the reins in 1998, John and Chris Harris took over, followed by Philip Lancaster, and it is he who we have to thank for the exemplary production of the last seven years of this publication.

To celebrate the twenty-fifth anniversary of the founding of the Finzi Friends it was felt that an anthology of articles from past editions of the *Newsletter* would make a fascinating book, recording so much of interest for the Finzi lover. Rolf Jordan agreed to edit and compile the book, and, typically, he has made it much more than simply a collection of past articles. You will find a complete Finzi world betwen these covers. I am also delighted to say that there is a real emphasis on Finzi's wife, Joy, who was such a great soulmate and support to him throughout his married life, and an inspiration and mentor to me, as to so many like me over the years. The book is made even more fascinating by many photographs which have not been in print before. This is a truly comprehensive volume which will be indispensable to lovers of English music who have an interest in, or a love of Finzi's music and his world.

I want to thank Rolf for the huge task which he has undertaken, for the assiduous editing of so much material, the gaining of authors' permissions, the whole typesetting and layout, and the professionalism with which the whole project has been undertaken. It has been a real labour of love. We all owe him a great debt of gratitude.

Paul Spicer
Chairman of Finzi Friends

Preface

This anthology is founded on articles from the first twenty-five years of the twice-yearly *Finzi Friends Newsletter*, the first of which appeared in January 1983. Along the way, several other sources have been utilised—including programme books, the memorial volume to Joy Finzi, and public and unseen archive material. There are brand new pieces too.

What if the spirit of Hardy's poem 'The clock of the years' really did wind the hands back to 1983? So much has changed since then, if you pause to think on it. One small facet is that music lovers collected and treasured LPs. That was soon to be swept aside by the compact disc and an explosion of recordings. A vast catalogue of neglected music has surfaced in the intervening years, and it won't be long before the complete output of Gerald Finzi has been released. Finzi, of course, is not alone. Ivor Gurney was barely known in 1983 (the present Poet Laureate, Andrew Motion, talked about him at the first Three Choirs Festival Finzi lunch), and only a fraction of the output of such composers as George Dyson, Herbert Howells, E. J. Moeran and Howard Ferguson had been recorded. The 'big name' Ralph Vaughan Williams has arguably become more popular than ever. The general listening public is now no longer afraid or dismissive of English music. Back in the 1980s, it was derided as 'all brass bands and ceremonials' or even worse, such as in that famous coinage of Elizabeth Lutyens—'cowpat music'. The 'squeaky-gate school' was to the fore, further polarising opinion. At least the public now knows Vaughan Williams's *The Lark Ascending* and Finzi's Eclogue thanks to the success of Classic FM (and whatever anyone says about commercial 'classical' radio, it *is* a useful service for novice listeners.)

This anthology does not replace the original newsletters. I have not systematically plundered every interesting snippet: to have done so would have meant a book twice the size. There are, of course, omissions—not everything has been written about yet, and I hope this volume will inspire and encourage readers to write their own articles, reviews and letters for future newsletters.

The result is a volume that will sit happily on the shelf as a companion to both Stephen Banfield and Diana McVeagh's individual biographies of Gerald Finzi. It is an ideal supplement—many items in their respective bibliographic sections are making a fresh appearance here, very often revised and rejuvenated, newly accessible to a wider readership.

It is not nostalgia that this volume deals with: it is the future. Posterity. Anybody who understands the message of Hardy's spirit should know that. These are important snapshots of performance habits and musical fashion, gossip, inspirational personalities and unique images. The reputations of all the cherished composers, artists, poets and musicians recorded in this volume have survived the weathers of fashion for twenty-five years since that first Newsletter, and that is most encouraging.

Rolf Jordan

A note on names

Church Farm was the Finzi's house at Ashmansworth, but many writers (including the Finzis themselves) refer to it just as 'Asmansworth'. Entries for the house are to be found only under 'Church Farm' in the index.

Christopher Finzi is more often known as Kiffer (an early attempt at pronouncing his own name that stuck), and both are interchangeable throughout this book.

There has often been some confusion about who the Finzi Trust, Finzi Trust Friends, and Finzi Friends actually are. The Finzi Trust was a charity formed in 1969 by Joy Finzi to further the works and ideals of Gerald Finzi, with a policy of encouraging young artists and composers. The Finzi Trust Friends was formed as an extension of the Trust in 1981, as a kind of 'Finzi Society' to further those aims. In 2001, separate charitable status was gained, and the name was changed to Finzi Friends. A fuller explanation is to be found in Appendix 2. For readers' peace-of-mind, all references to the Friends have been updated throughout this book.

I

At Ashmansworth

Church Farm

Clare Popplewell

Joy and Gerald Finzi first came to see Church Farm on a snowy day in 1937. The old farmhouse that stood where the nuttery now is was beyond saving, but this suited them as they had a yearning to build their own home, and they were delighted with the old farm buildings that could be used (the thatched barn and the flint garages in the yard). More importantly, the views were spectacular, and the semi-isolated position on the edge of a small village was ideal, outweighing even the fact that it was not good apple-growing country.

The architect Peter Harland designed a long narrow house. The music room and book room were at one end, separated from the noisier kitchen and nursery by bedrooms and sitting rooms. All the rooms facing the lighter side had large windows with uninterrupted panes of glass, and the eaves were deep enough to encourage house martins to come and nest against the wall. The house was shielded from the road and drive by a tall flint and brick wall, which used up the flints from the old buildings.

The Finzis' relationship with Harland was not one of complete accord. He insisted on positioning the house to face due south. Joy and Gerald felt that this would make the house too hot and sunny, and face it too immediately onto the road. Determined to get their own way they drove over from Aldbourne one evening when the pegging out for the foundations had been completed, and re-pegged the entire house to look out over the Hampshire Downs. It was a matter of enduring pride that there is only one crooked wall.

As the eight-foot-deep foundations were slowly dug through soil packed with flints and heavy with clay, there were unexpected hitches caused by finding remains which showed that the site had been inhabited back to Roman times. Gerald in particular was fascinated by the bits of crockery that were unearthed, and would spend hours piecing them together. This made them both think of the intransigence of their own building, and as a message to a future generation they laid a tin of objects applicable to their own time under the huge stone doorstep. In less than sixty years the house has already undergone many changes, and the doorstep is now part of the inner porch. The tin, however, rests undisturbed.

No sooner was the house habitable than war came. The ground outside, as the builders left, resembled Flanders, and the house was filled with refugees even before the luxury of paint and curtains. Despite this uncertain and confused situation, Joy and Gerald forged ahead with their own plans for the garden and orchards, which were to become, for both of them, an abiding interest, and which for Gerald would grow into a lifetime's passion.

Finzi Centenary lecture

Stephen Banfield

A lecture given at St James's Church, Ashmansworth on 19 May 2001, as part of the Newbury Spring Festival's 'Finzi Symposium' and to commemorate the unveiling of the blue plaque at Church Farm.

As the soul slowly begins to return to our ravaged land after its nine-month ordeal by flood, plague [the foot-and-mouth crisis] and transport, we may once again feel the urge to plunge into the depths of its country-side. And it doesn't get much deeper than where we are here. Approached on all sides—five of them—by what the Ordnance Survey quaintly used to call roads with 'Under 14 ft of Metalling, tarred', Ashmansworth is an obscure spot. Round the back, towards Inkpen Beacon, highest point in the south of England and although nine feet higher than Leith Hill still not quite struggling to 1,000 feet, you wonder whether the country lanes are going to make it at all through the thick beech woods or will peter out and leave you at the mercy of the Green Man. Up on the beacon, Combe Gibbet reminds us that in bygone centuries you were much more likely to have been abandoned to the mercy of the highwayman (though Combe Gibbet was never actually used as one), for I take it that Ashmansworth, unlikely as it seems, was actually on the main road from Newbury to Andover until the twentieth century or thereabouts, and it is at Ashmansworth that the road crosses the ridge of the chalk downs. It would have taken more than a highwayman to frighten William Cobbett on his rural rides of the 1820s, but even he had difficulties here. It was only when he encountered Hawkley Hanger at the opposite end of Hampshire, near Petersfield, that he felt minded to tell the world 'that Ashmansworth Lane is not the worst piece of road in the world.' No wonder that he developed something of an obsession with the red clayey soil that he found on the top of the ridge and always likened to that of Ashmansworth when he encountered it elsewhere.

Possibly the village awoke briefly in 1830 at finding itself so often the butt of Cobbett's comparisons; but it gives the impression of having, like a koala, spent most of its life asleep. The church can hardly be said to draw attention to itself, and perhaps travellers scarcely noticed when it acquired its stone Norman arch, its twelfth-century wall paintings, its thirteenth-century chancel, more paintings in the fifteenth century, its brick porch in 1694, east wall in 1745, pulpit some time in the eighteenth century, and then seemingly nothing more, until in 1956 a memorial with nice lettering by Reynolds Stone appeared in the churchyard. At Church Farm, opposite, life must similarly have followed the seasons with little by way of special event, though doubtless with pride that they had dug a well over 300 feet deep to find the water table, for they pointed this out to Cobbett, no doubt over a jug of mead as he recovered his temper following his muddy ordeal in the lane.

And then in 1938 the old derelict farmhouse came down and a flint perimeter wall went up, it was said by the locals because a nudist colony had bought the site. The new occupants were not nudists (as far as I know), but a retiring couple with two young children who had a replacement house built—nothing flashy, but spaciously designed by a posh architect. Soon a curious variety of artistic types would be stopping their puttering cars, some no doubt overheating from the climb up the ridge, to ask the way to Church Farm. Mr Finzi, it turned out, was a composer, as befitted his strange name, and for the next decade and a half—not much more than that—music was cultivated where animals and produce had hitherto been husbanded (actually produce was too, with

Gerald Finzi's apples, though that is not our point). But was Mr Finzi a famous composer, like Dr Vaughan Williams who occasionally turned up and wrote that new introit for the Coronation? No, it has to be admitted that he wasn't.

In fact Gerald Finzi's life, like that of Ashmansworth when it was bypassed even by the Andover road, was almost one of progressive obscurity. He was born into wealth, comfort and music in St John's Wood, London. Frederic Cowen, conductor of the Philharmonic, was the next-door neighbour; Edward German lived round the corner, where he was busy writing *Merrie England.* Mrs Finzi dabbled at composition and played the piano well while her husband was at his shipbroker's office in the City. From this promising start Gerald managed to deprive himself of nearly everything. As a youngster he refused to stay at school. By the age of eighteen he had lost every male rôle model, including his father, his three brothers, and his first composition teacher (Ernest Farrar, a pupil of Stanford), for all of them died young, two in the final weeks of the First World War. He never knuckled down to tutelage under the strict and impressive Edward Bairstow, to whom he went for lessons in York Minster whilst living with his mother in Harrogate during the latter part of the war and afterwards; and he cannot have let Bairstow help him towards a musical career path, for he next shut himself away (still with his mother) in an ancient mill in the Cotswolds for three years while he wrote what he later described as 'pastoral whatnots', much influenced by Vaughan Williams's *Pastoral Symphony.* London then called, but for a private existence only: no job, no institutional training, merely some lessons with the famed counterpoint historian R. O. Morris, whose name still strikes fear into the heart of the music student made to do score-reading and figured bass at the keyboard. A composer's debut with his neoclassical Violin Concerto in one of Vaughan Williams's Bach Choir concerts failed, and the work was withdrawn. Little else was heard, a gauche piano concerto, a troublesome chamber symphony and a solo cantata remained unfinished, a stint of harmony teaching at the Royal Academy of Music added insult to injury, and by the early 1930s a nervous breakdown seemed imminent. Marriage in 1933 rescued Finzi from that (as also from financial anxiety), and he and his wife Joy retreated to Aldbourne, a large but isolated Wiltshire village, before settling in Ashmansworth five years later as soon as the new house was ready. No sooner had they moved in here at Church Farm, however, than war broke out, the house teemed with refugees, and Gerald's potential big break, the first performance of *Dies natalis* at the Three Choirs Festival in

Hereford Cathedral, was cancelled at the last moment. Soon he had nothing more gainful to do than join 'Dad's Army', the Home Guard, waiting for his call-up. When it came, at the age of forty, he chose to bury himself as a London civil servant in the Ministry of War Transport rather than take a job offered him in the BBC under Arthur Bliss.

To any composer bound by the normal laws of ambition, competition and self-respect, this would have been the end of it as far as posterity was concerned: one more mute, inglorious Milton or embittered reject living out their time with or without private means, just like Sorabji, Darnton or George Lloyd. (Of course posterity never comes, and these composers now enjoy recordings or decent PhDs in the offing or on the shelves. Curiously enough, too, Darnton, whom Finzi couldn't stand, also lived at Ashmansworth for a while, one hopes at the other end of the village.) But this was not the end of it for Finzi. Finzi was different, and I like to think of him inheriting something of his Jewish forebears' brilliance and resourcefulness behind the pastoral smokescreen.

Be that as it may, when one turns the coin of obscurity and looks at what life was actually like here in Ashmansworth for the Finzis, it all feels rather different. I've been going through the notes I made when working on Gerald's biography to see what he was up to around 19 May each year of that preciously short time he and Joy and the family enjoyed between moving in in 1939 and Gerald's being diagnosed with Hodgkin's Disease twelve years later, and the even more precious, because even shorter, time they had together between 1951 and his death at the age of fifty-five in 1956.

Their social round started promisingly enough in mid-May 1939, two months after the move, with Ann Bowes-Lyon, cousin of the Queen Mother and a minor poet, staying the weekend, and Jack Haines, poet friend of Ivor Gurney, coming over from Gloucester on the Sunday to meet her. A year later things were very different. Hitler had just attacked the Low Countries, the 'phoney war' was over, and Anthony Eden had inaugurated 'Dad's Army' on 14 May. Gerald joined almost immediately, much to the amusement of his friends with their visions of his capturing German parachutists in nearby Doiley Bottom. Gerald himself was far from amused, to the point of insomnia as Boulogne fell to the Germans and he wondered what would happen to him, a Jew, should Hitler's forces actually occupy England. By mid-May 1941, however, England was still standing, though the Queen's Hall, prime concert venue in London, wasn't, having just been destroyed in the Blitz. Now Church Farm, full of refugees, was the administrative hub of Gerald's Newbury String Players, the NSP, his 'old ladies' as he called them with false modesty, who had given their first concert—the first of 379 during and after Gerald's lifetime—on this very spot in the church on 28 December 1940. Life went on during the war, and although in May 1942 Gerald was working in London at the Ministry of War Transport, he had somehow managed just then to put the finishing touches to one of his finest songs, 'O mistress mine', and to the proofs of his Prelude and Fugue for string trio. In May 1943 the NSP were performing Bach and Gurney respectively with Denis Matthews and Sophie Wyss at the Newbury Festival, which was how Finzi used his civil service leave, and the following year Leon Goossens appeared with them there. On 19 May 1945 the western war had been over for ten days with the German final surrender, and Vaughan Williams had just joined Finzi and the NSP at the Newbury Festival; it must have been a joyous occasion.

Now at last, with the house to themselves virtually for the first time since it had been built, the Finzis were in a position to exploit their rural environment, and by May 1947, two years later, Gerald was very much the antiquarian country gentleman, sharing his already encyclopaedic knowledge of eighteenth-century English composers with scholarly correspondents and, another year further on in 1948, helping Hubert Parry's daughter clear out Parry's library at Shulbrede Priory. Mid-May 1949 saw Finzi's creative portfolio very much on the rise, with baritone Robert Irwin staying at Church Farm to help him decide on the selection and order of Hardy songs for the cycle *Before and After Summer*, and the Clarinet Concerto by now two-thirds written. On 19 May 1950 Finzi finished composing his chef d'oeuvre, *Intimations of Immortality*, in vocal score—he had been working on it long before he even moved to Ashmansworth—but one year later its dedicatee, Adeline Vaughan Williams, had just died and Gerald's own fatal illness was at the point of diagnosis.

This did not stop the war poet Edmund Blunden and his whole family staying for a week at Church Farm at this time and John Betjeman coming over for supper. On 19 May 1952 Gerald will have been pressing his suit in readiness for the first orchestral performance of 'God is gone up' in St Paul's Cathedral at the Festival of the Sons of the Clergy the following day; and at the same point in 1953, the Coronation, complete with a Finzi madrigal performance in the Royal Festival Hall the night before, was only two weeks away, though with an intervening rush to St Andrews in Scotland, where Gerald was external examiner for the music degree course, still to come. The same examining routine had occupied the previous May and would do the next as well, to be replaced by further academic duties in 1955, when 19 May was the eve of the third and last of Finzi's public Crees Lectures at the Royal College of Music on 'The composer's use of words'. An insanely busy time for him, May 1955 saw Gerald also rushing to finish his Cello Concerto, writing and listening to the first performance of an orchestral variation in a multi-author set dedicated to the new music impresario Anne Macnaghten, having weekly radiation treatment in Oxford and worrying about his elder son Christopher, serving a two-month prison sentence as a conscientious objector. One year later his younger son, Nigel, was performing the Vivaldi A minor violin concerto with the NSP in Burghclere and Gerald was being consulted by a well-known London organist, Richard Latham, about the scoring of his new Te Deum on the one side and a colleague about a music director for Dartington Hall on the other. This was Gerald's last spring, and he had only four more months to live.

Now this sounds to me like a very full life, and an eminently fulfilling one. To be perfectly honest, it makes nonsense of most of the ideas associated with the picture of obscurity I provocatively painted earlier. But as a narrative pieced together almost entirely from private sources—letters to friends, Joy Finzi's journal—it also seems to mock many of the elements of public acclaim. Such acclaim did arise to a comfortable and moderate degree, but it was generally without being sought through institutions, which Finzi was often happy to let approach him rather than he them.

So we are here to celebrate a life, a lifestyle and a musical output that flourished despite some of the myths associated with it. One of those myths, exactly to overturn my opening remarks, is that of the rural visionary or husbandman. Finzi was not a farmer but a professional composer working at home from a study which he entered after breakfast every morning. Nor was he cut off here in Ashmansworth: he was on the phone, he had a radio and a gramophone, the comings and goings at Church Farm were by car, and he commuted to London by train during the war in much the same time as it takes to get there today. This was the twentieth century, though I doubt whether the conditions of communication in this country had ever been seriously different since the Norman Conquest, except for the length of time it took and the degree of security, for those who had two things, money and class. Finzi had both in sufficient if not excessive quantities. The money, much of it from Joy's dowry, secured his time, while his class, which I take to include literacy and liberality, secured the friendships which he used much of his time to cultivate.

What, then, was so special about him and where and how he lived that brings us today to this quiet though ultimately normal English spot with our blue plaque? I'd like to try to answer this by quickly taking a measured (rather than our earlier intimate) look at the second half of his life and output balancing the gloomy picture I painted of the first half. For it seems to me to show that he had the knack of taking both the long and the short view of career, output, creativity, relationships, value, fame, reputation, ultimately about how you come to terms with time. He tells us something rather particular about these things.

The scope of Finzi's musical personality may have reached the public slowly, but reach it it eventually did. *Earth and Air and Rain*, the best of his sets of ten Hardy songs, was published in 1936 but not showcased in performance, either live or broadcast, for Britten, slightly later, was the first English song composer to write for the performer and make a big event out of a new song cycle, though Finzi did achieve something comparable with his marvellous Shakespeare settings, *Let Us Garlands Bring*, written, or rather completed, for Vaughan Williams's seventieth birthday in 1942—this time broadcasts happened and helped. Nearly one third of Finzi's Hardy settings were not performed or published in his lifetime, and his touchstone work, *Dies natalis*, even after its delayed first performance in 1940, took a while to become recognised as the classic it is. Nevertheless, *Dies natalis* received a great boost when in 1945 Ernest Newman devoted three successive weeks of his widely read *Sunday Times* column to issues surrounding Finzi's word-setting. Newman put his finger on what many would still see as Finzi's indispensable contribution to music when he held him up as an example of how, in a composer 'with the requisite blend in himself of musical imagination and poetic sensitivity, a vast amount of our finest [English] poetry that has hitherto evaded musical treatment becomes susceptible to it'. To treat this, as it must have seemed in retrospect, as an invitation to continue swallowing whole Wordsworth's great 'Immortality' Ode was bold, and when the work appeared at the Three Choirs Festival in 1950 it was hardly hailed as a masterpiece. It sounded so old-fashioned that critics could write it off, as Desmond Shawe-Taylor did with the Cello Concerto at Cheltenham five years later, as something 'that only by courtesy can . . . be called a new work at all.' We'll come back to that.

Finzi's songs, true to Newman's prescription, had in the meantime been finding out many kindred spirits and making friends for him, sometimes in unlikely quarters (including Bernard Herrmann in the

USA), which was what he wanted and why he published them. Nor should we forget that his 'real' job (the wartime civil service post) had taught him speed and decision: as we have already seen, he accomplished an enormous amount, including conducting, committee and lecturing work and scholarly editing besides composition, in his last eleven years, and became (and has remained) the mascot of two constituencies he might not have anticipated wooing, clarinettists and lay clerks: with the Five Bagatelles of 1943 and concerto of 1949 for the former, and some spirited occasional anthems for the latter. Prime among the anthems is 'Lo, the full, final sacrifice', written for St Matthew's, Northampton in 1946 and vibrating with a mystical intensity that one sometimes feels only agnostics can conjure. His incidental radio music for *Love's Labour's Lost*, also from 1946, is less well known than it should be, and makes one regret that he was never professionally invited into a film studio, though he would probably not have coped with its rigours. Choirs he knew how to satisfy, which he continues to do with *In terra pax* (1955), perhaps his most perfect work, *For St Cecilia* (1947), and the unaccompanied Seven Poems of Robert Bridges.

I said earlier that Finzi knew how to take both the long and the short view. On the short side, much of his output, including some of our favourite bits, was written for those around him, ranging from the BBC radio public to his sister-in-law on the occasion of her wedding. But this arose more from a congenial than a utilitarian personality: he had a great capacity for cultivating friends, mentors and colleagues, both dead and alive. The live ones included R. O. Morris, Howells, Rubbra, Ferguson, Bliss, Vaughan Williams and Holst. Rubbra testified: 'I cannot remember a single occasion when, in contact with him, I did not carry away something of vital importance.' The dead ones were poets and, later, the eighteenth-century English composers mentioned earlier. His book collection grew to 4,000 volumes of verse and other literature, and it was eventually donated after his death to Reading University Library, where it survives intact in the Finzi Book Room. (His antiquarian music library went to St Andrews University.) Now it would be foolish to protest that there was nothing whatever of the train spotter about Finzi. Howard Ferguson used to say that some of the species of English apple—another collecting passion—he helped conserve and propagate would have merited their extinction. All the same, his bibliophilia was certainly not a sterile hobby or connoisseurship based on the first-edition precedence of 'a missing comma on the fly-leaf', as Finzi put it in a letter to Jack Haines. Books and scores were his imaginative life-blood.

Predictably, what emerged from his seclusion and ruminative digestion of culture and tradition was less his outpouring of song, the solo settings of Thomas Hardy in particular, as such, than the use of song for pursuing a growing love affair with tonal expression utterly daring in its conservatism. Finzi wrote about fifty Hardy songs, almost all of them with piano and mostly fitting his own baritone range (that of a voice 'small but disagreeable' like Gershwin's and many another composer's), and with God-given musical naïveté he managed to find a vernacular melodic match for the most unlikely verbal phrases and inflections. Phrases such as 'enlarged in scope'; 'season and season sereward steal'; 'So mean I'; 'It's gunnery practice out at sea'; even 'I have unbarred the backway' were set to insidiously memorable little snatches of tune such as you or I might hum to ourselves, and he did hum to himself, on country walks. Down they all went in his sketchbooks, usually with some fragment of accompaniment sufficient to fix the harmonic context (without which tonal melody is groundless), to be wrestled with later, sometimes years, decades, later, in his study, when his admiration for Brahms would seep through in the sonorous piano textures and developing continuum that he managed to fashion from them if he was lucky. Listen to 'In years defaced', one of his finest songs, with this in mind, and hear not only how many changes he rings on a simple motivic shape (the four notes of the title line), but how it comes in and out of focus or alters its shape, size and logic because of the particular words and phrases to which it is set, themselves the light and shade of rhetoric in a verse composition.

The congruence between Hardy's understanding of culture and civilisation and Finzi's would bear considerable scrutiny. Nevertheless, it was Britten, not Finzi, who went the whole philosophical hog when he set to music Hardy's 'Before life and after' as the last of his *Winter Words* songs, and Finzi's own most overtly and memorably philosophical vocal music inheres perhaps not in the Hardy songs, profound though they can be, but in his Traherne, Wordsworth and Flecker settings, respectively *Dies natalis*, *Intimations of Immortality*, and the song 'To a poet a thousand years hence'.

The first two of these works are about the joy and imagination of the child and their adult stifling and what that process means for our human condition. The third is an extraordinary love-letter written across time, a powerful token of the meaninglessness of death in the face of human creativity, handed on from Flecker's imaginary ancient poet to Flecker and thence, via Finzi and his performers, to anyone who has ears to hear, including Colin Matthews in his orchestration of the song as the first in the 'new' compilation cycle *In Years Defaced*. Matthews and his fellow-conspirators Judith Weir, Christian Alexander, Jeremy Dale Roberts, Anthony Payne and Finzi himself thereby add a new layer of greeting across the generations.

Two nights ago I was listening to a BBC Radio Four programme about mortgage mania, in the series 'Why did we do that?' One interviewee pointed out that with credit culture—it's debt culture really—we stopped teaching people that it was good to learn to wait, and lost the capacity to do so. But Finzi, when taking his long view, possessed that capacity to an extraordinary degree, however ironically in the light of his feeling that there would never be enough time to do all he wanted (as indeed there wasn't). When one is setting a poem to music about 'shak[ing] hands with a good friend over the centuries', as Finzi put it, which is the case with 'To a poet a thousand years hence', one develops patience with the march of stylistic fads and fashions and puts one's faith in the tried and tested elements of tonal expression wherewith, to quote him again, 'in each generation may be found a few responsive minds' if one has handled those elements with honesty and candour. He did handle them with honesty and candour, which is why, although it may have taken the best part of half a century for Finzi's biggest works, the Cello Concerto and *Intimations*, to be accepted as large-scale compositions of integrity and character, they are by and large now so accepted. If for some their down-home aspects still rule them out of court, on stylistic or structural grounds, for others, including many top performers, that is no longer an issue, for their feeling and power are genuine. I'm not sure Finzi quite expected this acceptance, though as I have suggested he would always have been willing to wait for it.

'They also serve who only stand and wait', runs the last line of a Milton sonnet set to music by Finzi. Such waiting is the opposite of careering, to take the double meaning of that word. And those who wait have time to listen, 'Heark'ning in the aspect of th' eternal silence' as Robert Bridges' words at the end of *In terra pax* put it.

I'd like to end by remembering this work. *In terra pax* describes an agnostic's visionary comfort on a starry hilltop on Christmas Eve while the bells sound in the valleys. Finzi had had such an experience—though at New Year—consorting with bell-ringers in the Cotswolds as a young man, and after conducting the first performance of the full orchestral version of the work in Gloucester Cathedral in 1956, thirty years later, he took Vaughan Williams up nearby Chosen Hill to show him the spot, catching chickenpox from children in the sexton's cottage and dying within three weeks because of his destroyed immune system. Hardy would have appreciated this as a supreme example of life's little ironies, missing perhaps the more positive dimension of hilltop appointments with destiny and the 'eternal silence', shared by humanity from Moses' day to ours across many faiths and cultures, Finzi's included. The stars haven't changed much in all those times and places, and pose the same challenge to human understanding that they did 10,000 years ago.

Anyone who can help to tell us this, through communicable music or poetry, has a place in the scheme of things. Ashmansworth Church today should feel happy that after a mere 1,000 years, with the little blue plaque on the house opposite, it now has a new fellow-witness: their respective symbols of Christian faith and human art from now on shake hands across the lane to try to fathom creation.

Memories of Church Farm

Malcolm Lipkin

I met Joy, Christopher and Nigel Finzi in 1958, and first visited Ashmansworth in the summer of that year. On entering the music room, I was immediately aware of a very special peace, but it was only after working on several of my own compositions there, over the next five years, that I understood the nature of this tranquillity. It was the light—particularly that of a late afternoon or early evening in spring and autumn. The lowering sun shone through the window in front of the writing desk, illuminating the bookshelves and filling the room with a deep glow, while at the same time colouring the magnificent southward vista of the hills from the other window. The positioning of these windows by Gerald and Joy Finzi was surely an inspiration, and the magical effect of the light will always remain with me.

Thanks to the hospitality of the Finzi family, I wrote several works at Ashmansworth, completing my *Sinfonia di Roma* there in the autumn of 1965, and beginning Psalm 96 for chorus and orchestra in 1969. However, composing in the music room was not necessarily a leisurely occupation. One weekend, when I thought I had come from London to enjoy again the quietude of the countryside, I was told by Christopher that the Newbury Players required a short piece for horn and strings within eight days, and I was set to work accordingly! Thus was my *Pastorale* created in a single day. My String Trio, completed in 1964, is dedicated to Joy Finzi, and for Christopher's marriage to Hilary du Pré I wrote my Suite for flute and cello.

I cannot fail to acknowledge the influence of Gerald's fine library of English literature, which opened my mind to the poets, especially those of the seventeenth century. From hours of pleasurable browsing there evolved my *Four Departures* for soprano and violin, to poems of Herrick, and *The Pursuit* (Symphony No 2), inspired by some lines of Marvell.

Lucy Edgeley

Daughter of Edmund Blunden (written after a long talk with her sisters Margi Blunden and Fan Marquand, 7 February 2006.)

As we meander through memories of our childhood visits to the Finzi home we find it impossible to separate people from place. Our own home was in Hong Kong, and our two short stays cannot have added up to more than two or three weeks, but those weeks were magical, and the wonderful world of the English countryside in June (surely it was June) was, and is still for us all, there, at Ashmansworth.

It must have been Joy who started the magic. There she was to meet us at Heathrow, tall, beautiful, with her mass of hair and large beaming eyes, and there was her Bedford van, the side doors kept open as she drove down ever-narrowing winding roads, and at last turned into the drive—and in front of us was that beautiful plain house and the enormous tree.

Joy had such vitality, strength and calm that life in her sphere became exciting, full of possibility and yet ran in a happily ordered fashion, boundaries wide but clearly set. The arrival of the Blunden family (six of us, including baby Cathy) at Ashmansworth didn't seem to cause any strain, though it must have done—how did that delicious food appear so effortlessly? Oeufs en cocotte with fresh chives, homemade bread, instant whip with coffee added, muesli (almost unheard of in 1957)—everything tasted so fresh and was so different, and was served on pottery dishes, not china. We were given jobs—to pick gooseberries for fool, to collect eggs, to help wash up—and we loved to be helpful. Joy gave Dad a haircut, drew his portrait; we were lent the boys' Aran jumpers on a chilly day, and knew that we were privileged.

An ideal world for a child, and no doubt for a poet too, even one brought down to work, as Dad was on our first stay. He was locked up with Gerald in the music room—a room we children were wary of, as we knew that we must not cause disturbance near it during the day, and that in the evening we might have to endure a violin recital there by one of the Finzis' protégés (we weren't a particularly musical lot—indeed Joy, we think, was rather concerned by the ordinariness of our upbringing. Were we being educated as poets' daughters should be? Her concern was not expressed to us, but we recognised it and didn't mind. Did Mum? I doubt it; she loved Joy and was only glad of her support and interest.)

Gerald is there in our memories, but in a shadow—quiet, always working, kind but remote. Nigel is there too, but something of a mystery—a film star, Joy said, in dark glasses—and perhaps it is her view of him that stays, for in reality he can't have been around much. Much clearer is Olive, Joy's right hand in the house and kitchen garden, with her husband Jack an essential support outdoors.

But our hero was Kiffer. He told us wonderful tales of secret passages in the house, of spies in the war, of dark doings down the well. He organised us—to search for eggs in the hedges, to help in the henhouse with washing and grading—we must earn our keep, and our yummy English sweets. He showed us his hives and gave us beeswax to chew. He had us running races and playing croquet. One day he must have felt the need for a break from child minding, and cleverly challenged us to a day of silence. We more or less managed it, and he paid us handsomely.

Alas, three years later, on our second visit, our hero had grown up—and fallen in love. There was a girl in his loft bedroom—Hilary had arrived—and neither he nor she had time for anything than each other. Bitter disappointment for the Blunden girls. But we were older too, made the most of the opportunity to observe a love affair at close hand. Sometimes our prudish attitudes were challenged. In the kitchen, the grownup talk was often of the romance, and we missed little.

Hilary's brother came for the day; we were all sent out to play, and we liked him. Another day we went down to Weymouth to see Hilary and Kiffer off on the ferry to Jersey. On this second visit, Ah Ling, Cathy's amah, an elderly, warm and wise woman travelling out of the east for the first time, was with us and Joy looked after her with great care and fondness.

And then the house. The kitchen we remember as quite narrow, cool, with the path from the kitchen door leading to sunshine, fruit cage, vegetables, herbs. The other downstairs rooms were less important to us, but upstairs was better than Enid Blyton—so many rooms, the secret passage from the attic (which was later turned into a bedroom by Kiffer, with a ladder-like stair—an early loft conversion), eiderdowns on high comfortable beds, low windows with swallows nesting under the eaves, and the little bookroom, a glorious overgrown cupboard lined with the children's books. Books borrowed must be treated with care, and returned to their proper place; everything in Ashmansworth seemed to have a proper place, so this was not difficult.

And waking up, the air was a little chilly under the early sun, and the scented air could have been sold to us under the label 'English Heaven'. We had to get outdoors. Out to the wide lawns, the old stone terraces, the deep deep well. There was all of England in our view, and we rolled down the slopes of grass, wandered in the apple orchard (the trees, though we hardly knew it, were of old and rare varieties), and out in the field where the chickens pecked and clucked. Did the sun shine every day? Even Joy could not have arranged that. And if it rained, we were still happy.

We were taken to the tiny ancient church, to a village cricket match and a fête. In Newbury, Dad bought paintings, the old watercolours that he collected, and we went to a wonderful cake shop. All of this was new, nothing like it in the colonies.

Two weeks or three, no time at all in a lifetime. But say to any of us 'Ashmansworth' and we breathe fresh air, see green vistas, taste new-laid eggs. It all seems too perfect, as I write it down, but so it was then. It, no doubt, was not such an easy matter for Joy, especially after Gerald's death, but even then warmth and calm reigned in the house, and outside was freedom, beauty, discovery. How fortunate we were, and are to have such memories.

Lady Bliss

An attractive connection between Arthur Bliss and the Finzi Friends is the portrait of Arthur in Joy's book *In That Place*. It was drawn during one of our happy visits to Ashmansworth. Arthur and Gerald were comfortably talking in the book room while Joy's pencil was busy. There is another drawing of Arthur, made on an occasion when he was playing chess with Christopher. While he was pondering his next move, he may have been stroking one of the Finzi cats purring on his knee.

We all loved and envied the Finzi cats—soft pampered creatures! Twice a week, Joy baked a batch of wholemeal bread. It was perfectly delicious but it was not baked primarily for the Finzis and their guests—oh no—it was a necessary part of the cats' diet. Each cat had its very own place in the house, inviolate. The king cat had the best place, a shelf, just at the right height, above the Aga in Joy's kitchen. There was a saying in those years: 'All good Americans, when they die, go to Paris'. Well, Arthur and I used to say: 'All good cats, when they die, go to Ashmansworth.'

I remember too, the excitement of the garden well on dark nights. Gerald used to remove the grill from its top with a ceremoniously muttered abracadabra and then flick a lighted sheet of newspaper into the dark opening. All the children, leaning over the edge (but firmly gripped by the grown-ups) watched the flame go down, down, down and down—and shivered at the menacing hiss as the firebrand reached the water. Ah, for cats and visitors, Ashmansworth was a heavenly place.

II

'The most honest of friends'

Remembering Gerald Finzi

Christopher Finzi

Talk for Finzi Friends given at Church Farm, Ashmansworth, 29 June 1996.

As I become older I increasingly understand that judgements reveal more of the judge than the judged, so my opinions of my father will be more telling of me than of him. I find it almost impossible to separate first-hand recollections from those handed down by word of mouth. Although I was born in 1934, I don't have any genuine memories until 1939, the year our family moved into Church Farm, just before the outbreak of the Second World War.

Dad joined the Home Guard and used to go to parades and drill at Ashmansworth House. After a while he was called to war work and was offered a post at the BBC, but felt that this was too soft an option, so applied to the Ministry of War Transport. He was proud of the fact that he was selected for a responsible post, having no qualifications at all, for he had never sat an exam, musical or otherwise. He went to London on Sunday evenings, returning here on Friday evenings. Apart from his holidays I would have seen him for only two days a week, and in 1943 I went off to boarding school (Dunhurst/Bedales) where I stayed until I was seventeen, so really only spent the school holidays here.

The fact that the war was not a frightening experience must largely be due to Mum. She never flapped and always motivated people. As we were new to the area she was put in charge of billeting refugees because she didn't know anyone and was therefore impartial. We took in three East End refugees who were followed by two Germans and then Lydia, Frank and Vera. Vera was a friend of Dad's older sister Katie, Frank being her second husband and Lydia, his cousin, who was a Czechoslovakian Jew. Frank was about ten years older than Dad, his original name being Strauss which he changed to Strawson. Nigel and I always knew him as Gubsy. He hadn't done a 'proper' (Dad's expression) day's work in his life. At university he read philosophy and had come up with his own original thinking: that any fool can make money. So he set off as a young man to somewhere north of India, living in a grand hotel straddling to boundary of two states, where he played golf every day, but in the bottom of his caddy there was a false compartment which he filled with diamonds. At the far end of the course he pulled a lever, the diamonds dropped (presumably in the rough) to picked up by an accomplice. Thus he made his money by smuggling. When he returned to England he used his money cleverly by financing Victor Gollancz and shrewdly investing the rest. I remember him sitting cross-legged on the sitting room floor with the newspaper and share certificates around him, deciding which to sell and what to buy.

Lydia Riesenecker had been a neighbour and bridge partner of Richard Strauss, which makes me wonder whether Frank was any relation of his. Eugène Ysaÿe, the ageing violin virtuoso, had fallen desperately in love with Lydia, when she was eighteen, and insisted he couldn't perform without her presence. She told me that on a good day he could bring audiences to raptures of excitement or tears of sorrow; but on a bad day a modern music student would be ashamed of the playing. It was all or nothing.

One of the Home Guard exercises was that the platoon was divided in two, one half guarding the village and the other infiltrating it. Dad dressed up as an old woman with a veil (he looked so like his mother) and hobbled up the road on Joy's arm. He was the only one to breach the defences! The Home Guard started out with hardly any equipment but as the war continued more was released, until Gubsy, a frail fellow, found it too much to carry. As the parades were half a mile away in the village, Vera followed him with his equipment in a wheelbarrow. Unfortunately he couldn't reach his back, so she fixed the extras on him at the parade ground, and divested him of them for the return journey.

Given the right conditions, Gubsy was a very good shot and helped

Ashmansworth win several competitions. He had to be lying down with his elbows planted on terra firma. Alas, he couldn't reach the ammunition pouches, so Nigel or I had to accompany him to keep him supplied with bullets! Another often-told story was that during the 'any questions' after a lecture on the Bren gun, Gubsy (who was in charge of the vegetable garden here) asked 'can anyone tell me when to plant my broad beans?'

We did have some experience of the war, but it never seemed threatening. We had no curtains, so wooden frames covered with black material had to be fitted into the windows at dusk and I used to hold these in front of me so the Germans couldn't see me. I remember a German aeroplane being shot down—it limped over our house and went down with a big bang. Nigel and I rushed to the crash scene on our bikes and came back with the pilot, who had baled out. Mum gave him a hearty breakfast and he let us play with his empty revolver whilst she telephoned the police, who came to collect him.

We were one of the few people with a telephone, so if there was an air-raid warning, we were telephoned, and Nigel or I biked down to the Coopers (the next farm) to pass on the message. The thatched ridge of his barn was worn through, so when he was milking in the evening light poured through the gaps. He took little notice; when we returned with the 'all clear' message, he was still milking away, a few cows further along the row.

One day towards the end of the war, Dad came home mid-week, and the following morning took us out onto the front lawn, saying there was something we might like to see: the invasion of France! It seemed to go on all day—endless heavy aircraft towing gliders in circles overhead, as they formed into great columns that droned away southwards.

There were three German prisoners-of-war who came here every day from a camp at the bottom of the hill: Fritz, who had been a master builder in Germany, and two others. They built all the walls and terraces around the house, and levelled out the front lawns with the heaps of earth and rubble left over from the house building. We all had a chatty lunch together; it was a breaking of boundaries between nations.

During the war, Dad was occupied on Saturday mornings with sorting out the week's post and preparing for the Newbury String Players' afternoon rehearsals. His search for new repertoire for the NSP was the path that led to his discovery of eighteenth-century music. It was the perfect time to pursue his new interest, as it was possible to buy original editions cheaply. This trail of discovery helped to mitigate his return to the city at the week's end, for he enjoyed trudging around the London bookshops during his lunch hour. The excitement when he returned with the first of his Stanley original prints was memorable.

Our life after the war was well ordered with a constant routine. Dad rose early in the morning and went straight to his study for half an hour to look over the previous day's work. He found that if he worked on a problem last thing at night, it was often resolved in his subconscious during the night's sleep. We all had breakfast at about 7.30, and then back to his work until lunch (with a break for a mid-morning cup of coffee in the kitchen, and dealing with the post).

After lunch he took a nap. Being an extremely light sleeper, he was easily woken and at night wore earplugs and goggles, made for him by Lottie (Joy's old nurse), which had raised centres that didn't brush his eyelashes. He liked to be read to, and Joy (later on, my brother or I) read from his current book. After a few minutes, he would drop off and very silently we would tiptoe out so as not to waken him. He generally spent the rest of the afternoon in the garden, and after tea went back to his study. We had fairly early suppers (probably due to us children), and the rest of the evening was spent reading or doing other things. He always liked to look through the day's composing just before going to bed.

So it was an organised but very free life, with few restrictions. If we wanted to see Dad we just rushed into his study and felt completely free to say whatever we wished. The house was designed with his workroom at one end, our nursery at the other, and the living rooms in-between so he couldn't hear too much noise. Mum suffered terrible attacks of asthma, the worst of which kept her in bed all day. The sight and smell of the smouldering fumes given off by the Potter's herbal asthma powder, as she gasped for breath, remain a powerful image and memory.

Gerald's relationship with Joy made for a wonderful marriage. He was the volatile element, with much nervous energy, which she contained and supported unswervingly. He was also very aware of her formidable talents and was always pressing her to do her own work. He once locked her in her studio over the garage, only to dash up after a short while to ask her to come and type a letter for him.

After reading Stephen Banfield's biography, I have been reconsidering Dad's relationship with his own family, and the fact he felt so out of place with them. It was a sad family situation: his father died of cancer when my father was eight, and his three brothers didn't survive a great deal longer. His older sister he loathed (and I use that word without reservation), and he felt his mother had the brains of a chicken. He was so miserable at prep school that he feigned fainting fits, the last one in a bath, with his nose just sticking out of the water; the school decided that he had to leave, as they could no longer take responsibility for him.

His mother took him to Switzerland as she felt the air was cleaner there, and on the way back they arrived in Paris just as the Germans were advancing. As the city was almost deserted, she thought it would be a good time to show him around, and Dad remembered the sound of distant gunfire.

I recollect Granny clearly; she was half German and spoke with a strong accent. At an advanced age she broke her hip, but being an ardent Christian Scientist would not have it seen to, so it left her with a pronounced limp. We visited her frequently in the village of Clare near Sudbury. According to Dad she was a brilliant pianist, and could play anything—but understood nothing. She did write a couple of piano pieces which I think Stephen Banfield has retrieved.

Occasionally we saw Dad's older sister Katie in Essex whom he felt was entirely superficial. He said that there are two kinds of people on this earth: those who do a thing for what it is, and those for the effect it will have on others. He regarded her as one of the latter. She must have been a sporting lady as she used to play football with us, and I am now ashamed to say that because of his dislike of her we used to kick her rather than the ball, which shows misguided family loyalty.

Mum's sister Mags (Margaret), who had a farm in Enborne, was a frequent visitor, and Granny came to stay from time to time. I remember Dad hiding behind the dining room door with Mags in a stylised embrace (no small feat as she was as tall as Joy), so when Granny shut the door she let out a screech of horror at the scene revealed. At supper once, he told us of a tea party with the vicar. He was horrified when the vicar licked his plate 'just like this'—immediately demonstrating the action with relish!

His impish sense of humour spurred him to send a memo around the Ministry of War Transport saying that as Winston Churchill was to pay an informal visit the following Saturday, everyone was to leave their office tidy and clean for the weekend. A large contingent turned up for work on that day, armed with their cameras. As far as I know there were no repercussions! He made friends with several people at the Ministry, including Gilmour Jenkins (later Sir Gilmour), Principal of the Ministry, whom he introduced to Ursula Wood. They became good friends, both before and after her marriage to Vaughan Williams.

My father had three older brothers—Felix, Douglas and Edgar. Felix was ten years older than he was, a year younger than Katie. Felix was quite a brilliant young man—an engineer—he designed an aircraft carrier before the First World War, sending the plans to the Admiralty. He went to India to work as an engineer on a tea plantation and committed suicide out there. Dad remembered being in his nursery one evening when his mother came in asking for Felix, and searching in the cupboards and under the beds. The next morning she received the letter telling her he was dead. Granny was an intuitive person who acted on her instincts.

There's an interesting aftermath to that sad event. A retired Indian Army officer, who lived in Ashmansworth, had a great friend from India, a Dr Winchester, staying with him. The name rang a bell with my father, remembering it on Felix's death certificate; and though never mentioned, Dad's suspicion that it was suicide was confirmed. It was a tragic consequence of being in a fatherless family: I suppose during adolescence he became worried about wet dreams and masturbation, went to see his doctor, who told him to 'pull himself together'. He left for India with an unbearable sense of guilt that he could only solve with an overdose.

The second brother, Douglas, died of pneumonia at Bradfield College, and Edgar (the closest in age to my father) was killed in the Fleet Air Arm at the end of the First World War. He was a draughtsman of considerable talent who had cartoons accepted by *Punch* before he was sixteen; but he and Dad were never really friendly.

The period of our closest collaboration was after the war, when I had finished school. Although I went to live in London, I came home frequently and helped Dad prepare his Boyce volume for *Musica Britannica*. I did the donkey-work for that, copying out the scores and writing in the continuo part (which he of course corrected—a wonderful lesson in itself) and generally researching portraits and other relevant material.

Later on I spent much time with him going through the solo part of the Cello Concerto, showing what was possible and what would not work. He got the idea of the double octave pizzicato link between the second and third movement from our sessions. He was under great pressure to meet the first performance deadline, as well as being under the cloud of illness.

For a long time he'd had a little hacking cough, which didn't really concern him, then, a small lump on his neck appeared, so he consulted Dr Scott (of the architectural family, Gilbert Scott), who was also a very great family friend. Dad said he always knew as soon as Tom put his hands on him that it was something serious—he could tell from Tom's reaction. He had to have the lump removed and analysed, which is how the illness was diagnosed.

It was a 'relation' of Hodgkin's Disease, which probably now could be cured by chemotherapy quite easily. No-one knew—not even his oldest friend Howard Ferguson—although we as a family knew, and would talk about it quite openly. He said one of the awful things is that you blame everything on your illness, but of course you are getting older anyway: when he found it hard to climb over a gate he felt it was most likely due to old age. The illness meant that he had to have radiotherapy quite often, and that was even more destructive than the illness itself. He went to the Radcliffe Infirmary in Oxford, where he was under Professor Witts, the great authority on blood at that time (it was a leukaemia-related disease). He was attracted to Witts the first time he went to see him, as Witts said, 'I just want to make one thing quite clear: I know no more about this illness than you do. I have statistical information on what I think might happen, but I know nothing more than you do.'

His statistical information was quite accurate, he told Dad he would live at least five years but not more than fifteen; in actuality he lived, I think, eight or nine years. But it took a terrible toll, periods of going to Oxford every day to have x-ray treatment which left him feeling awful and washed out.

It affected our relationships, because I've certainly seen it from another angle. The problem of adolescent sons and fathers is not an easy one for either the father or the son, but because we had that extra consideration to take into account, in some ways it made life easier. I think it made that period of breaking away—which is always difficult—easier, because we had to make allowances and they weren't asked for in a self pitying way at all.

Nigel and I started to take part in the Newbury String Players as instrumentalists, which was great fun. Dad was not a good conductor. He really didn't have natural physical co-ordination. He was not the kind of person who could cope with a bouncing ball very well. He did play the violin as a young man, but had to give it up because he was petrified that a string was going to break and hit him in the face; he couldn't bear the strain of it. He wasn't a particularly good pianist. He could get around but he wasn't at all outstanding. His one great boast was that he had played the Grieg Piano Concerto. Actually, I think he had played the orchestral part while a fellow student had played the solo part. He always used to brag about the fact that Britten had been his copyist. When he went to London, Britten as a young man had done some copying for my father; and when Britten's name cropped up at social occasions he would say (with a twinkle in his eye), 'Oh yes—he was my copyist!' He had a great respect for Britten's music, but he didn't admire it.

In his life, apart from my mother, the most important relationships he had were with Howard Ferguson and Ralph Vaughan Williams. Howard and he were inseparable friends from their first meeting, when Howard was only eighteen, until my father died. In fact, Howard lived down in Flintwall Cottage for six months at the beginning of the war.

Vaughan Williams, in a sense, replaced the father he never had. He used to have a play-through of every new piece he wrote, and invited a few people—one of whom was my father—and asked for comments. He wouldn't take any notice of anyone, but my father would not hesitate if he thought something was poor. I admire my father for not being one of those adulating people who knelt to the Great Master: he was very critical of a lot of the things he wrote, and I must say that time has proved his judgement to be sound. That is also a characteristic of his relationship with Howard Ferguson—in fact Howard said that he cannot imagine how they could have been so ruthlessly honest. I think in later years Vaughan Williams came to trust my father as being one of the last remaining people he could rely on from a judgmental point of view.

I recollect Vaughan Williams very clearly. I used to go with him to concerts when he needed someone to take him. We had a wonderful time. I remember a Stravinsky concert at All Souls, Langham Place, which included a couple of Bach arrangements for orchestra. Vaughan Williams sat there looking more and more grumpy; in the end he rose up after these two orchestrations and said, 'If he dislikes Bach that much, I don't know why he bothers to orchestrate him', and stormed out just as poor little Stravinsky was getting up out of his seat. I thought there was going to be a terrible collision, because Vaughan Williams was not a small man, by any means. We went to see the first performance of *The Knot Garden* by Tippett, and *The Carmelites* by Poulenc. He was great fun to go with, but I don't think he listened to a great deal. When we went to *The Carmelites*, he said it was the most terribly boring piece of music he'd ever heard. I tried to come up with some defence, and although I didn't think it was particularly good myself, told him I thought it was sincere. He turned, and said, 'I take that for granted'.

When we went to the Tippett opera, he couldn't understand what was happening at all, so gave up after a bit, and decided to make up his own story as it went along. There were two podiums on each side—from which people came up and went down and said things across to each other and occasionally met in the middle—and he decided that the left one was the gents' loo, and the right, the ladies' loo, and wove some fantastic story around that. I do think, however, he respected some of the music.

He used to come to Church Farm a great deal, and wrote three movements of his Eighth Symphony here. When you were in the room with him, you would have thought he was a painter sketching a picture. It wasn't neat, it was all brushing bits around the page—very rough and ready. In his older years, he used would write for piano with scoring instructions, or short score, and then send it off to Michael Mullinar or Roy Douglas, to decipher the scribbles and write it out in full. He would look at it again, and make any adjustments, which took a lot of the hack-work off his shoulders. In the evenings, he would sit by the open fire. He was a large man—there used to be several 'shelves'—each with a cat on it. He could accommodate three with ease. I remember one day asking him how work had gone, and he replied that he had spent the whole morning writing bad Elgar and the whole afternoon scrapping it.

One night after my father had died, he came down from London and my mother took him out to see the dawn. He had arrived at about midnight, in mid summer, and they set off at about three in the morning to go up to the top of the hills to watch the sunrise.

We had other frequent visitors: Robin Milford, who used to live the other side of Newbury; and Arthur Bliss—I think I acquitted myself quite well playing chess with him.

Lots of performers used to come in relation to the Newbury String Players, such as Julian Bream. My father was a stickler for punctuality—he hated being late himself, and he hated anyone else being late. Julian was due to come at 11.30. The clock reached 12.30, then 1.30 . . . eventually he turned up in an old banger. My father had a photograph of Sibelius looking rather imposing on the stairs, and I think he had that in the back of his mind. Thinking he was going to make a rather impressive stance, he came down the front stairs rather stiffly, trying to be the grand old man: Julian came rushing in saying, 'I am so sorry I'm late and I can't talk properly because I bruised my lip kissing a girl last night'—and my father immediately burst into laughter. We spent the rest of the afternoon sitting in the rotunda, with Julian playing the guitar while we all listened.

We had Henry Holst, the violinist, to stay; all the soloists generally used to come and stay with us as well as the students—Anna Shuttleworth was a very regular player—and the wind players; Alexander Murray who became the first flautist in the LSO; Jimmy Brown who played with the ECO for years. Colin Davis gave a performance of the Clarinet Concerto in Enborne church, which my father mis-conducted so they had to start one movement again. Conducting to him was rather like stripping in public I think—my father was intensely shy and he really could not do it properly—it was almost too much for him.

I have talked about living friends and dead friends. Thomas Hardy must be the most important person in his life that he never met, even though their lives did overlap. I have often thought about what it was that gave the tremendous pull that Hardy had for him. In many ways they were completely opposite, and in others very similar. They were opposite in that Thomas Hardy's life really reached its greatest intensity fairly early on and sank down into a rather sad ending. My father was exactly the opposite. His early life was not happy—he felt alone and isolated until he married—and the last twenty-odd years of his life were happy beyond compare.

So in some ways, they worked from the opposite ends. But they did both have intense recollections of childhood. For all its sadness, and maybe because of it, my father's strong memories of being a child remained. He always said he found it so sad when people had lost touch with their childhood—bankers who could only think about banks, who'd lost all their instinctive impulse and become as dull as ditch water. Thomas Hardy certainly was the same. He was writing poems right to the end of his life that were seen literally through a child's eyes; they weren't by an old man looking back; they were a child writing with eighty years' experience. I think they both had a certain fatalistic approach in common. My father certainly loved the man, and had tremendous admiration for him, but again was critical as well, he wouldn't hesitate to say what he thought was weak. I remember him saying, 'Who else but Thomas Hardy could start a poem saying, "Who now remembers Almack's balls"?'

I often wonder what would happen if Dad were to come back now—how he would cope, how he would find things? I think in many ways he would be horrified. Don't forget, when he was alive there were no supermarkets, there were no international corporations. I remember—to illustrate my point—that there used to be a large American base at Greenham, and one day a young American hitched a lift from him, and began talking about how backward everything was in England: 'no-one's got a refrigerator, no-one's got a car.' I could feel Dad's hackles rising, and he said, 'Well, Bach and Shakespeare didn't need refrigerators.' The young American replied, 'Who are they?' As far as my father was concerned that was the end of that; it was not worth continuing the conversation.

I still remember harvesting the corn in stooks, with horse-drawn binders, and I remember the advent of the Coopers' first tractor—the

Coopers are the only people now in this village who remain from before Mum and Dad arrived—everything else has changed hands since then. Again, I think he'd have been quite shocked coming back to the house he built. So much of it is similar and so much of it is different. A whole third has been added on, and some more is going to be added soon. That is what happens with the next generation. He would have found it hard to cope, and I think part of his appeal—and it's the same with Thomas Hardy—is that they were voices against the inexorable rollercoaster of so-called progress. First of all of the Victorian era: almost everything about Thomas Hardy was the eclipse of the agricultural ethos by the industrial outlook. My father's attractiveness is that he stood, and stands, outside the thrust of our present direction. I think that is another thing that united him and Hardy. The feeling of trying to save some of the precious things of the past—which of course you can't do—you can't selectively turn the clock back. He would have found the house strangely different. I don't know how he would have coped with great-grandchildren, but I think on the whole he would have been glad; he was very keen on the continuation of generation to generation, although he had such a rift in his own.

Sybil Eaton

My first recollection of Gerald is from 1915 or 1916 when I used to meet him, always with his mother, in Minster Court [York] on his way to a composition lesson with Edward Bairstow. He looked very young! I saw very little of him at that time as the family lived outside York, but I heard a great deal as Bairstow was keenly interested in him.

In 1916, I moved to London with Editha Knocker, my intention of going to Auer in Petrograd being smashed by the war. Gerald turned up before long, bringing me his compositions to bow (I am fearful as to how I did it in those days). I remember his frustration with the ceaseless sound of traffic when composing, instead of the peace of a ploughed field.

Some time later, he was on the committee of the Painswick Music Club and engaged me to play, insisting that I play the newly written Moeran Sonata; never having heard of Moeran, it was good for me to be pulled out of the rut of Handel, Brahms and Kreisler pieces.

Then came his engagement to Joy, which produced an immortal remark. I asked repeatedly what she was like, but he seemed to find her quite indescribable. Eventually, he came out with 'Well, she is not Harriet Cohen!'

I cannot remember the year when Gerald honoured me by writing his Violin Concerto. The first performance was with Malcolm Sargent at Queen's Hall.[1] It had a particularly beautiful slow movement, which was later published. I remember how much Gerald appreciated Vaughan Williams's real sympathy with him when the orchestra scoffed at something new, having so often experienced the same thing. Gerald used to come to me for rehearsals, and to my surprise, he varied the tempo for the opening bars. When I protested, he said 'My job is to compose the music, yours is to find the right tempo.' His view was confirmed by Vaughan Williams when I later played his (shamefully neglected) *Concerto Accademico*,[2] with the composer conducting. At the first rehearsal, he stopped me because he wanted a quicker tempo for the first movement; but at the second rehearsal he stopped me again, saying that he liked my tempo better! Obviously I am wrong in my very strong feeling that there is only one right tempo for everything, but all my life I have had a sinking feeling at the question 'how fast should it go?'

One day, when Nigel Finzi was three or four years old, I was rehearsing with Gerald at Ashmansworth when Nigel, having been fairly obstreperous, became still—obviously rapt in the music. I remarked on this to Gerald, and he said, 'Nigel, get your fiddle out.' Nigel dived under the piano for his half-sized fiddle and proceeded to put it on the wrong shoulder. When this was put right, he put his bow on the wrong side of the bridge! When all set, with Gerald at the piano, he then drew the whole bow on open strings with the ease and poise of a virtuoso. Joy took some photographs, which she kindly sent to me, and I still treasure them to this day.

The recollection for which I am most grateful is being told by Gerald that I had played out of tune in the slow movement of his concerto. He was the most honest of friends; I wish more people had been as honest as him.

Howard Ferguson

Though we had already met once in 1926 at the house of R. O. Morris in Glebe Place, our second meeting a few weeks later was far more significant. It took place just outside the Albert Hall in London, where Richard Strauss had been conducting a programme of his own works. The

[1] May 9 1927
[2] Now retitled as the Violin Concerto in D minor

presence of the Master should have guaranteed the solemnity of the occasion; but things started off badly when the fortissimo organ solo at the beginning of the *Festliches Praeludium* proved to be a quarter of a tone sharper (or was it flatter?) than the entry of the full orchestra that immediately followed. The highlight of the evening came, however, in one of the noisier climaxes of the *Alpensinfonie*, when the thunder-machine was seen to topple over and crash into the middle of the startled orchestra. (I say 'seen' advisedly, for 'The Storm on the Mountain' blotted out everything else.) As the audience left the hall afterwards, Gerald and I cannoned into one another by chance, both of us helpless with laughter; and from that moment our friendship was sealed.

For the next eight or nine years, until he moved into the country, we met regularly, to go through each other's compositions, talk endlessly, and play through every sort of music. Being the less fluent pianist of the two, Gerald would station himself at the extreme top of the keyboard and add whatever vocal or instrumental part came his way, several octaves too high, rather loudly, and with a distinctly capricious sense of time-values. The din must have been appalling, but how we enjoyed ourselves!

Simona Pakenham

In 1947 my husband, Noel Iliff, a drama producer at the BBC, was asked to choose a Shakespeare play for Saturday Night Theatre, reduce it to an hour and a half and commission a composer to provide the music. I was given the job of adaptation and, as a bonus, the choice of composer. I was half way through the lengthy process of writing my Ralph Vaughan Williams book and my mind instantly flew to the great man. We were doubtful that he would accept.

Before the BBC had time to make an approach I went, as I often did, to a lunchtime concert at the National Gallery where I chanced to hear a song-cycle—*Dies natalis*—by somebody I had never heard of—Gerald Finzi. During the Intrada, before the soloist, Eric Greene, had even opened his mouth, I knew that this Finzi, if he were alive, rather than Vaughan Williams, was the natural-born composer for *Love's Labour's Lost*, the play we had chosen. It turned out that he was alive because he took a bow, to enthusiastic applause, at the end of the work. I rushed to the BBC and told Noel to cancel, if not too late, the request to RVW.

I have totally forgotten the process by which they persuaded Gerald to agree to the commission and I did not meet him for some weeks. Before that I had emerged from a concert to find all my joints seizes up and upon getting home, a doctor was summoned and I shortly found myself in a huge bed in a nursing home in the Cromwell Road diagnosed with rheumatic fever. I was told I could not put my foot to the ground until my temperature had been normal for a week.

At least I had the adaptation of *Love's Labour's Lost* to keep me from despair, but I could not go far with it unless I had some conversation with the composer. Having seen him briefly at the National Gallery I was prepared for the Italian-looking chap with the shock of black curls. He seemed unfazed by the situation and we found we had marked all the same places in our copies of Shakespeare. He visited me several times and so enchanted my nurse that she did not chase him off when he sat on the bed.

It was two months before I was allowed to move out of my bed and my legs would not support me. As soon as I could reliably stand, Joy Finzi invited Noel and me to Ashmansworth. My most vivid memory of that visit was of waking to the smell of roasting coffee beans. Kiffer and Nigel were there—medium-sized boys. I remarked on their beauty to Joy. 'Yes, and don't they know it!' she said.

I did not breathe a word about my book in progress. Since I never expected even to send it to a publisher I had kept it secret from everyone but Noel, so I cannot remember what prompted Gerald to declare 'the opinions of the ordinary listener are of no interest to any musician!' my heart took a dive and I went home with the intention of putting my manuscript on the bonfire. It was Noel who dissuaded me. Then, years later, when RVW had (almost) admitted to enjoying my book about him, I told him of this remark. 'Typical Gerald!' was his reply.

I had made the perfect choice of composer and the production was enchanting—but radio gets little notice from the press and it vanished almost without trace. Eventually a suite was made of the music, but without the voices of the actors it loses its character. I long for Stratford-on-Avon to stage a proper production.

John Carol Case

As a young singer at the outset of my career, I was lucky enough to be asked to sing in the opening series of concerts in the newly built Royal Festival Hall during the Festival of Britain in 1951. It is possible I am the only singer left who sang in the RFH before the platform was built; it was never intended that performers should climb steps up to a platform but walk straight on to a mosaic stone floor—excellent for sound, but you could not be seen by the audience! They went to a great deal of trouble over sound, but no-one had given any thought to sight lines. So I had to stand on a five-foot-high box (very unnerving) to sing my chosen songs with orchestra, Gerald's *Let Us Garlands Bring*—very new in those days.

A knock at my dressing-room door afterwards revealed a tall lady, two boys, and a gentleman who announced 'I am Gerald Finzi!' I had no idea that he even knew about the concert, let alone that he would be there with his family. He thanked me for my performance and asked me to come and sing the cycle with him conducting his Newbury String Players: this first meeting with Gerald began five marvellous years of music-making which only ended with his death.

It was a tremendous opportunity for me, because through rehearsing and performing under his direction a number of times I was able to understand exactly what he wanted, and can say that my recording of the cycle, with the Philharmonia Orchestra and Vernon Handley is a faithful recreation of his wishes.

I remember a piano rehearsal of the cycle with Gerald playing, and he suddenly stopped during the final page of 'Fear no more the heat o' the sun' (the section beginning 'No exorciser harm thee'), and he said 'Why did you sing it like that?' I was totally nonplussed and must have shown it for he went on; 'you sang it in strict time'. I replied that 'I would never dream of anything other than strict tempo unless there was an indication like "ad lib" or "a piacere".' He then said 'Ah, but if I wrote a direction like that you would probably do too much! Let the rhythm of the words dictate the rhythm of the vocal line; there are only sustained chords in the accompaniment.' It's interesting that Gerald felt he could trust a singer to do just enough to point the words without destroying the overall tempo and flow of the music.

Gerald was kind enough to work with me on all his then published songs, *Earth and Air and Rain* and *Before and After Summer*, and I felt very privileged to be asked to create, with Howard Ferguson—who was a tower of strength—the first performance of Gerald's posthumously published *I Said to Love* at his memorial concert. With no Gerald to guide me, I tried to remember all the things he had asked me to do in others of his songs.

The great strength of his vocal music is his extraordinary ability to allow the rhythm of the words to control the rhythm of the music, yet never to the detriment of a tuneful vocal line. This is why I so much enjoyed singing Gerald's songs, and was emboldened to ask him to write a baritone cycle equivalent to his wonderful *Dies natalis*. His reply, with a charming smile, was 'There is not enough time.' I thought he meant he was too busy, but he knew his life-time was limited, never giving any indication of this to anyone outside his immediate family.

Anna Shuttleworth

My first meeting with the Finzis came through an invitation by Amaryllis Fleming, a fellow cello student at the Royal College of Music, to play at the Newbury Festival of 1945 in Vaughan Williams's *Tallis Fantasia* with the Newbury String Players (I was about twenty years old). As we had rehearsals on the previous day, the Finzis arranged for all the visitors to stay the night, either in their house or with friends in the village at Ashmansworth. On this first visit, I slept in a small house down the lane, but had the chance to meet everyone. I especially remember Jean Stewart and Ralph and Ursula Vaughan Williams spending the evening with the Finzi family.

I felt at once that somehow I belonged there, musically, spiritually, artistically and intellectually—in every way. Their way of living was so 'rich', not with money, but with warmth and friendship based on similar ideals about music and life. I don't know that they felt this especially about me, but they seemed happy that I showed a genuine desire to come down whenever possible to play in the NSP concerts, and stay with them over many memorable Sundays.

Gerald somehow tapped my subconscious at a very deep level (perhaps through my Polish-Italian-Jewish great grandmother) and although he was a far from frightening figure, I often dreamt about him and admitted this to Joy and the boys, who teased me about it!

When I visited Ashmansworth, Gerald sometimes drove the car, which seemed to have control over him. I remember wildly perilous trips to the bus stop at the bottom of the hill, where he would always kindly wait until the bus came. In the early wartime days, there were some very snowy winters. I always remember the excitement of going up the hill without getting stuck, though Gerald hoped to be snowed in so that he would not have to go to his wartime job for a few days.

One Sunday, Gerald asked me to play the slow movement of his (as yet) uncompleted Cello Concerto, and asked my advice about bowing and some other details, as I had by now played many concertos with the NSP: Haydn, Leonardo Leo, Boccherini, and what Stephen Banfield called his 'eighteenth-century godchildren'; the Garth cello concertos (there were six altogether), and Stanley's concerti grossi.

Gerald's conducting was always with big sweeping movements, broad and generous, as was the violin playing of the leader, May Hope. To Gerald, most music was 'song', so that little articulation or rhythmic stress was demanded from the string players. The cellists were usually placed in a straight line along the back of the orchestra. In the churches we were some distance away from Gerald, so our visibility was often poor. The result was that the cellos were often accused of playing 'late'—but sometimes they were indulging in gossip. Some of the charm of these concerts was the magical settings, the meeting of old friends and the love of music generated by everyone involved.

Gerald was not always the most punctual of mortals. I can remember once sitting outside in the car with Joy, Kiffer, Nigel and all the NSP music and stands waiting for him. It was rather late, so Joy honked the car horn, and some time later Gerald arrived and said, 'Every time you hooted, I sat down and counted to ten!'

Joy was always looking after everyone in every way, whether encouraging people to collect mushrooms in the fields on the other side of the lane, telling one about a book or a work of art, or feeding one with delicious homemade food. How she ever found time for her own fine art I was not quite sure, because at the same time she was looking after two very energetic lively boys, running the house; defending Gerald so he could compose in peace in his room, and dealing with the bulk of practicalities of the organisation of the orchestra—telephoning, dealing with orchestral parts and so on.

Before one Enborne Church concert (a regular pre-Christmas event), I arrived with the most awful flu—I went to bed after the rehearsal with a magic pill, which Joy promised would make me perfectly well again, and so it did: with a whizzing head I played the concert at what seemed like 100 mph. We used to go for marvellous picnics on top of the Downs, where the boys dashed about setting light to the brushwood, and nobody seemed to mind. Some years later, Joy drew a portrait of my mother, which she gave to me.

I did not get down to Ashmansworth much during the summer of 1956, as I was so busy with many broadcasts and concerts (with chamber orchestras such as the Kalmar) and a Casals summer course, but I do remember one weekend visit. Gerald was trying to finish some of his Hardy songs with John Carol Case—I was only allowed to hear them through the floor—and Joy was trying to defend him from all interruptions. He seemed unwell, and when I asked Joy about it I got a hedging answer.

On 5 July, Gerald sent me an inscribed copy of the Cello Concerto, with a letter:

> My dear Anna
> This is a plaything for your idle moments! I remember you trying through a few fragments years ago and now that the fragments are all joined together I hope you'll like it.
>
> We had another lovely Bucklebury Concert on June 24th and wish you had been there. Now we're rehearsing new things, until the break up at the end of the month. Lots of concerts already mounting up for the next season.
>
> I hope all's flourishing. We all send our love
> Yours
> Gerald

He did not live to see the coming season, of course. Joy wrote shortly after he died to explain his illness and stress the importance NSP had for her husband:

> One of his anxieties in these last years was the future of Newbury String Players. He felt so strongly that this sort of music making should and could exist everywhere, and that Newbury String Players, with fifteen years of existence and experience, should continue, even under new influences and conditions.
>
> Christopher wants to try and conduct these next three concerts, and I think with his and your musicianship we could maintain our standard of musical vitality despite his technical immaturity.
>
> In this way, by continuing, we can best create a living memorial to the faith in the importance of Newbury String Players to the community.

In late August 1958, Joy rang me up to come and play some unaccompanied cello suites to Uncle Ralph Vaughan Williams at Ashmansworth—it was a beautiful day. Not long afterwards, a card came from Ursula:

> I am so glad that you played to us that Sunday, it was the last Bach Ralph heard, and like the rest of that golden week was such a last time as one would choose for all loved things.

Another parcel came on 28 October:

> I want you to have this—partly as a thank-you for playing Bach to Ralph

> that August Sunday—and because I think you may like to have something which belonged to him, also because I think I'd like to give you a present just now, with my love, because I have been thinking of you so much.

It was a blue pill box with white china birds on it. Inside, on a label on a cracked little mirror:

TRIFLES SHOW RESPECT

The NSP gave an 'In Memoriam' concert for Vaughan Williams. The programme included the *Tallis Fantasia* and an Adagio by Christopher Finzi, suggested by a phrase sung by Jesus in Bach's *St Matthew Passion*, 'Take, eat, this is my body'. I was sorry he did not continue to write music. Wilfred Brown also sang *Dies natalis*—it seemed a truly fitting tribute to two composers I had the wonderful honour to have known.

Mr. Gerald Finzi,

Ashmansworth,
Near Newbury, Berks.

Calling card, 1940s

III

A kind of fostering

Gerald Finzi and Robin Milford: two letters

Gerald Finzi first came to know composer Robin Milford (1903-1959) during the 1920s, but a deeper friendship developed in 1938, when they lived in close proximity to each other. Milford was the son of Sir Humphrey Milford, the head of Oxford University Press, initially coming to the public's attention with his oratorio A Prophet in the Land, *given at the Three Choirs Festival in 1931. Although he wrote many large-scale work, such as a Violin Concerto, his reputation rests on his many fine miniatures and works for amateur musicians. His best-known work is* Fishing for Moonlight *for piano and strings, first performed by Newbury String Players in April 1956. The following letters give an example of the encouragment that Milford found so important, which would also inspire Kenneth Leighton in his early career.*

The Way House, Hermitage, Newbury, Berks; 20 June 1938.

Dear Gerald,
An invitation[1] to you both is being sent from Miss Willis for Saturday. Please don't expect the musical part of the Ballet to be awfully good.

It is very nice of you to have rung up again & offered to come & see me.

[1] For a performance at Downe House School, where Milford was composition teacher.

I think, however, I may go off to my parents for a couple of days, but don't know. I never can tell beforehand now what I shall do, or seldom.

I am better; in fact I've done a little composing again, but I don't think it's going to be much good. You see I have conceived a distaste for my previous music, & I think it has been a long time growing on me. Sometimes I like a thing of mine, & then I play through something like your 'Ditty', & I realise that that is the kind of music I should like to have written, or the VW 'Love bade me welcome'. All, yes, I think all my stuff sounds meretricious, not first rate, artificial in some way or other, & often vulgar, or worse, commonplace. Also often slightly mawkish.

I like music to be clean & fresh, as yours is (what I know of it) or Sibelius or the earlier VW, or Bach or Mozart. I have a spiritual affinity with Tschaikovsky & I hate that.

Well, enough of this. The lesson to learn is SUBMIT, always, (as far as one is personally concerned) to everything. Only then can I achieve peace of mind, I believe; but then what is left? How can I teach, indeed what can I do? As my mother said, very pertinently to me recently when I said I felt I was no good as a composer, 'Well, you can't do anything else', & that is true.

And then I become a washout for my family too, which is worst of all.

However, I am better, & perhaps I shall achieve some sense of direction again by & by though I am very, very confused at present.

Now, for heaven's sake don't answer this! I know you think well of my work, & it gives me pleasure to know this, though curiously enough it gives me little confidence if my friends like my work. I feel they are biased. This is terribly ungrateful, & I think a little warped; but there it is. Anyhow it will save you feeling you have or ought to write to me!

Very glad you enjoyed Glyndebourne so much. We shall look forward to seeing you at Downe on Sat.

Now I'm going to continue correcting Vln. Conc. parts. Old habits die hard!

Yours ever, Robin Milford

Beech Knoll, Aldbourne, Wilts; June 22 1938

Dear Robin

I'm looking forward to Saturday v. much & only wish that Joy cd come too. However, she'll see something of the rehearsal on Thursday which I shall probably have to miss. Sat: will hardly be the time for a talk, so I'm going to write, as I'm certain that there are one or two things in your letter that need putting right.

Firstly, isn't it a mistake to think that only friends like your music, or rather that they like it just because they are your friends? In my own case, I knew your work from the days of 'The Moor'[2] & the double fugue[3] long before I knew you, or anything about you, and I don't think you have any idea of the number of people who know & love your work. Even in the case of VW, you're no great personal friend, & he has had scores of pupils before & since your time, but I don't think there are many about whom he feels so positively.

Of course, this doesn't mean that everything you write is sacrosanct! Like everyone else, you've got your dull pages, movements & works. (Are there more than a dozen works out of Mozart's 600, or the masses of Schubert, that are really worth dying for?) But it's work which 'stands for something' & for which no apology is needed. Aren't you rather inclined to think that because you cant do what Sibelius can do, or what Walton or VW, or anyone else whose work you may admire, can do, the fault lies with you? Surely it's the other way round & it's precisely because you can't do what they can do that you are yourself. Or to put it more concisely there's no shape without limitation & it's your limitations which make you RM (if you want to see your antithesis look at Bax, who has no limitations of any sort &, as a result, has no qualities either.)

Another thing that I can't make head or tail of is your idea of a spiritual affinity with Tschaikovsky. Some of that element is in all of us (to some extent) yet, honestly, I can't think of anybody's music in whom such a strain is less obvious than in yours! The bane of introspection comes far more naturally to me than to you at least, so I shd have thought judging from my music & then looking at yours. So whilst you're thinking of Sibelius, early VW & so on, you might remember that others are thinking of a care free, delight full art that is yours & not, alas, theirs! You don't think, by any chance, that this loss of direction is due to your trying to accrete something that really doesn't belong to your nature? I don't mean that one has to endlessly go round in a circle chasing one's tail, but there's no doubt that certain grafts take on certain stocks & others don't. However, there wd be a lot to say about this & you'd best be reading Wordsworth, Hardy or Keats rather than an overlong letter!

[2] A Ralph Hodgson setting published in 1925.
[3] For orchestra, 1926.

Anyhow, it's just a thought thrown out, probably without any foundation & forgive all this. In this case there really is no need to answer, but your

letter stimulated argument & as it may be some time before we meet I thought I'd get if off my chest.

Yours ever, Gerald Finzi

I'd like you to accept these songs [*Earth and Air and Rain*], as I think you'll like some of them, & with others you'll see that introspection is much more a fault with me than with you. Of course don't acknowledge them, but rather forgive me for sending them.

Gerald Finzi as a tutor of composition

Anthony Scott

'Hello! Is that you, Tony? How are you, and how's the work going?—and how's Ruth?' This was the almost invariable greeting to me from Gerald Finzi from since our first meeting in 1937, up until 1939–40, and even during the war when we had to go our separate ways—and also from Joy, in the same words. This welcoming recognition of my existence—in fact, of my purpose in life to be a composer from a man whom I so much admired—sustained me through many years of depression following the return of scores with the rejection slips. Even after Gerald's death, Joy continued with much the same greeting to maintain my confidence and impulse to write and used her influence to secure performances of works she had asked me to write.

I am writing about my experiences under Gerald Finzi's tutelage because, as far as I know, I was his only private pupil, although I believe he deputised at the Royal Academy of Music for a term to teach Howard Ferguson's pupils. He deprecated the description of what occurred as a 'teacher-pupil relationship', and said 'these sessions are to be as one composer to another: I look at the music you show me, and I put in a stick here, suggest a path there, just to guide you, a handrail to steady you'. He would not accept any fees for the many hours he devoted to helping me, and it was indeed help, not only in my music but also with my personal problems and those of my family.

I must first explain how this musical friendship came about. My wife

Ruth and I, in our twenties, rented a small farmhouse near Newbury, between Thatcham and Bucklebury Common. This was a few years before the Second World War. I had finished studying with Herbert Howells and Henry Ley (organ) at the RCM, and we left London for the country where I intended to devote myself to composing.

In 1937 George Weldon, later to become associate conductor of the Birmingham Orchestra, was conductor of the Newbury Amateur Orchestral Union whose lively musical activities owed much to the timpanist, Peter Davies and to Mrs Neate, one of the violinists, whose son Joe later married Mags, Joy's sister.

It became known to the orchestra that there were several composers living in the Newbury area, and the Committee decided to put on a concert entirely of the music of 'Local Composers'. The concert began with Robin Milford's fine overture, *Sir Walter Raleigh*. Amongst other composers' works were Gerald Finzi's *Earth and Air and Rain*—my very first experience of his music, and my *Fantasia for Strings*. At this time I was hopelessly in love with the music of Frederick Delius, and the piece was written in an idiom strongly influenced by his music, but with his chords stretched to a tauter and more acerbic idiom. At the rehearsal, a female music teacher took exception to the Fantasia because it, apparently, broke the laws of harmony and counterpoint. Among the violins I noted a tall, attractive and rather heron-like figure: Joy, who joined issue on my side against the music teacher.

We three composers exchanged compliments after the concert, and arranged to meet later on. Gerald, perhaps out of kindness, expressed a wish to see the score of my *Fantasia*, and suggested that I bring more scores for him to see at Aldbourne. This was rather awkward for me as I had not written much at that time, but I found a set of songs, piano pieces and fragments of a new work. Eventually, I had to confess that I was facing an impasse, that, at least for a time, I was musically constipated.

He must have thought I was worth an attempt at resuscitation, for he invited me to come to his house at Aldbourne once a week, refusing to take a penny for it, on condition that I brought some music with me. These weekly meetings with Gerald were tremendously exciting and challenging to me. I gave full rein to my gift of hero-worship and submitted meekly to and accepted, uncritically perhaps, his personal theories and sometimes eccentric opinions. For our sessions were not only musical, but branched out into philosophical and topical—generally moral—problems. I had glimpsed a world of cultivated but free and happy discourse from my reading, especially of de Quincey and his Lake poets, of Samuel Butler and, later, Virginia Woolf and Edith Sitwell. Several books by composers appealed strongly to me at that time, for instance Debussy's piquant essays *Monsieur Croche*, van Dieren's *Down Among the Dead Men* and Constant Lambert's *Music Ho!*. And now, incredibly, I seemed admitted to this Arcadian way of life which Ruth and I were able to share with the Finzis in their lovely house. The latter was an attractive Georgian building, with stables and a coach house now converted to a badminton court, a most important item for me, as I shall explain later. The large garden had a great copper beech giving the house its name, Beech Knoll, and a fruit cage which was a permanent structure of gas piping to hold the nets, and a track from just across the lane giving a pleasant walk across the downs to some barrows or tumuli. Joy suffered from asthma, severely at this time before efficacious drugs were invented, and I realized the attacks at night were a trial for both of them. Before going out I would hear Gerald say: 'Now, Petsy, have you remembered your puffer?'

In those days the Finzis could afford a cook-general, Violet, who under Joy's guidance cooked delicious and, to me, unusual dishes such as vineleaf fritters. During the war, when Joy and Gerald were established at Ashmansworth, Ruth moved to a cottage in the village. Our four boys were frequently together: Richard and Michael were invited to join Christopher and Nigel's club. Gerald and Joy had an antipathy to façades or anything that seemed a sham in architecture or furniture to disguise its real function, and also in art and music, any kind of applied or superficial decoration would be anathema. As in music, so their personal and social relationships could be nothing less than open and truthful, though not hurtful, friendships. The organist of Gloucester cathedral, 'John' Sumsion, a friend of the Finzis to whom I was introduced, liked to divide people according to their positive and passive personalities, and called them respectively 'dynamos' or 'waitamos'. Gerald was very much a 'dynamo' and Joy, though not perhaps a 'waitamo', had a more reflective and less emphatic stance in discussion, and her pleasure and amusement at somebody's foibles prevented her from seeing people or their behaviour in black and white stereotypes.

At Aldbourne there were two grand pianos in a large sitting room, and should I fail to bring any new music, Gerald would order Joy to keep guard over me—if not actually lock me in. Then, with the help of one of the pianos, I generally succeeded in getting several bars of music down on paper, aiming, to please my tutor, to introduce a linear character to the music. Joy would give strict orders for us to break off our studies at around noon and then repair to the badminton court, which I think was made in the old stables, and have a foursome if there was a guest to be roped in, or singles. Then to lunch.

It was about this time that Gerald was composing 'Come away, come away, death', later to be the first of *Let Us Garlands Bring*. The poignant beauty of this song with its sinuous melismata was quite piercing and revealing to me, and a precursor of his music to come. Gerald soon realised that I had lost musical freedom and was bogged down in composing harmonic progressions. What I needed, he saw, was to introduce lines through these harmonies like steel wires through concrete.

He found an original and clever solution to my problem. He gave me a series of the two-part Bach inventions for clavier and set me an exercise which consisted of adding a third part to each invention. I liked doing these exercises, and I found that the effect was startling; I began to think in lines and threaded them though the harmonic progressions which appealed to me. This was a very different approach indeed to the arid exercises in sterile 'paper work'; so-called harmony and counterpoint. My efforts with the three-part inventions would be rewarded with a visit to the fruit cage, where we would gorge on black and white currants, gooseberries or raspberries, whichever was ripe. Other important periodical events were visits by composers, either singly, or two or three together, in order to play and study each other's works. These times were very interesting and educational to me. The best evenings were when Edmund Rubbra brought a new symphony. He performed it very well on the piano, but sang an inner part, perhaps the viola, in a moaning kind of voice suggesting an ancient reed instrument—a crumhorn or chalumeau.

Frequently Gerald would break off from the piece of mine he was discussing to talk about music he had been listening to or perhaps was sparked off by a passage in my manuscript which recalled some contemporary composer he had in mind. It seemed to me that after the early fifteenth and sixteenth century, and later more classical composers, his heart lay with Elgar and Vaughan Williams. He loathed Wagner, and Richard Strauss even more. He said that, whereas Debussy in revision attempted to remove all superfluous notes, Strauss tried to add as many as possible. He listened to Berg and the Schoenbergian School, most especially Berg's operas and Violin Concerto. Of Walton's music he especially admired the Viola Concerto and the First Symphony: he said that Walton was the Isaac Newton of music. Indeed the sustaining of those splendid arches of sound in the symphony's first movement, with such logical intensity, certainly merits the comparison. I shared his admiration of the Viola Concerto, but also agreed that the subtleties and over-sophisticated scoring of the Violin Concerto seemed an anguished attempt to recapture the unforced ecstasy of the former work.

Another composer I remember he often talked of was Ernest Bloch whose work he admired; he was almost guiltily distressed that Bloch had to spend many of his composing hours chopping firewood and other chores. It was the same in his relationship with Edmund Blunden, the poet: he considered that artists should be protected by a state pension in the dearth of private patronage. Lennox Berkeley sometimes visited the Finzis when they had moved to Ashmansworth, their relationship being one of mutual respect rather than affection. He used to qualify Herbert Howells as a sad case of a composer whose early promise, as shown in his brilliant chamber music and lovely settings of French chansons, was not fulfilled, with the exception of *Hymnus Paradisi*—which brings me back to my own musical blockages. He sometimes spoke about poets—and a few musicians—who had a wonderful flowering of poetry in adolescence, but with the onset of maturity their outpourings dried up. Eventually I realised that he was kindly trying to persuade me, with such subtlety, to face the fact of sterility. However, we persevered and I was able to repay him, in small part, by ferrying many loads of hand-made bricks from the Hermitage Hand Made Brick and Tile Works up to the site of his new house at Ashmansworth. My wife and I also crammed our little car with books for his new library, the book room. This was under his music room to give him extra privacy.

In this little account of my tutelage under Gerald Finzi, I make no apology for discursiveness because one could not learn music from him without learning a great deal about life. Music was at the centre, and all activities radiated from this and, returning, enriched the music.

But to return to my musical problems: Gerald honoured me by writing a lovely theme for me to write a fugue upon. To my surprise I found that I could write a fugue. Gerald I am sure, was delighted and pleased with his pupil, especially when it had become a Prelude and Fugue for organ and vindicated his unconventional method of teaching. OUP accepted it for publication, but persuaded me to insert a new section in the fugue to balance the larger prelude. Gerald never quite accepted the insertion as he felt that it did not fit the tranquil mood of the original.

My tutelage did not end here. Our two families shared holidays, twice before the war, and sometimes after, at a windmill on the North Norfolk coast at Burnham Overy Staithe, where a creek from the villages of North and South Creake flowed into the sea. It had been converted into a liveable dwelling (though with no electricity or mains water, but with an old well and hand pump, an outside loo, and oil lamps) by Hugh Hughes, a Cambridge architect, and his wife Mary, Ruth's cousin. In the upper sitting room, Hugh had attached a sloping wooden desk for him to draw on at standing height against the wall. Here Gerald would place his manuscript and work, sometimes on his editions of Stanley and other contemporaries of Handel—such as Arne and Boyce—whom he thought were unfairly overshadowed by him.

The children shared a big room near the top of the windmill; and the lower floors, being divided, housed the couples or single people, such as Ruth's cousin Cicely, or Sissy, who was sweet but eccentric. The floors being connected by trapdoors, our moments of intimacy were apt to be interrupted by a head popping up through one of these doors on the way to its room.

Joy would find a pair of scissors and several baskets and we would all troop off to the salt marshes to cut samphire (the poor man's sparrow-grass) for our supper, perhaps with shrimps. I remember one shrimping expedition in particular. Gerald and I had stayed behind to mend the musical box, and walking up the creek to meet them, saw to our alarm that the tide was coming in fast. At last we saw them advancing, the tide at thigh height, hitching up their skirts; Sissy with her voluminous petticoats and 'bockers, and Joy more heron-like than ever.

I think Joy kept a child's sense of innocence and wonder all her life. Nothing in nature or human nature became stale to her but had its element of surprise. It went with her amusement at the comic side: the men with beer-bellies ('how many pints does it take?'), at the quaint remarks of WI stall holders and the rasping jargon of auctioneers. Reading an account in the local paper of a farmer convicted of bestiality with one of his cows, Joy, her eyes round with innocent wonder, exclaimed: 'But my dear! However did he manage? Oh, of course, the milking stool.'

At the windmill, we all came under Gerald's life-enhancing spell—it was impossible to become tired or bored by him. All the children gathered round him to hear his stories about an eccentric but loveable colonel in India who lived in Poona. I also remember his solicitude and practical care of any of us who were not well. After the war, I continued to bring all my compositions to him for his advice and so that he would know that his tutelage had borne fruit.

Memories of Gerald Finzi

Kenneth Leighton

During my time as an Oxford student (1947-51) under the wise and generous guidance of my tutor, Bernard Rose, there were many musical highlights, and some of these remain in my mind as deep and vivid experiences. In spite of extensive classical studies during my first two years at Oxford, I was steeped in music, and particularly English music. Edmund Rubbra was there and came along specially to hear me play a new piano sonata. Then there was a chance to hear Vaughan Williams's new symphony (No. 6) in the Sheldonian. But perhaps the most 'intimate' discovery I made was in playing through the songs of Gerald Finzi, often in the company of fellow students and even with croaky attempts to sing them myself. I loved them all and I particularly recall the deep impression made on me by 'Channel firing'. This song opened up for me a new dimension in Finzi's musical thought. I never had any difficulty in responding to the pure lyricism which imbued not only the vocal line, but top, bottom and middle of the accompaniment too. It was the pathos, I think, and the compassion which spoke to me more intimately than the work of any of the other English composers of the time. And there was also the wonder and the ecstasy of *Dies natalis* which has always been a peak for me. Much later I conducted performances of both this and the Cello Concerto in Edinburgh.

To be introduced, in 1949, to Finzi in the flesh was therefore a thrilling event. It happened through Bernard Rose, who asked Finzi to look at the score of my Symphony for Strings, which I composed in the winter of 1948-49 while I was still reading Classics. I was really quite astonished when the next thing was an invitation to attend a rehearsal of this work by the Newbury String Players under Finzi, and I remember that bright sunny afternoon and the warmth of the string tone as if it were yesterday. It was certainly one of the most thrilling events of my musical career, to hear an orchestral work of mine played by such good musicians, and rehearsed with such care and understanding. Gerald was immensely kind and enthusiastic; he took me aside to explain how certain little passages could be scored in a 'slightly safer manner', and he also expressed a sense of disappointment that the tension of the music should be so quickly defused at the passionate climax of the slow movement. Such was his insight that he had immediately touched on points of self-doubt deep in my own subconscious.

From that time forward until his death, I knew that I had in Gerald a most wise and firm source of encouragement. My next major work, *Veris gratia*, was composed especially for him and the Newbury Players and contains, I think, in its final movement, a clear though unconscious tribute to his melodic style. I remember the first performance (with Anna Shuttleworth and Tony Danby) vividly, and it was clear that Gerald loved the piece: it was later dedicated to his memory. He performed it with Jacqueline du Pré as an amazingly powerful cello soloist, and brought Vaughan Williams along to hear it in London with the Kalmar Orchestra. After that, Gerald and sometimes Vaughan Williams came to listen to almost all my London performances, including my more 'advanced' Violin Sonata. As a result of my year in Italy with Petrassi, the style of my music had changed considerably, but Gerald's interest and enthusiasm burned as brightly as ever, and his letters were always packed with sound advice and a deep understanding of the real problems which face a young composer. The main thing for him was to search always after one's true self and to avoid taking too much notice of the current fashion or 'ism'. When deeply cast down by the harsh words of a review, he first taught me to recognise the completely shallow and ephemeral nature of newspaper criticism. As for his belief in the search for self, I hope that I have shared this all my life.

In the years that have passed, I have come to appreciate even more the beauty of Gerald's music, particularly in the larger works like the Cello Concerto. As a man, he was for me the symbol of all that is best in English music, and it is a privilege to have known him and to have witnessed so intimately his complete truthfulness and glowing artistic integrity.

Gerald Finzi's letters to Kenneth Leighton

This series of letters represents the complete remaining letters from Gerald Finzi to Kenneth Leighton, then in his early twenties. Sadly, the Leighton half of the correspondence does not appear to have survived.

Ashmansworth, nr Newbury, Berks; 8 January [1954]

Dear Kenneth
The Oboe Concerto is safely here and I've had a quick run-through. There doesn't seem to be anything which the strings can't tackle, though

it's a bit more difficult than the earlier works from the point of view of intonation and the idiom is perhaps a bit harder for the sort of audience we get. However, that doesn't matter. It might be a good idea to have the string parts duplicated now and let them have a set, so that I could begin to get the players used to the work, even though it's so far ahead.

If you haven't another suggestion I'll write to James Brown and see if he'll be back from Holland by April 27th. Someone told me that Tony Danby had improved enormously, and so I wouldn't mind asking him if you preferred it. But Brown is first rate.

We could leave the final decision as to whether to do the Harp/Viola work, or this one, until later and I should certainly like to see it when you get the score back from Harvey Phillips.

By the way, we should be quite safe for cellos as we always have a minimum of 4. Christopher, who is now at the RAM under Douglas Cameron, gets down for all the rehearsals and concerts and is a real asset now.

I imagine that Parkside Road is . . .

[The rest of this letter is missing.]

Ashmansworth, nr Newbury, Berks; 8 March [1954]

Dear Kenneth
Yes, our letters crossed and we were very delighted to hear about the arrival of Angela. We send our especial greetings to her and our congratulations to you and Lydia. For all the disturbances and the new commitments I still think that a new life is the most perfect and most hopeful thing we ever experience, and our own experiences in having brought up our two boys are something we would not have missed for anything.

Yes, I should much like to see the Harp/Viola work. It might possibly do for Enbourne in Dec or Stockross next year, and a look at it will give me an idea as to whether the strings can handle it. This schism between "amateur" and "professional" music making is a real problem. It would be a dreadful thing if music had to be limited to what amateurs can play! On the other hand I can't feel that lofty 12 tone theorists, whose music is too rare to be played, are really doing much good. Personally I think that great work can be created out of any language—whether 1/2 tone, 12 tone, or plain diatonic, given the right men to use it, and that men are not great or small by virtue of their language, not according to their stature.

Yet there does come a technical limit beyond which the amateur can't go. I don't think I could ever get them to overcome the Bartok Divertimento, for instance, and that's straightforward enough, and a splendid work.

That limitation is always a worry with an amateur body.

Our greetings, Yours, Gerald

Ashmansworth, nr Newbury, Berks; 3 August 1954

Dear Kenneth
Your delightful card arrived by the same post as your letter and I'm glad to think of you having a good holiday in Italy. I hope to get to the Prom to hear your Concerto, though I'm not yet sure. But I want to: I heard the last broadcast under very peculiar conditions—on Iona, where the 3rd programme is not meant to reach! But what came through seemed lovely.

I only hope that the BBC won't ask for the material of the Oboe Concerto before Sept. 25th. The position is this. We had our last concert of the season last Sunday week and then closed down until Sept. 25th. I asked everybody to hand in all the music, except yours! We have been working on it for half an hour or so nearly every week and have broken the back (oh, those colloquial expressions: I wonder how you will explain that to Lydia!) of the 1st and 2nd movements. Jack Kirby has been playing oboe on the fiddle and I don't think there's the least doubt that we shall be able to do it, given the right occasion.

But I wanted the players to keep it going during the holidays, so that they shouldn't be too rusty when we start again, and now that they are all scattered it would be difficult to get in the parts. It's the 1st violins that I'm short of. I have here Bass, 2 Vcl, 2 Vla, and 2 seconds 1 first. If the BBC asks for the material later on, then, of course, I can easily let them have it.

I don't know why they should want to put it into an "experimental" rehearsal. Can't they tell it's a good work without that!

Yes, thanks. John Russell's concert came off well. It was a remarkable piece of courage and generosity on his part and I was delighted on his account that he got such a full hall and warm-hearted audience—and, above all, fine performances. Press rather superior, but that doesn't worry me!

You are lucky to have escaped this dismal wet weather. Day after day has been depressing and sullen and only now do we seem to have signs of a break.

Greetings and I hope, perhaps, a meeting at the Proms.
Yours ever, Gerald

Ashmansworth, nr Newbury, Berks; 13 December 1954

Dear Kenneth
I was glad to have the 'Christmas Carol'. Actually I had already seen it and given my copy to the conductor of a local choral group, in the hope that we could one day do it with our strings. So it's good to have another copy for myself.

I don't think there are any comments I could make on the choral writing. The whole thing comes very naturally to you. Choirs would like singing it, because—quite apart from the actual content—everything is so happily "placed".

No doubt theory-ridden creatures will tell you that it ought to be 12 tone, or that you mightn't to use melisma or that there's not enough 14th century style about it etc, etc. But your capacity for writing rather as the birds (about which you are writing) sing, is worth all the theories put together.

We had Fred Grinke staying here and it was nice to have news of you through him. Thanks, too, for making such a good job of that violin piece. Overlong, I agree, but it might not be so if used as the centrepiece of a larger work, as originally intended. I must put it aside and think it over.

I hope Lydia is not overwhelmed by this beastly weather, probably even worse in Leeds than here. Our warm greetings to you both.
Yours, Gerald

Ashmansworth, nr Newbury, Berks; 29 September 1955

Dear Kenneth
I was waiting for your return from Italy before writing. The question of a teacher in Italy is a bit of a difficulty. The grant of £100 for a three month sojourn abroad, for the purpose of study, might have been alright 40 years ago! Unfortunately, scholarships and grants don't rise with the cost of living. The young composer in question has managed to get another £50 out of some old lady, but, even so, it doesn't seem possible. He can stay at the British School in Rome, which will be a great saving, but my feeling is that what he really needs at his present stage is a strong dose of straightforward counterpoint, such as could be given to him by any competent teacher over here. With costs so high, lessons relatively expensive (not

that they aren't worth it) and the language difficulty, I'm inclined to think that he'd do best to do academic work over here, and use the £150 on a 'holiday' abroad, with the chance of hearing new 'facets' of music in Italy.

I was with the Rubbras yesterday—ER has many Italian connections through his wife—and showed him your letter. The boy lives in Oxford and is going to try and get some temporary lessons from ER and talk the matter over with him.

I've posted off the Oboe Concerto to Wilkinson and do hope something happens about it. I mentioned the Oboe and Cello work, too, to Evelyn Rothwell.

The Oboe Concerto looks like being a bit too tough for amateurs to tackle. We've brought it out several times and had a go at it, and even had an oboist down, but I think it's just beyond them. If I had a picked body there would be no difficulty; and it's lovely for the soloist.

Greetings to you both, Yours ever, Gerald

Ashmansworth, nr Newbury, Berks; 29 August 1956

Dear Kenneth
The main difference between 'N' and 'M' is that in the former, because you have to place the tongue on the roof of the mouth, you get a slightly more pinched tone. It's also more tiring for high notes and long stretches. You can do it with either open or closed lips, though I don't think that makes very much difference to the actual volume. With 'M' you have to have closed lips and it's more relaxed. ('Ah' is the same as 'M', except that you have to have open lips and you can get more volume.) If you keep your direction of 'half closed lips' it's no good saying 'M'. I think a more closed vowel like 'E' would be a mistake, too penetrating, rather like the oboe tone. I should stick to 'N' with half closed lips, or if you want something quieter, "Bouche Fermé" (M).

I like the Carol very much. The very sort of thing we want for Enbourne, by the way, and there's just enough (and not too much) humming. Round about the 20s there was a spate of that sort of thing. Granville Bantock and others used it for huge stretches in long choral works, and tried to get variations of colour by means of N. M. Ah. E. OO. O. etc etc and at the end one felt wearied beyond words and never wanted to hear another 'hum'! But V.W. in 'Ca' the Yowes' and Holst, too, sometimes did it beautifully and in short stretches, as in your carol, it can be lovely.

I meant to write to you long ago, after reading that nauseating and quite untrue criticism of your Cello Concerto by Colin Mason. These little miseries, who spend their time putting a microscope to 3 bars of Schönberg and imagining that they are getting inside music, are something of a menace. They try to narrow the language of music down to one particular idiom. I take it that the experience of art implies a widening of understanding and there's no reason why we shouldn't appreciate Schönberg or Walton, or Rubbra, V.W., Elgar, you, or anyone else whose mind is worth knowing.

The real danger is when younger people come along and write in a language not necessarily natural to themselves, because they can't get a hearing if they don't, or they get jeered at by pip-squeaks like Colin Mason if they are spontaneous.

Well, the main point is that a reasonably intelligent audience appreciated your Concerto immensely. And as for the 'dead language', since 95% of the musical world still uses it and still understands it, it looks as if it's still alive enough!

Greetings to you both, Yours, Gerald

A composer's view: second thoughts

Jeremy Dale Roberts

Although he has sometimes been perceived as a composer who rather preferred to keep to himself—he certainly had a mistrust of what we would now call the 'scene'—Gerald Finzi was actually well in step, if not in sympathy, with the times he lived in: informed, curious, and trenchant in his opinions—(The 'Walking Manchester Guardian').

He was also genuinely interested in the music of other composers. Not all composers are: for instance, Delius, who in his declining years, as Eric Fenby reports, had constantly to be drip-fed 'Delius'. Gerald, on the other hand, would take endless pains when he could to encourage others, both practically—through performance with the Newbury Strings, say—as well as morally. (This, in notorious contrast with the mean-spirited attitude of Benjamin Britten). I am one of the many beneficiaries of his goodwill—and at this late stage in my life I am in a position to recognize and cherish the seam running through. But I should make clear that my connection with him as a young composer—I was only sixteen in 1950 when I first came across the Finzis—was very slender: I had scarcely begun, and his time was running short.

I don't think I ever had the occasion to formally show my efforts to him, in a 'one-to-one situation'. As far as I can remember, I used to bash stuff through on the piano in the sitting room—with the rest of the family hanging about—and he would make the odd comment. I never got to enjoy the sustained regime which Tony Scott has described so vividly; and I was nowhere near so accomplished and productive as the young Kenneth Leighton. In his memoir you will discover Finzi's 'method'—he, who had such mistrust and loathing for academe: as he said to Tony, 'These sessions are to be as one composer to another: I look at the music you show me and I put in a stick here, suggest a path there, just to guide you, a handrail to steady you'. And I realize, after a lifetime working with other composers—first at Morley College, and then for many years at the Royal College of Music—that these have been my precepts, always.

I don't need to point out that coming across Gerald Finzi as I did, carried with it the 'whole package': I mean the family, Joy and Kiffer and Nigel; also Ashmansworth; and a whole radiating tissue of connections and coincidences. I have written elsewhere of the impact that first encounter had upon me. Tony also in his memoir speaks of the 'Arcadian way of life' he found there; and from a perspective of fifty years it has acquired a kind of nimbus, warm and hazy—not unlike Samuel Palmer's Shoreham Valley. But that was only disclosed to me somewhat later. I first encountered the Finzis in the hurly-burly of a rather rackety summer school at Cowley Manor near Cheltenham, now a 5 star de luxe hotel, boasting Elizabeth Hurley as one of its regulars. I am a West Country man, and my godmother, Diana Oldridge—a remarkable woman who had run the Stinchcombe Festival before the war, emulating Vaughan Williams's Leith Hill Festival, and who knew everybody - Holst, VW, Howells, Robin Milford, as well as Finzi—had urged me to go along, hoping that it might help to prise me from my shell. I came from a rather conventional background; and although I was encouraged by my family I had no musical companions; and as a pianist (quite promising) who dabbled in composing (couldn't stop, really) I needed to stretch myself a bit. They were all there: Kiffer and Nigel, 'Shush' (Richard Shirley Smith), and the Scotts, Caroline and Johnny—it sounds like Enid Blyton, but it was actually more like *Lord of the Flies*. Total anarchy in the dorm.

At the end of the two weeks or so, Joy and Gerald made an appearance, to retrieve their children: it was the run-up to the Three Choirs Festival at Gloucester—that annus mirabilis which saw the premieres of Howells's *Hymnus Paradisi* as well as Gerald's *Intimations*. It was my first glimpse of them, and I remember being somewhat overawed when I was introduced—Joy so tall, and kind of vague and bemused by all the turmoil, and Gerald an energetic bundle beside her—the first COMPOSER I'd ever seen.

That summer in Gloucester—forever milling about the Close with my new friends; the excitement of attending rehearsals; all this whole new world of music spread out before me; and at night, the floodlit cathedral sending its mysterious shadow into the sky like the northern lights; the little parties Alice Sumsion used to arrange after the concerts—remains one of the most potent memories of my life: the moment when I finally grasped the key to wherever it was I was destined to go.

And the people! Many of the gentlemen still wore morning dress, and the ladies rigged out in hats and gowns. 'There's Mrs Elgar Blake!', someone would say, as a rather nondescript woman passed; and the jostling parade of some of the great names in the 'English Renaissance': Ivor Atkins and Sir Percy Hull, with their Three Choirs connection; Boris Ord of Kings. And of course RVW, the presiding spirit of the place, who was down to conduct the *Pastoral Symphony*. Hurrying round a corner with my godmother to catch the morning rehearsal of *Intimations*, we bumped smack into Herbert Howells—a dapper little man, carrying a huge music-case (the full score of *Hymnus*), also scurrying somewhere, like the dormouse in *Alice in Wonderland*: my first introduction to someone who would later provide my entrée into the Royal College.

Like all Three Choirs Festivals, musically it was a fairly gluttonous occasion: but for a boy of sixteen who had never attended an orchestral concert in his life, it was quite simply intoxicating: and the fumes of that intoxication still hang around. It would be fair to say that on their first appearance *Intimations* was rather upstaged by *Hymnus Paradisi*: the more sober message and colouring of Finzi's work overshadowed by the blazing luminosity and fervour of the Howells. I was also more seduced by the latter; but in a way, that was not surprising: from childhood my musical taste had been orientated towards French music—Debussy, and especially Ravel; and what Frank Howes called the 'contrapuntal impressionism' of *Hymnus Paradisi* I found irresistibly appealing—quite apart from its searing incandescence.

This is fairly blatantly exposed in a little motet in eight parts I composed in 1953. It is a setting of the Funeral Sentences: 'I heard a voice from heaven saying unto me: Write, from henceforth blessed are the dead which die in the Lord. Even so saith the spirit: for they rest from their labours'. Howells included a setting of this text in *Hymnus*; mine was written as a kind of appendage to an a capella setting of the requiem mass: it was the best bit, and I threw out the rest.

I said that my musical taste had tended towards French music: a result of having had a wonderful piano teacher who sniffed out my attraction to that kind of thing, and my disdain for 'Minuets in G'. This is not to deny that English music had ever meant anything to me: I had performed the John Ireland Piano Concerto in my last year at school; and I will never forget the experience (in 1946) of listening to the first broadcast performance of Vaughan Williams Sixth Symphony on a tiny radio, sitting in the half light on the side of the bed, in a Betjemanesque seaside boarding house at Ilfracombe. But it is true to say that meeting the Finzis, and all those successive Three Choirs Festivals—not to say the pressure of my godmother—did bring about an adjustment, if not an indoctrination, which affected my thinking about music for a long while.

Fast-forward to 1952, when I was offered a place at the Royal Academy of Music to study composition. Another indelible memory: on my very first day, walking from Baker Street Underground, past Madame Tussaud's, along Marylebone Road, running straight into Kiffer, lugging his cello—I don't think either of us had been aware that we'd land up at the same dump. The relief of finding a familiar face!

In those days, in many ways, the Academy *was* a bit of a dump: it prescribed an extremely conventional, parochial, musical education. The aural training was a joke, and the history too; and quite soon Kiffer and I, bored out of our minds by Maurice Cole's atomisation of Berlioz's *Symphonie Fantastique*, decided to skive off. And maybe our truancy provided some of the most irreplaceable items in our growing up: we careered around the town, running after buses, trying to squash as many things into the day as possible—the art galleries of Bond Street, first sightings of Francis Bacon and Graham Sutherland; endless matinée showings in the Academy Cinema—(I can't remember how many times we went to *Monsieur Hulot's Holiday*). And—as far as I was concerned—the alarming novelty of nut rissoles, when Kiffer dragged me to Showen's vegetarian restaurant in Tottenham Court Road.

Quite soon, Kiffer suggested that I should come down to Ashmansworth for the weekend. And so it began. And I came, as a visitor, gradually to know them all: Mags, Joy's sister; the helpers, Olive and Jack; Liddy, one of the refugees from the war years; all the Scotts, the family of Tom Scott, their doctor. And although these may seem peripheral names, they are woven inextricably into the texture of Ashmansworth. I'd like to claim—like Shush, who also came from a 'professional' background—

both our fathers were doctors—and certainly caring and supportive families—that we found in the Finzis a kind of fostering, and an ambiance, that we were incredibly fortunate to have been drawn into. And for me, just at the right time. Joy, especially—who had, I think, the most perfect taste I have ever encountered—was 'on a mission', as we would say today: to make good what she saw, or felt, was deficient; to provide and enable; to steer in what she felt was the right direction. And I was perfect material: slightly wet, a bit of a dreamer, public school. I think they all felt I needed to be taken in hand! And so, the Aran sweaters: everyone was wearing Aran sweaters; the slightly prickly Harris tweeds, the colour of manure, that my mother was prevailed upon to order for me; the disgusting protocol of NOT using soap, 'in order to preserve the natural oils of the body'; and the even more disgusting routine of washing ones hair in olive oil.

But much more important than my obvious infatuation with what appeared to me a wonderfully alternative 'lifestyle', was the steadiness of purpose that was instilled into me, by the simple assumption, unspoken but clear, that I was a musician, a composer, and that I did not need to explain myself.

I used to bring down my efforts, and play them through. The first solid work I produced was a song-cycle to words by Denton Welch, which made a wee bit of a stir when it was performed by Norman Tattersall at the SPNM in London. Quite co-incidentally, I had been attracted to this writer some time before I came to meet Howard Ferguson, who had also used his words in his *Discovery* set. When I, rather gushingly, enthused about the poetry (and even more the Journals), Gerald said 'the product of a diseased mind'—which rather put a damper on things. I think I was aware from the start that the grain of our thinking, and our respective characters, would not always match. He definitely 'had a thing' about French music: although he had a lot of respect for Ravel (whom on the other hand, in one of his letters to Howard, he calls 'a brave little composer' (sic), and real love for Fauré, he had little time for Debussy, whom at that time I venerated above all. When, a couple of years later, I came back from my national service with a big song-cycle, on words by Verlaine, de Banville and de Musset, he said 'Why on earth do you want to be setting all that French stuff when you've got all this great English poetry about you?' Notwithstanding, he was immensely helpful in recruiting for its performance Sophie Wyss—Britten's muse, before Peter Pears came on the scene—who had performed several times with the Newbury String Players. He obviously felt that there was something slightly toxic in the French strain: when I returned to resume study at the RAM, he became very troubled at the prospect of my going to study with Lennox Berkeley (a Nadia Boulanger pupil): almost as though I need to be protected from the pernicious strain. He suggested instead Alan Bush—which would have been death: a sort of grey communist composer. Why he didn't suggest Howard Ferguson is odd; but maybe not all that odd . . .

When I went down to Ashmansworth I used to spend a lot of time bashing through scores: for me the Music Room was a treasure trove—it seemed to have everything, even the Op. 11 Piano Pieces of Schoenberg. Gerald used to say—I was quite a good sight-reader—'I wish I could play the piano like you': decrying what he regarded as limited or 'unpianistic' in his own writing for piano. Nonsense, of course! What he was really saying, in code, was: 'Mind you don't fall into the danger of facility and luxuriance'. I was still playing a lot of Ravel, Rachmaninov and the romantics: but it was Gerald who helped me get over my John Ireland phase—Kiffer and I were having a go at the Cello Sonata: he evidently felt there was something sentimental and lush in the music, almost vulgar: what we would call 'cheesy'. Certainly when I got to know Gerald's music more—I used to play and sing the songs in that curious bleating, unreliable way that composers have—I found it quite bracing, almost a reproof: its lack of frills; spareness and candour; the perfect judgement of sonorities; fastidious, compact, contained, and all the more eloquent and powerful for it. I was faced with a whole new set of values, which affected not only my music, but my taste and whole approach to aesthetics.

I don't think he held virtuosity in high esteem, regarding it as meretricious, a form of camouflage: maybe this was a part of his prejudice against 'professionalism'. (Mind you, he could turn a pretty impressive virtuosic caper when he wanted to: the Toccata; even 'The rapture' in *Dies*). Unfortunately, perhaps as a result of starting off as a performer, this was something that always engrossed me: not so much the 'flash' factor, but as a game of wit and sorcery. I had written a Rhapsody for the Right Hand when a boy, for I'd broken my left wrist in the gym: an obvious crib from Ravel's Concerto for the Left Hand! And it has remained a topic of fascination for me: I have been extremely lucky in my career to have been able to collaborate with some tremendous players: I wrote a colossal set of Studies and Variations for piano (like the Diabelli or the Etudes Symphoniques of Schumann) for Stephen Kovacevich called *Tombeau*, in which I was delighted to put my mate through all sorts of hoops. And when years later I wrote a large collection of bagatelles for members of the Arditti Quartet, I had the same fun, making them sound like a sextet, a little Chinese orchestra, a consort of viols, and drums: the art of illusion, seeing just what I could get from the barest minimum.

I was always concerned that the virtuosity should have some kind of integrity: I wasn't just interested in a 'cheap thrill'. So when I came to write my 'Capriccio for Violin and Piano', the piece in which I'm told—the composer never knows—my individual voice began to emerge, I was at pains to contain the bravura and fantasy within a context of quite strict musical thinking. Almost all the material comes from the first page, the little flickering figurations for the violin. I think Howard, who gave the first performance with Yfrah Neaman, was quite happy with the dedication.

From what I've said it might appear that I felt Gerald to be repressive: I certainly needed discipline, but also encouragement—and this he gave me a hundredfold, simply by taking me seriously, caring about my 'mistakes'. And of course it was wonderful for me to stay in a household in which the focus was upon work, 'making', harvest. And then the recreation, all those expeditions: over to Burghclere for the Stanley Spencer murals; driving up to London in the van; a quick dash into the booksellers to pick up a massive order for the bookroom; on to the Leicester Gallery for the Alan Reynolds; high tea in a café; then on to the old Stoll Theatre for *Porgy and Bess*, the original American cast, with Cab Calloway as Lucky Dice.

But I shouldn't forget that, while all this was going on—and the extra-curricular activities that Kiffer embroiled me in too—I was also being pulled in other directions. My composition teacher at the Academy was William Alwyn, a lovely man, and a very good composer of his kind: late Romantic, a cross between Bax and Walton, at that time chiefly famous for his film-scores. He and his wife welcomed me into their family too; and I was able to see Bill's astounding collection of Pre-Raphaelite paintings—top-drawer stuff, bought for a song, long before Andrew Lloyd Webber got his grubby hands on them. In our lessons, it was quite plain that Bill had little time for Vaughan Williams and the 'English School'; so I had my first lessons in diplomacy and keeping my mouth shut.

I saw quite a lot of Howard Ferguson, to whom I had been introduced socially by the Finzis. I didn't study formally with him; but I used to go up to West Hampstead and have supper—WHAT supper!—and he'd look at my work; and also, eventually, talk about his own. We'd play piano duets—Schubert, Fauré—and he would browse for hours through the keyboard works of Couperin, John Blow, the *Fitzwilliam Virginal Book*: already the scholar was coming to the fore. And next day I'd trot off to Foyles or the music publishers and get the scores for myself: I was so hungry and receptive, I was like blotting paper. At the time I got to know him well, he was just starting on *Amore Langueo*, his large-scale choral setting of the mediaeval poem; and I have some marvellous letters, written to me while I was on national service in the Middle East, chronicling how the work was progressing. Needless to say, I started on my own 'mediaeval' oratorio, based on Langland's *Piers Plowman*, the text of which Howard and Gerald calculated to last a good nine hours. End of story. But nothing is wasted: I still have the stream of postcards of the Luttrell Psalter from the British Museum and the big two volume Skeat edition which Howard sent out to me; and my imagination, my inner life, is still illumined by what Howard unfolded to me.

When I got back to the Academy after my two years away, my old teacher Bill Alwyn had left, and I ended up going to study with Priaulx Rainier, a remarkable woman of South African extraction, who had studied with Nadia Boulanger, and a passionate admirer of Stravinsky. While sympathetic and perceptive as to what was innate in my makeup, she challenged me on a lot of things: and so the process of 'leaving the nest' musically got under way. Her 'culture' was quite distinct from that of Ashmansworth: she had a studio in St Ives, was a close friend of Barbara Hepworth; at her rather ghastly parties in Ladbroke Grove you'd often brush up against Michael Tippett or Howard Hodgkin. She also knew Jimmy Ede of Kettle's Yard very well. All these things rubbed off; and for a while my music was deeply imbued with the filigree and sprung rhythms (and the quartal harmony) of Tippett's *Midsummer Marriage*.

These features were displayed in another 'early work', my Suite for Flute and Strings, which I dedicated to 'My friends, the Finzis of Ashmansworth', and it was performed several times with the Newbury Strings—lastly, and unforgettably, by Hilary de Pré. It is in four movements, each enshrining in turn one of the family—though by the time I had completed the composition, Gerald was dead.

It was a terrible shock to me—as it was to everybody when they heard—when Kiffer rang me one morning to give me the news. We had seen something of the Finzis a few months earlier at the Three Choirs; and when they all came over one afternoon for tea, my father observed afterwards how extremely ill Gerald had looked. It was shocking to realize what the family had all been living through: that ever since I had first entered that extraordinary world—which seemed so sunny and buoyant—they had each one been contending with this shadow.

It must therefore have been an ambiguous gift when I had some time earlier presented him with a new song, one of a set of three entitled *Beautiful lie the Dead*, each dedicated to one of my mentors (Alwyn, Finzi, and Ferguson). He never heard it sung. I have a very precious memory of one particular performance: late summer at Ashmansworth: VW and Ursula were staying—he was working hard on his Ninth Symphony—and every morning, around four or five am, I'd be woken from my slumbers (I was sleeping on a little truckle bed in the kitchen, among the cats, the Aga, and all the carboys of mead bubbling away): I'd hear the gentle sound of piano notes trickling down from the room above me, penetrating my sleep, as he searched and padded about, and then went back again. Imagine!

Another houseguest was Marion Milford, Robin's niece, who sometimes sang with the Newbury Strings: she had what used to be called a 'nice' soprano voice, slightly brittle. As usual there was quite a lot of music: I think we ran through all Robin's songs, some Rubbra, and a bit of Howells—and my little songs as well. I have this picture of VW slumped on the settee, with Joy and Ursula on either side of him: saying 'Let's have it again' and then again! And so it went on: he took an interest in my work—didn't much care for the French song-cycle!—and Ursula in time became one of my very closest friends. (She was my landlady for many years).

I'm going to end with two letters from Gerald: both written in the last year of his life, when he had much more important things to do than bothering himself about a young student composer. So many facets of his character are expressed here—his humour, his deep concern for current affairs, his/their generosity spreading to all members of my family.

27 April 1955 [1]

> I ought to have written to you long ago, even though you will have had a letter from Joy in between. Your Mother sent me the 'Piers Ploughman' text, and though I told her I thought it was much too long, I had meant to write and tell you direct. Blame we Ancients for not being able to get through all the things to be done. Now I see that Howard has done all that needs to be done, though I fancy that even his three and a half hours was a generous estimate on his part. Even Mahler and Bruckner get a bit

[1] Written while I was on national service in Cyprus.

exhausting after the first hour and a half! But I think it was brave of you to tackle such an enormous job, and I hope something comes out of the smaller conception.

I'll put your letter to Kiffer on one side till we visit him. I'm afraid it can't be forwarded as he is only allowed one letter in and out a fortnight. He was first at Oxford for a week or so, and then via Brixton and Wormwood Scrubbs he got to Lewes Jail. Lewes is the prison for under twenty-ones, as it is supposed to be bad for young people to be with old offenders, though why it should be supposed that the under twenty-ones are less corrupting I can't imagine. However, Kiffer's strong character will stand up to all that, though he is finding it pretty horrifying, and you mustn't think he has chosen an easy way out.

Even though he is likely to be left alone after his three months, the months of suspense beforehand, the courts, the publicity, the enforced living with some of the lowest scum you can find, is not an easy thing to go through. And then, when he is out he'll have to face a good deal of veiled disapproval—mostly, I suspect, from women who have never had to be conscripted! But it's curious what a lot of support he has had from old soldiers, scientists, etc., and of course the Quakers would see him through anything. One of them, seeing Kiffer's case reported in the paper, with his speech from the dock, insisted on sending a cheque towards his fine. And, oh, the numbers who say I wish I had had the courage to do the same thing.

Well, I suppose it's difficult to fight the State, and though I don't go with Kiff the whole way, I do admire him for choosing prison in preference to two years in an army band, playing for dances and officer's messes, and pretending that that is national service!

I can't quite understand about Jonathan's Grand Tour.[2] I suppose this is when he is out of the army. Anyhow he is a lucky chap to be started off (at 21) with a cellar. I once took V.W. out to dinner at Layton's; and Layton (whose Father had been V.W.'s O.C. in the R.A.M.C. during the First World War) was so impressed (by V.W., of course, not me!) that he opened a bottle of port from Disraeli's cellar. What will Jonathan open on such an occasion?

It was sweet of your Mother to have offered the caravan, and I hope all will be well and that we can go, as I shall certainly need a break between Cheltenham and Hereford.

Yours, Gerald

[2] The author's brother.

31 December 1955 [3]

Dear Jeremy,
Jonathan is coming for a night or two next week, when I expect we shall hear more news of you. Meanwhile, your nice long letter was very welcome; and you must imagine a nice family group, typical of an R.A. picture of about 1899—called, of course—'News from the Front'—as gnarled and spectacled Grandad, fragile white-haired Grandmother, two offspring and a cat or two, gather round to read it!

. . . I like the song very much, and thought it very nice of you to have sent it—one of your best, I thought—and the texture gaining in clarity through not being too elaborate. The vocal line is good too, and I shall look forward to seeing the others, perhaps when you are at home. It's good to know that you have some time for getting on with music, and that the two years won't be such a waste of time for you as they are for so many.

Yes, things sound pretty unpleasant out in Cyprus, and I am afraid expediency is our only "moral" ground for being there. If the Russians did the same—well, of course, they have done the same—shouldn't we all be bubbling over with indignation. It's the great case against conscription, whatever the country, that one is forced to do utterly immoral things according to the policy of the moment. I think one should at least have the option of making one's own decisions on these matters.

Alas, I couldn't get to the Macnaghten concert and haven't heard any reports. It would have meant giving up another day out of a week from which too many days had already been taken. I gather there was a good audience and many more than at the previous two.

Isn't it rather a pity to concentrate on French songs, which the French can probably do better. I was sent a volume of English songs by a Danish composer, and felt he had made such a mistake! Alan Bush may be the right man for you. He will be a disciplinarian, but that should help you in the end. In spite of what you say—(or perhaps you don't know the difficulties of others)—music flows pretty easily from you, and the danger of over-flexibility is quite as great as constipation.

We all send our love and every happy wish for the New Year.

Gerald and Joy

I am aware that under the title 'A composer's view: second thoughts' I could have given several quite different lectures: for instance, my feelings now about Finzi's music. They have obviously fluctuated, from youthful

[3] His last New Year's Eve.

adoration to choosey, sometimes nitpicking condescension: for a long time I refrained from listening to it; I had to get it out of my system, move on. But like the Prodigal Son I came back: and the work that I've done for the Finzi Trust, editing some of the great, larger works like the Cello Concerto and *Love's Labour's Lost*, have brought me closer to him—almost at his elbow—than I ever was in his lifetime. And personally, apart from my respect for the superlative musicianship, 'professionalism', sometimes even virtuosity, that I've learned to recognize in his scores, it has long been a deep source of nourishment for me, to partake of his 'clear and gentle stream'.

But I make no excuse for what has turned out to be a bit of an ego-trip: I have been glad to seize the opportunity to revisit my early days: and this is really just a late thank-you-letter to Kiffer, without whose friendship all those years ago none of this would have happened.

IV

Wife and mother, artist and organiser

Starshine over distant fields

Michael A. Salmon

My memory of our first meeting remains vivid. I had discovered Church Farm on a lovely July afternoon in 1969, while searching for Gerald Finzi's headstone in the little churchyard at Ashmansworth. The sexton, who was digging a grave nearby came over and asked if he could help me. He whispered conspiratorially: 'Mrs Finzi lives over there, you know.' He pointed to a long low house just visible above the brick and flint wall opposite the churchyard. Tall, impressive, dark-haired and almost Pre-Raphaelite in appearance, Joy immediately put me at my ease. 'Ooh, we have a visitor; how nice; let's have some tea.' I think we talked for almost two hours and I remember that as I left she said 'we must talk again dear, I have something I would like to discuss with you.' I drove along the narrow lane leading from the Ashmansworth to the Newbury-Andover road wondering what on earth Joy wanted to discuss with the total stranger who had turned up unannounced at her front door. It was perhaps two weeks later that my dilemma was answered. A letter arrived from Joy inviting me to join the fledgling Finzi Trust.

After Gerald died, Joy lived on at Church Farm until 1974. She told me that after his death she had found it almost impossible to work in Gerald's music room and that it was many years, perhaps ten, before she could bring herself to use it regularly. Her confidence then slowly returned and in 1966 she was able to write: 'things move inexplicably—threaded to unseen impulse & I'm beginning to emerge from the dark shadow which fell on me in 1956. I strangely feel new beginnings - a new born strengthening confidence – tentative & easily abashed – but there.' 1966 was a defining year. Church Farm now housed a growing population. Kiffer had married Hilary du Pré in 1961 and their family, together with other friends, filled the house. Joy, in a letter to Alice Sumsion, wrote: 'I always felt [the house] was like an ark . . . it has filled up with strangers.' Now was clearly the time to move on. Joy removed, firstly to Yew Tree Cottage near Newbury, and then in 1974 to Bushey Leaze, an even more beautiful cottage set amid rolling fields at Chieveley. The outlook was so important to Joy that within a very short time she had the hedge separating her garden from the neighbouring cornfields removed. One could then see for miles.

In July 1975 I received an invitation to spend the weekend of the 14th at Yew Tree Cottage. This was the anniversary of Gerald's birth and I felt strangely privileged to be with Joy at that time. On arrival I found her busily preparing lunch and I was immediately banished to the sitting room with an enormous glass of vermouth. I remember watching a squirrel performing acrobatics in the little tree outside while Joy summoned up sorrel soup, an omelette of chanterelle mushrooms, and plums in a delectable honey and fruit syrup. When I said how much I had enjoyed the soup she said slowly: 'you really shouldn't have too much of it dear'. I was mystified. After lunch we talked, consumed far too many chocolates and drank herbal tea before I was ordered to take a walk through the surrounding countryside. That evening we sat by a roaring log fire talking about Gerald and his music. Joy allowed me to record the conversation and now, thirty years on, as I play through the tapes I can hear her slow, measured voice, her slight wheeze, breathlessness and cough, and the hiss and crackle of the fire in the background. As we talked I learned wonderful things. I told her that I thought my handwriting was similar to Gerald's. 'Gerald's writing was like a person walking up a hill,' she replied, 'Gerald had a very curious, rather large, emphatic walk, especially going uphill. His writing is like him walking up a hill.' Later. I asked if Gerald had ever been to Italy, the land of his forbears. 'No dear, he never wanted to go abroad. He was very English; almost violently insular. He wasn't interested in going abroad.'

In 1928 Gerald was suspected of having tuberculosis although the diagnosis was never confirmed. I was fascinated to learn that he was admitted to the sanatorium at Midhurst, as my father was Resident

Medical Officer there at the time. In those days patients were advised that total rest was necessary to help their recovery, but this often meant boredom beyond belief. It was a stultifying passage of time. 'The whole idea was to turn you into a cabbage', said Joy, 'the highest point of existence was going out for walks and cutting a walking stick out of the hedge. Gerald did absolutely nothing at all. It was total stagnation. I think it was probably rather good for him, but utterly frustrating. He came out and then wrote the Grand Fantasia which was very different from anything else he had written. I find the actual Fantasia very exciting. I rather enjoy it.'

We talked about Gerald's early life and then about his musical teachers. Inevitably we got around to one of his prime mentors—R. O. Morris. 'He had a cynical mind,' said Joy, 'I was terrified of him. He was a fascinating man. I felt he was a kind of spring under tension. He was a man under enormous pressure. He used to be a writer for *The Times* crossword. He was analytical. I don't know what the qualities were that made him such a great teacher, but Gerald thought it wasn't just by chance that so many went to him. Anyone who was constipated in their writing was inevitably sent to R. O.' I was interested in the fact that Finzi sometimes took years to compose a piece, even one of no great length. Why was this? Joy thought for a moment before saying: 'Yes, that's right. He believed enormously in the power of the subconscious. He never believed in forcing ideas. If he had been working all day at something and it wouldn't resolve itself he found that if you thought about it last thing at night, before you went to sleep—the last thought—and took it with you into sleep, then when you woke up in the morning it would have resolved itself. In a sense it is what he did in life.'

Was Church Farm the Finzi's first home? 'No,' said Joy. 'When we were first married we lived in Downshire Hill, Hampstead. He had a little house there. It is extraordinary now to think that one could buy a house for £1,500 then. At about the same time we found a house at Aldbourne in Wiltshire, near Marlborough, on the Wiltshire Downs. We tried the practice of going there for the weekends and odd things, but it became apparent that this was a nightmare for Gerald. We were forever packing up or unpacking things, in fact the whole disturbance of going to the country. I think it was after only two years that we sold the house and went to live entirely in the country.' Joy was quiet for some time after this before telling me that she had discussed the move with Gerald, arguing that the most important thing was for him to write music rather than 'knowing the right people or going to parties . . . he was a man with such wide interests and London was so full of distractions. For someone who wrote with great difficulty he was not able to get the right isolation. Gerald hated being in a village. He always had a desire to live somewhere high. He thought that he had this feeling of claustrophobia because some time in his childhood he was shut in a cupboard as a punishment. He even had this sense of claustrophobia when putting on a sweater, which he had to do very quickly. It always made him long to live on a hill.'

And what about Church Farm? After a long spell of searching the Finzis were sent details of a property at Ashmansworth. It lay out of the village, but curiously, the estate agents had not mentioned the view, merely pointing out that the property was ripe for conversion. They visited the house on a January day with snow still lying about. The building was so derelict that the owner wouldn't let them in and said that it was not for sale. Joy telephoned the agents in Andover and was informed that it had just been sold. Gerald was very depressed as he had set his heart on rebuilding the property. However, a visit to Andover the next morning revealed that although a speculator had just purchased the property he might be persuaded for a sum of £100 to sell it to them. 'And that', said Joy, 'was how we got Ashmansworth.'

I asked Joy about her first meeting with Gerald. 'Gerald was at the Bach Festival I think, in Oxford, and he met an old school friend of mine. They talked about the countryside and how Gerald liked to escape from London. She mentioned that we had a cottage which we lent or rented and Gerald came down to the cottage which was on our land; and that was how we met. I went up to the cottage as I always did to see if the tenants had got everything they needed and there was Gerald. We used to go and play tennis at the VWs. The VWs loved playing tennis.' Did Gerald play tennis well? 'Oh, very badly' He had very little control over his body—very bad co-ordination. I mean even when conducting you'd feel that his arms might go round the wrong way. He found driving cars an awful strain. He never used to drive very much.'

I have always loved the poetry of George Meredith and wondered whether Gerald had ever considered setting him? Joy said that on one occasion she discussed 'Love in the valley' with him, but Gerald felt that Meredith had missed something and that there was no great depth of feeling. 'Feeling is greater than experience and that you must always remember. One cannot shout it out enough.' As I changed the cassette in my little tape recorder Joy became strangely animated. Peering at its rotating spools she said: 'How very clever; just a collection of someone's memories without a brain to recall them.'

That night at Bushey Leaze, I lay in bed looking out over the cornfields. The entire night-time scene was flooded with moonlight and innumerable stars. I have never forgotten it. I awoke the next morning to the sound of birdsong. The sun was streaming into the room and sparrows darted about the eaves. Outside in the garden, we watched the first swallows that had just arrived from Africa.

I visited Joy at Yew Tree Cottage and Bushey Leaze many times after that and each time I learned new facts or met new people. She showed a particular interest in the fact that I was at that time conducting a research programme into the treatment of migraine. I told her that many of the bizarre happenings in Lewis Carroll's *Alice* adventures were representations of the author's own migrainous symptoms. This hugely interested her and she became quietly thoughtful. Eventually the silence was broken and she said: 'Of course dear, there were no drugs in his day, but he could have used this.' I was somewhat perplexed when she walked over to a table near the window and came back with a paper bag, from which she took a crystal pendulum. On returning home I sent Joy the typescript of a lecture that I had given to the Baconian Society in 1975, in which I had discussed the association of Lewis Carroll and migraine, as well as theories about Napoleon's last illness. She replied in a long letter which ended with the message: 'I have been struck with the aspects of the doctor & observer & the artist who also sees the physical presentation as a record of unseen causes, and has discovered that the whole passage of life is laid down in the hills and valleys of the face. How you see enables what you find.' We discussed all this at my next visit, when I told Joy that a colleague of mine, a Professor of Psychiatry, had made a brilliant study of the creative mind of various musical composers. She must have misunderstood me, for in a subsequent letter she wrote:

> I told Diana [McVeagh, then working on Gerald Finzi's biography] that you said that you knew a good hypnotist. I wondered whether this could be rather fascinating in trying to bring up things that I have forgotten and which have got overlaid by stress. I have observed a very fascinating session in the Plaza in Newbury by a young man who has since become a professional. I did not take part in it because I wanted to observe for myself and therefore had not the slightest inclination when the bulk of the audience put their hands on their heads & couldn't take them down again. He was marvellously deft and seemed able to do anything he wanted. I should find it very interesting to see if I could willingly enable Diana's questions to be answered in part. I have observed how strange it is what one remembers and what one does not, and I suspect a lot of

> forgetfulness is a binding up by scars and stresses. But as one nears the portal the view becomes longer and the willingness to explore perhaps more fruitful.

Joy did not really believe in birthdays or Christmas. However, towards the end of the year her friends received a card heralding the New Year, as well as one of her poems. In 1979 I told her that I was engaged to be married and she immediately said 'Oh, how wonderful dear, you must bring her over.' Two weeks later Susie and I drove over to Ashmansworth for tea. We had a marvellous afternoon and as we left Joy presented us with her copy of T. H. White's *Once and Future King* and a photograph of Gerald taken by his mother on St Catherine's Hill, Winchester, in his twenties. A letter followed two days later; in this Joy wrote:

> What really happy news! This brings my blessings to you both and the new way. Life is so brief and so fragile that it is lovely to know that you both can make something of quality together to enhance living. How lovely to be playing the Introit at your marriage—it will be 'an entering in' as Gerry envisaged it. This does embellish the taking of hands together.

One of Joy's greatest qualities was her ability to organise people. She was a true anticipator, enabler and arranger. On one occasion we discussed a work by Finzi that I longed to hear—*For St Cecilia*. The score was sitting amongst a jumble of books and miscellaneous ephemera at Bushey Leaze and she handed it to me, saying it was high time that someone recorded it. Some time after this she introduced me to Richard Hickox who later visited me at the hospital where I worked. We discussed English music while sitting in the rather cold surroundings of an Out-Patient Clinic, but it was there that I suggested that he might consider the *St Cecilia*. In 1978 he phoned me to say that he was recording it in London, in three weeks' time. Joy attended the recording session, and as we drove through the grey suburbs of London, a traffic jam engulfed us for ages. She regarded the busy streets, the grey monotone of the buildings near the Kingsway hall where the recording was to be made and said: 'this really is a very small place—it has very little quality.' At the hall we joined Howard Ferguson and others as the opening fanfares of this wonderful work lit up the drab surroundings, and I remember how delighted we were with Philip Langridge's performance as the tenor soloist. She was remarkably silent on the return journey but a letter arrived a few days later. 'Most grateful thanks for dropping me so near my lodging on Friday night—and for being the instrument that originally promoted the recording sessions! It was an enormously exciting experience and I am persistently hearing odd snatches of *St Cecilia* which even persist through dreams!'

In 2001, the centenary of Finzi's birth, time had now come to move on, and I felt it necessary to tender my resignation from the Finzi Trust, thirty-two years after Joy Finzi first asked me to join in its formation. Contemplating my resignation I thumbed through the pile of letters and cards that Joy had sent me over this period of time, and pondered over three lines written by her in 1979: 'But no more on such an occasion—when you can shut the door and go out into the sun. I doubt whether you would have turned down the Ashmansworth turning if all sorts of doubts had not prompted you!'

Extracts from 'Joy Finzi 1907–1991. Tributes from her friends'

Howard Ferguson

It only struck me after Joy's death that she and I had been friends for over half a century. We first met in March 1933, when I visited Gerald at a cottage at Lye Green in Sussex where he was having a working holiday. The cottage belonged to Joy and her sister Mags, who lived nearby in an attractive old house called Bingles, and there we were invited to join them for a meal. Both sisters were tall and strikingly beautiful; but whereas Mags's main concern was with horses, Joy had studied sculpture and pottery at the Central School of Art and Design, played the violin, and shared all Gerald's interests. It was no great surprise, therefore, when he told me a month later that Joy and he were engaged.

It was the best thing that ever happened to him. When I wrote to Joy to tell her so, she replied from the Aran Isles, where she and G. had gone for a celebratory holiday:

> Dear Fergie,
> I wanted to write and thank you for your awfully nice letter before leaving but didn't have a moment. I appreciate it so much, and am so glad you feel happy about it too. It's a great and glorious thing to Gerald and me . . .
>
> Excuse pencil—the ink has run out and the boat doesn't come in until tomorrow!

Six months later they were married at Dorking Registry Office, where the only witnesses were Ralph and Adeline Vaughan Williams.

On returning from their honeymoon in Scotland they moved into 30 Downshire Hill, Hampstead, which was not far from 8 East Heath Road where I lived with Harold Samuel. This made weekly visits easy when Joy decided she would like to sculpt my head. The two of us would retire to their well-lit basement (where the modelling-clay could be kept damp), and there she worked concentratedly for an hour or so, saying an occasional word to keep me awake. I was never allowed to look at the work-in-progress. But one evening, after about ten sittings, I was led up to G.'s workroom at the top of the house, the door was flung open dramatically, and there I was in the dark, lying on a sofa with a powerful light trained on my white plaster face and a rug draped over some cushions to counterfeit my body. It was an eerie sight.

After their removal to Aldbourne, Joy embarked on her largest carving: the magnificent alabaster fish that later rested on the piano at Bushey Leaze. It took her several years to complete, for sculpture is a slow business and difficult to combine with running a home, bringing up a family, and looking after a composer husband. Moreover, G. and J. had always planned to build a house of their own in the country, and were soon on the look-out for a suitable site. Eventually they found exactly what they wanted at Ashmansworth, high on the Downs south of Newbury. There was already a farmhouse there; but it was in such a bad state of repair that the only thing to do was to pull it down and start again.

Their architect friend, Peter Harland, was persuaded with some difficulty to design the home they wanted rather than the one he would have preferred to build; but for some reason he absolutely refused to orientate it in exactly the direction they wished. To circumvent the problem, G. and J. drove up to the site one evening after the workmen had left, and quietly shifted all the pegs that showed where the walls should go. Later they told me gleefully that Harland never noticed what they had done.

While the house was being built they most thoughtfully lent me the gardener's cottage that was already there, for I was at the moment homeless following Harold Samuel's death in 1937. It was a perfect way of being able to sample the delights of nine months in the country, even if it didn't decide me to settle there permanently.

No sooner was their house completed in 1939 than war broke out. Joy coped indomitably with moving in, looking after evacuees, and even organising Newbury String Players, the little orchestra Gerald got together to make good the wartime lack of music in country districts. (Later she told me that over the years they had given more than 400 concerts in churches and village halls throughout Wiltshire, Berkshire and Oxfordshire.)

To replace time-consuming sculpture she discovered what was, I think, her true métier: portrait-drawing in pencil. The beauty and subtlety of her work in this field can be seen from a book of fine reproductions of some fifty of her portraits entitled *In That Place*. Particularly striking are the two of Ralph Vaughan Williams, one now belonging to the National Portrait Gallery and the other to Trinity College, Cambridge. But equally sensitive are the other drawings of musicians, writers, artists, and friends of all ages. They were generally done in only two or three sittings, which may partly account for their extreme vividness.

Throughout their married life Joy was an unfailing support in all Gerald's undertakings. Indeed, it is hard to imagine how he would have accomplished them, had she not been at hand and all too willing to subordinate her own interests to his. Typical of their 'combined operations' was the long saga of Ivor Gurney's unpublished songs and poems. After Gerald and Joy had rescued trunksful of them from the loving clutches of Miss Marion Scott, Joy made annotated lists of over 200 of the songs as G. and I gradually played through them; later she typed out the complete poems—hundreds of pages of them; and finally, after both Miss Scott and Gerald were dead, and the manuscripts had become the legal property of the Gurney family, it was Joy who persuaded an unappreciative relative to hand them over to the Gloucester Public Library instead of burning them in the back garden. How pleased Gerald would have been to know that the job he began so many years before had at last been satisfactorily concluded.

Lucilla Warre-Cornish

When I was a child in the late 1920s, living at Hilles, my home in Gloucestershire, Gerald was living nearby in Painswick. He often used to come over and see us. He was one of a group of close friends of my parents[1] who were often at Hilles, amongst them George Villiers, Neville Lytton and Charlôt Geoffroy-Dechaume. He was great fun for us children. Amongst other stories he told, one was that he had been a highwayman and he even sent a bit of rope by which he had escaped from

[1] Architect Detmar Blow and his wife Winifred.

Reading Gaol. I remember how bitterly I resented being told by an older child that of course he wasn't really a highwayman. Once when I was about eight he sent a telegram: 'COMING WITH JOY'. We imagined teasing him saying, 'Well where is Joy?' Then they arrived, and Joy was a real person. We were enchanted by her beauty and warmth and we all loved her. We continued to see them often and it was always a delight. She was such a wonderful person, so beautiful in every way and everyone loved her.

Caroline Taylor

When we were children, 'going up to the Finzis' lifted our spirits immediately. Whether we climbed the hill to Ashmansworth by car or took the bus to Doiley Bottom and walked up the lane, it involved an elevation to another world.

During the war my father, Tom Scott, was one of the few doctors left in the area, and my mother, Buffy, not only added two more babies of her own to her pre-war trio but had the house filled with pregnant women from the East End, nervy fighter pilots and war widows, or Londoners with yet more babies. Ashmansworth was a haven and a quite different way of life for us all—though it too had its excitable refugees. It smelt of honey and wood and clean linen; of apples and books and carbolic soap. Joy and Gerald—wholly inseparable in my mind until years later—seemed a core of stability, preoccupied by things of the mind (in spite of the meals and Gerald often in London and the bees and the visitors). We were left to our own devices—and got up to terrible conservational things with Kiffer and Nigel, like saving the poor moles by dropping all the mole-traps down the well; we had 'interesting conversations' with grown-ups; sang carols on Christmas Eve; played stringed instruments badly with those who played them well; ate strange foods—yoghurt from the back of the Esse, ginger from the window-sill, honey with our cereal—and learnt to wash up 'under a running tap'. Before Christmas a grave voice asked hollowly down the chimney what we wanted in our stockings; Joy took us for magical picnics carrying huge bowls of sloppy fruit salad. After the war we danced country dances with Royal Shakespeare actors at Stratford after seeing *King Lear*; we went to Three Choirs Festivals and operas in odd places; my youngest sister was Joy's goddaughter and remembers above all her thoughtful kindness.

I only learnt when Gerald died how much he had meant to my father;

and I learnt the same about my mother when Joy died. As for the five of us, we certainly would not be the people we are if Joy and Gerald and Ashmansworth had not become part of our lives. We will always remember the thrill of it.

Ursula Vaughan Williams

When I met Joy in 1942, she was in her middle thirties. She looked then, as she did as she grew older, like one of her own drawings, clear and delicate with nothing vague or blurred in feature or in movement. She had already achieved her individual way of dressing, in any variation her clothes were recognizably hers—a long, wood-violet coloured wool evening dress, the little jackets with interesting buttons, the longish skirts—it is impossible to imagine her in any other sort of garments, for they suited her perfectly. She had a way of taking anything as it came, and she never seemed in a hurry, whether she was shutting up the chickens and ducks for the night, packing music stands and picnic supplies for many into a van, choosing plates in the reject china chop in Worcester—one of that festival's extra-curricular pleasures—or cooking at the Aga and talking to her guests as she stirred a saucepan's delicious contents. All were done with what seemed an easy and observing care, and an air of detachment.

When Ralph and I lived at Hanover Terrace we had a happy arrangement with the Finzis. We were their town house and they our country lodging. Thus we saw each other often and shared both London pleasures and country expeditions. One night, when we had all been at a concert, Ralph suggested that it would be a good idea to drive down to Ashmansworth, instead of going to bed and going there in the morning. Joy was the only driver and she agreed that she was not too tired for such a venture, so we set off in the June darkness and arrived in time to see the first light and to hear the earliest bird-song as we had our cups of tea by the open window, watching light broaden over the wide view.

We shared many first performances of both Gerald's and Ralph's works, with their attendant agitations and the hours of elation, discussion and fatigue which follow after the concerts are over, sitting in their house or in ours, long and late, or at the Three Choirs, where every evening ended with some sort of party.

One odd visit was to see the Boughtons at Newent. We were all four amazed when Rutland said that he had done everything he wanted to do in his work and life. We did not know that Gerald and Joy already knew that Gerald's future was to be short—but even so, it seemed an extravagant claim for anyone to make. We shared, with an American friend of theirs, the golden afternoon in the overgrown and flowery graveyard at Chosen Hill, after the first performance of *In terra pax*, when Gerald described the snowy Christmas he had spent there with bell-ringers, hearing bells 'in steeples far and near' ringing across the Cotswold woods and the fields below. It was that visit that precipitated his death, for the cheerful children belonging to the churchwarden had chickenpox, and Gerald, with no immune system, caught the infection. We had already gone to Majorca for a holiday when he died, but Joy managed to write a long letter and arranged a special delivery so that we heard before we saw the newspapers. Palma was full of migrating swallows that day, perhaps, we thought, the ones we had seen so little while before, leaving Gloucestershire.

Two years later Ralph and I were staying with Joy and she drove us to many of Ralph's favourite places—Yarnbury and Old Sarum; Salisbury Cathedral, floodlit for the first time that year and looking magical. We picnicked by the White Horse one day, with Ruth and Tony Scott, looking over harvest fields, and later drove through Dorset and to the Chesil Bank—a grey sea, and almost rain, a feeling of autumn already in the air. But the week had been full of bounties, Joy had found all the right places, England at its most satisfying, the country as town dwellers like to think of it. Later I knew that one of life's kindnesses is that last times are not known until death changes them into mirage and to memory.

Alan Ridout

My first meeting with Joy was in 1958, when John Russell conducted a work of mine for organ and strings in St Paul's Cathedral. She was playing among the second violins, and spoke to me warmly and generously afterwards. It came as a complete surprise, however, when in the early 1960s, at Howard Ferguson's house in Hampstead, I saw one of her drawings—a portrait of his old Irish nanny, Pu. I found it very difficult to square this masterpiece with the apparently simple-hearted lady I had met previously; and, as I yearned to have such a drawing near me, I wrote to Joy to ask whether an exhibition might be in prospect. Her response disconcerted me: she said that she would like to draw me. This was not at all what I wanted, so I let the matter drop.

The next time we met was at Howard's house in Cambridge, and this spelt the start of our friendship, for Joy invited me to visit her at Bushey Leaze.

I always felt that she seemed to shy away from expressions of affection, with the result that the moments of meeting her were something of a disappointment. If it happened to be at Newbury station, Joy simply sat in the car wearing a slightly startled expression; and she was not really comfortable until one had got past initial greetings. Such contained emotions were wholly belied by the power of concern and sympathy she showed in letters or on the telephone. She could be an extraordinary support if one went through difficult times; and there was, indeed, something of the healer about her.

Bushey Leaze was very much her creation—the domain of an unusual individual. Books and pictures were everywhere; but it was the mixture and emphasis of them that gave one clues: Edmund Blunden, Sylvia Townsend Warner, Valentine Ackland, Ivor Gurney, newsletters of the Voluntary Euthanasia Society, many topographical books and, amongst the art books some surprising names, for example the American Andrew Wyeth. There were books too where beauty of printing and lettering were paramount. One would feel that acute selection was followed through with a long-term fidelity; and the same was true of visual things, a special interest being shown in the works of Benedict Rubbra and the glass engravings of Laurence Whistler.

The house and garden seemed a magical and happy place, steeped in her presence and in the presence of friendly spirits. A wooden seat out of sight of the house came to have a palpable enchantment for me: 'Nirvana' I called it. I spent hours and hours there each time I visited Joy, and I never wanted to leave the spot.

And then, that view! The field unhedged and unfenced but extending the garden and sweeping to an everlasting distance, a rich ploughed tilth in winter, and bursting with wheat in summer.

Joy's sequence of rituals each day was intriguing, and one or two of them seemed amusingly dotty. I often wondered if she donned her polka dot headscarf before anything else when rising, so permanent a part of her did it seem. Then the funny little home-made pâtés and concoctions which began at breakfast; and the statutory, but hugely enjoyed, elevenses, when her handyman neighbour Bert called, he wielding a large cigar (brought from Dubai by Nigel) whilst expressing his daily disgust with the closely-read gutter press. The final ritual of the day was the drinking of vast quantities of peppermint tea, strongly believed by Joy to bring about deep, peaceful sleep, but consumed in such amounts ensured at least two night-calls.

Such wondrous logic seemed somehow indicative of other more eccentric habits, of which her consultation of the pendulum was perhaps the most startling. Although she could give examples of its striking success—believers in such things always can, being oblivious of how selective their examples are—it seemed to me potentially dangerous. When she started announcing the date of her own death, I felt the time had come to make a point: I could not resist phoning her a couple of days after the event had been predicted to ask her how she was. By then her 'deadline' had mysteriously changed of course; and she never lost faith in her whimsical pendulum.

Meanwhile she continued to express a desire to draw me, and I continued to sidestep. She cornered me in the end, however; though, in her note on the drawing in the volume *In That Place*, she stated, amongst an endearingly characteristic congestion of errors, that I had asked her to do it! Joy's working-methods were quite eerie. Her hand on pencil and paper seemed to be moving so lightly that it was as if she was dreaming. She appeared to live my life through each stage of the drawing, the first outlines looking to me like those of an infant; then I saw myself clearly as a young boy; and then as a youth. All the time she kept saying, 'most extraordinary: I don't understand it.'

I composed as she drew; but once, exhausted, I stopped the composition I was engaged on, and, feeling it would make no difference, started thinking about something else. She too stopped almost immediately. 'It's gone,' she said, 'something in your face has disappeared.' I could barely believe such a perception possible.

When the drawing was finished I had two odd experiences. One was that I suddenly saw my father in it—a likeness that had never hit me or my family before. The other was when my awe-struck mother (herself a painter) said, 'she has drawn you as you really are, not just the way you look.'

If I say that I think Joy had genius as an artist, it is not on the basis of what I have written. But some of her drawings—the portrait of Vaughan Williams in the National Portrait Gallery, and of Sir Adrian Boult, and the overpowering double-portraits of Lucy Boston with Elizabeth Vellacott and Dorothy Neate with her grandson Mark—seem to me to be very great indeed. They are much more than mere likenesses, for they express not only the essence of the sitter's personality, but also something that is resonant of eternal values.

Everything else about Joy, if of less significance, was nevertheless individual. She was concerned, caring, good humoured, amused, and vastly interested—'how very interesting' was constantly on her lips. She spread a bubbly happiness around her while alive; why should she not do the same now when we remember her?

Myfanwy Thomas

It is good to have this chance of sharing thoughts and memories of Joy, to whom my late sister Bronwen and I owe so much. Joy made the last ten or so years of our mother, Helen Thomas's life so happy, full and varied. Moreover, she encouraged Mother to write her memories of writers she had known for *The Times*. They often went to the theatre in Oxford and Stratford, and Joy arranged for Mother to come to a number of the Newbury String Players' concerts. I remember them going off to see David Warner's *Hamlet* at Stratford. I sat up for their return with hot soup at the ready. Midnight passed, then one, then two. Eventually I heard a car stop and whispering and laughing at the front door and in they came like two guilty schoolgirls: 'Good heavens, is it that late?' Joy's car had suddenly started smoking and they had to hang about in deserted Wantage while a kindly garage mechanic put things right. Joy was a great sharer of everything: friends, time, encouragement, pleasure—she brought Sylvia Townsend Warner to meet Mother and they were soon animated friends, corresponding regularly. It was Joy too who introduced Mother to Laurence Whistler and Theresa, who was writing a biography of Walter de la Mare. Mother was able to give some useful memories of the de la Mare family in their early days, when he had just started to write.

Two young men who used to record rehearsals of the String Players, wanted to record the human voice, and nothing daunted, Joy arranged for them to come to our cottage and to record Mother reading aloud some of my father's poems. The first attempt was disastrous—a ticking clock, traffic passing, our old spaniel's snores, and the pages of the typescript being turned sounding like a waterfall. So all had to be done again, by which time Mother's sight had worsened for reading, but she knew most of the poems by heart! Joy arranged to have a limited number of gramophone records made from the tape, and she dealt very efficiently with packing and sending off records ordered. She was a perfectionist in every way—even her typewriting was meticulous and always pleasing to the eye.

When, soon after our mother's death, I knew that there must be a Laurence Whistler window here to both Edward and Helen, Joy acted as my go-between, as I had not met Laurie then. I remember so well my hesitant letter to Joy asking if she felt she could approach Laurie about a window, and her enthusiastic phone call the moment she had my letter, telling me she had written at once but that I must not expect an answer for some weeks. But he wrote by return of post! Joy was our help and mainstay through all the period between 1967 and 1971, when the window was being planned, made and installed. Always encouraging and buoyant—a great help to me when all my family feared I'd end up in prison or the workhouse! It was Joy who saw the letter to possible subscribers through its printing, who drove me to Winchester to choose the trees for the background in the churchyard, and when the time came, helped to address the envelopes to our list of about 500 possible subscribers, and lick the stamps. It was a friend of Joy's who sent the first cheque for £100—we were on the way! A wonderful gift of friendship—Joy gave to so many of all her store of energy and vitality and encouragement in so many ways. Interested in everything that she came across, never surprised by the strangeness of human nature, and always finding qualities to enjoy in the oddest of characters. Joy wrote poems for me on Mother's and Bronwen's deaths and on the making of the glorious window. Artist, sculptor, wood-carver, poet, dressmaker, musician—so many gifts shared with so many people.

Richard Shirley Smith

My mother remembered that when I was six, sitting at a different table from her in a busy café, Joy unconsciously took me under her wing. Now, half a century later, I can see how enormously her example has affected my work and life. Making a third scallywag with her two sons at kindergarten, I had the good fortune to be invited to stay at a house where creative work was all-important. Joy was a woman of vision, applying great imagination and artistry to that most life-enhancing house and garden. She was a humorous and loving mother, and, of course, greatly enabled her husband's inspired work. Gradually I saw that her own art was diverse and of the finest. Her exquisitely finished woodcarvings based on plant forms and her penetrating portrait drawings of for instance Helen Thomas and Sylvia Townsend Warner, could not possibly have been better. Her *A Point of Departure* poems inspired me to do my best early engravings when she brought them on a visit to us near Rome in 1961. Five years earlier she and Gerald had driven me over to Great Bardfield, just before I started at the Slade, to meet their friend and my future tutor, John Aldridge.

All of us who struggled to do creative work were actively encouraged. At all ages we were whisked off to never-to-be-forgotten exhibitions, operas or plays—not to mention the Three Choirs Festival; thus Joy also keenly supported performers. Occasionally little phrases would express her dismay—having spent time in a materialist household: 'a swift repetition of meals', or watching a massive hardwood cornice constructed around a private swimming pool, 'purposeless wealth'. Unwrapping a Christmas present of favourite chocolates she would say aloud, 'Who shall we give these to?' In the same unselfish way a valuable Naum Gabo sculpture she had inherited went to the Kettle's Yard, Cambridge and her working art books she gave to me. Of course I learned much from them. It was drawing that interested her, especially where ideas and observation combined: da Vinci, Goya, Palmer, Blake, Redon, Morris, Beardsley, Ravilious etc.

Joy, like Gerald, was appreciative of both old and new art forms, taught us to make the most of the precious moment and that imagination and craftsmanship were essential. Joy was very patient in putting up with all kinds of silliness as I grew up and when things went wrong, was wonderful with discussion and advice. In all her tireless organisation of the Newbury Strings, the Finzi Trust or the Reading University Finzi Book room, there was always the vision of transience and mystery.

Robert Gower

Life with Joy was never dull. On our frequent journeys around the country—Joy loved the travel and relished fresh experiences up to the last—she would frequently exclaim, 'I've seen that face before'—and then a racking cough—'I don't understand it: quite extraordinary.' Or we would pull up at traffic lights parallel with another car. Joy, in the front passenger seat, could be seen peering with an artist's intensity of gaze at the unfortunate driver to her left, drinking in the features she observed.

The faster we went, the more she liked it. I spent a long while trying to persuade her that we did not return from Rochester to Bushey Leaze in an hour, or from Brighton to Bushey Leaze in an hour and a quarter, tales she would loudly proclaim with an assertion that 'our roads are really marvellous, dearie'.

And the meals—Joy seemed to subsist on air. Apart, that is, from the noxious garlic fish pâtés on which she breakfasted daily and the odour of which hung round the car (for she would take it with her when travelling) in a most depressing way. But, Joy, faced with salmon, would suddenly develop an appetite, whilst a box of Bendicks Bittermints was likely to shift rapidly. A glass of dry vermouth ('Howard's favourite tipple') or white wine did not go amiss, but if it was especially good, the level sank a notch faster and a refill was always welcomed. Perhaps it was this inherent sense of fun (naughtiness?) which warmed the hearts of the young in Joy's presence. They felt an identification of spirit—and how Joy found herself in demand from musicians, artists, writers as a mentor and comforter. I constantly marvelled at the genuine interest Joy shared not only in my work, but in contemporary developments in the musical world—no pulling down of the shutters in old age here.

Through Joy, I encountered the work of Benedict and Tessa Rubbra, Mike Mitchell, Laurence Whistler, Richard Shirley Smith, Eric Gill—and learnt of kindred spirits in other art forms. How my life has been enriched as a result.

It would be wrong to describe Joy as religious (there was general surprise when we learnt of her enthusiasm to visit neighbours Bert and Jessie to watch *Songs of Praise*), but she had a strong belief in the structured path of predestination—sometimes consulting her pendulum if the need for confirmation of her view was felt necessary. She was invaluable in speaking out to those who were caught in indecision about matters professional or personal: 'of course he should marry her', 'that work will simply never make it', 'the job is intended'. All was said in the kindest, but also the most definitive of tones.

It was characteristic of Joy to be totally unforthcoming about her own work. She rarely referred to it, except to complain about the distress drawing caused her in the effort to capture the true likeness. I saw this for myself as she sketched me. Rarely did I see Joy worked up, but here she was in some state of self-directed anger and emotion: one saw a brief insight into her artistic temperament. *In That Place* testified to her exceptional gifts for revealing character in her portraits—the eyes have it. Her poetry was as important to her, in my mind—though I could not personally place it in the same league. Regularly she would send a New Year card with her verse printed, with an accompanying wood engraving: how good it was to receive this personal greeting—and how characteristic of Joy to be slightly out of step with the mainstream.

With her headscarf and padded coat, ancient shoes and trousers ('they were Nigel's, dear') Joy made a striking figure. But the strong impression she leaves is through her kindness, her unfailing gifts of hospitality, her honesty and dependability, and through her artistic commitment—all qualities she shared universally. How many owe so much to her. No wonder she was so much loved and will be so greatly missed.

Jeremy Dale Roberts

One of Joy's most remarkable capacities—innate as well as learned from her life with Gerald Finzi—was as an 'enabler'. It would be impossible to count the artists, craftsmen and musicians—amateur and professional, of all ages, even deceased—who had their work eased by her and encouraged, both practically and, more deeply, by the sense that it was valued. Whilst all of us who were in her debt bewailed the sacrifice of her own creative work—those huge, reproachful blocks of wood standing year after year on the terrace at Ashmansworth waiting vainly to be transmuted into exquisite winged shapes or fronds—Joy calmly went about her business: eliciting, organising, gently pushing. Her most famous achievement in this respect—an exploit which required all Joy's human qualities: tenacity, nerve, as well as tact—was the retrieval and securing of Ivor Gurney's manuscripts. But I am also thinking of all those bits and pieces she collected around her over the years with her marvellous eye: pictures, obviously; the work of children and students; the gorgeous crochet counterpanes made up by Olive from the village. Clearing her throat she would say, sometimes a little vaguely perhaps, but with quiet conviction and satisfaction: 'It has a quality'.

A never-to-be-forgotten scene, in the sitting room at Ashmansworth, sometime in the autumn of 1956: the tenor Wilfred Brown and Howard Ferguson unfolding the last sheaf of Finzi's songs to a group of friends. Poignant, but somehow bountiful. No-one could fail to hear Gerald's salute to his wife in his setting of Bridges' 'Since we loved'.

Paul Spicer

I think the thing I valued most about Joy was her absolute objectivity. Her judgement was never clouded by sentiment or emotion, and it was this feature of her personality which came across most strongly, even on our first meeting back in 1979 when Robert Gower and I went to see her at

Bushey Leaze. We wanted to talk about Gerald and his music and about the way he composed, and we were astonished by no-nonsense answers. Having recently been to see John Ireland's doting housekeeper, Norah Kirby, this was a sea change, and a welcome one. Joy was game for anything until the last year or so and was always very keen to share her enthusiasms, especially if this meant that she could be driven somewhere for the day. When I was at Ellesmere College she would ring me up and say, 'Dearie, you know that there's a Piper exhibition at the Tate on at the moment—you are coming aren't you?' And, of course, I would find some plausible reason for needing to be in London for the day and go over and drive her down. We would never look for more than an hour as she didn't think we could take more than that in. We would then drive back and I would be fed with delicious grapes and wicked chocolates. It became quite a pattern for a while.

There is no doubt that Joy altered the course of my life. She had very distinct feelings about the way things should go for me after the first Finzi Festival at Ellesmere, and she was always a tower of strength during the time I was going through the change of career from teaching to the BBC. Bushey Leaze, though, was also a haven for composition and she was a tough taskmaster keeping my nose to the grindstone and always having an interesting comment to make when I came through for a vermouth at 'break time'.

I loved the aspect of her personality which insisted that there was never a problem, only an opportunity. She was a compulsive optimist, and we used to laugh at committee meetings for the festivals when we were agonising about where the money was to come from and she would sit there saying, 'Don't worry, dearie. It'll come'—and somehow it usually did! In reality, money meant little or nothing to her—she didn't have much, but what she had was always a means to an end, usually charitable or creative.

I think I probably learned from Joy, more than anything else, how to observe. Her drawings show what a great observer she was, and once I had got to know her, I would often sit watching her watching others—it was fascinating seeing her eyes drinking in the details and seeing the play of expressions on her face as she was variously amused or interested by someone. She loved to watch fashion, the great drug, and its effects on people, and she also was a great observer of the size of men's tummies and the amount they protruded over the belt! She was always advocating pre-breakfast swimming as an antidote, as she had been so impressed by a coach driver she met who she found to be unusually slim for a middle-aged man and asked what his secret was, given his sedentary job. He turned out to be a regular early morning swimmer and so his virtues were laid at the doors of a number of her protégés and family thereafter.

The Bushey Leaze experience was unforgettable with the log fire on a winter's night after a good hard day's work, sitting around chatting about anything followed by the inevitable 'good night' tea (mint). Then to the 'great bed' with its two electric blankets and raised feet, so that one could wake up and look out over the fields to the 'heaven's gate' in the distance. Those crisp, frosty nights with the sky filled with stars and the ruts in the field picked out by a bright moon are wonderful to remember, as, equally, are the wonderful summer days when the garden was looking at its best, and all the birds from the locality would come to be fed with food prepared with much more enthusiasm than Joy would ever show for preparing food for herself.

There is no room for all the experiences or impressions I could give in even my brief acquaintance with Joy in this short piece. All I can say is that I am a wiser and better person for having known her and that I owe to her a great deal of what I have managed to achieve during the last twelve years, especially her enthusiasm for the Finzi Singers project for which she has my undying gratitude. Thank you Joy!

Andrew Burn

I first met Joy in 1978 when I visited her at Bushey Leaze on a wind-swept winter's day. We spent the afternoon in front of the roaring log fire talking about Gerald's music; it was to be the first of many memorable visits and a friendship of thirteen years in which Joy influenced in so many ways the person I am now. For that I shall be eternally grateful.

I always felt that there was something remarkable about the atmosphere of Bushey Leaze, stamped as it was with Joy's personality. It had an extraordinary peace and, typical of Joy, the fencing was removed so that the garden merged naturally into the farmland beyond. Its quietude seemed to emanate from Joy herself; one almost felt she had some intuitive rapport with natural life, some atavistic resonance with the past, which were embodied in the character of cottage and garden. Was that why the garden was so profuse with flowers and herbs, and redolent with wildlife, particularly birds whom Joy delighted in feeding first thing in the morning? No houseguest was offered breakfast before them and their tameness was a delight. Frequently, she reminded me of the timeless, eponymous sage of Edward Thomas's poem 'Lob'.

Joy had great skills in introducing people whom she instinctively felt would enjoy each others' companionship—in current jargon she was brilliant at networking. In 1979, she wrote to me explaining that she'd recently had a visit from Paul Spicer and Robert Gower who, like I had done, had come seeking knowledge about Gerald. They'd suggested organising a festival to mark the twenty-fifth anniversary of Finzi's death; instinctively she felt that the chemistry between Paul, Robert and I would be fruitful and brought us together. From that intuition came the 1981 Ellesmere Weekend, the subsequent triennial Summer Festivals of British Music and her invitation to us to become members of the Trust.

Similarly, what was such fun being in Joy's company was the way she whisked you off to see people whom she thought you would enjoy meeting. Shortly after meeting her I discovered Edward Thomas's writing and poetry; so, on my next visit I found she'd arranged a visit to the poet's daughter Myfanwy. There were many meetings like this; from them came rich friendships made through Joy; among others were the composer Malcolm Lipkin, the master printer Mike Mitchell, the painters Richard Shirley Smith and Benedict Rubbra, and the potter Tessa Rubbra, Ben's wife. Two friendships in particular started by Joy that I fondly recall were with Hugh and Eileen Waterman, now alas both departed this life. Hugh was a retired farmer and a remarkable sagacious mind. How did Joy know that Hugh, who had originally studied English, would be exactly the person to help my attempts as a tiro writer on music, as well as stimulate my burgeoning interest in countryside life?

During the 80s the Trust initiated several recordings of music by Howard Ferguson, Michael Berkeley, Malcolm Lipkin, Kenneth Leighton, Herbert Sumsion, Ivor Gurney as well as Gerald himself. Joy relished and was fascinated by the sessions; she would listen silently and intently, only stirring to pass mints, grapes and biscuits around to grateful musicians during playback sessions. She had an instinctive ear for music of worth; but she could be ruthlessly critical. Once, during the recording sessions of Gerald's Prelude and Fugue, she leant over to me and said in so many words that she didn't think much of it. This was typical; there was never adulation of Gerald's memory to the exclusion of being aware which pieces were or were not the best of him.

I owe many things to Joy: through her eyes I learnt to see the natural world of the countryside more sharply; she led me to poets, painters and writers who, in her splendid phrase, 'had a quality'; often though they were little known and unjustly neglected. She stimulated my visual senses, encouraged my writings, gave me confidence, and all in all, values for living that I'll take with me down the years.

I'll always also be grateful to Joy for her generosity and hospitality. As with others Bushey Leaze became a bolt hole, where I, then latterly my wife Caroline and I, could recharge the batteries and escape the pressures of everyday life. She was unfailingly welcome, knew exactly what was needed and invariably shooed one out into the fresh air to walk and gain peace of mind. During our friendship I came to know the countryside near to the cottage in all seasons, all weathers and always came away refreshed. I was lucky enough to have been drawn by Joy at Bushey Leaze; the portrait is among my most treasured possessions, evoking as it does the concentrated quiet in which she worked, a silence disturbed only by the cracking of the fire in winter, or the sounds of birds and breeze in summer.

I've come full circle, back to Bushey Leaze, to Joy 'in her place', and perhaps to my most abiding memory of all: early morning in spring and summer; sunlight streaming into the cottage; the fresh scents of honeysuckle and roses in a garden with tits and finches, vivid in plumage and song, a pheasant strolling across the lawn, swallows wheeling in and out of the shed; a woodpecker, brilliant in its livery, attacking the coconut shell hanging from the feeding table. In the midst of this Joy, feeding and conversing with them as they flocked around her. They, like us, will miss her.

A farewell tribute to Joy Finzi

Diana McVeagh

Music, friends, the countryside: these three strong strands in Joy's life were woven together in a farewell tribute. Since Joy had donated her body to medical research, and was in any case a non-believer, there had been no funeral or cremation that those who mourned her might attend. But there is an elemental human need to mark such a passing, to be with other like-minded people, to share some kind of ritual; to pause, and feel a personal grief gathered into communal mourning, a private emotion given shape and form by ceremony. So on 14 September 1991 a large gathering of Joy's friends, drawn from many of the arts, came together to celebrate her long, vigorous and productive life. Newbury String Players first played in St Martin's Church at East Woodhay in 1941. To that village, on this bright early-autumn day in 1991, her friends came, driving up little lanes, parking in a field, crossing the grass to the church, and packing it so that late-comers were sitting even in the porch. NSP reached its natural end some years ago, but the energy and enthusiasm from that music-making has passed into the Finzi Trust, the Finzi Friends, and the English Musical Festivals. All who spoke or performed in this tribute were closely bound up with these activities. All the music brought its web of association.

Finzi's *Eclogue* opened the concert, played by Robert Gower in his own organ arrangement. Some will have recalled the work's first performance by Kathleen Long, at Gerald's memorial concert in January 1957 at the Victoria and Albert Museum, when their sons Christopher and Nigel played in the orchestra under John Russell. Then the Rector of Ashmansworth, Tim Horsington, welcomed everyone to the church. Next, Raphael Wallfisch and Clifford Benson played an *Elegy* by Kenneth Leighton, the composer who as an Oxford student won the support of Gerald and Joy, so that NSP performed his *Symphony for Strings* in 1949, and received in gratitude the dedication of his *Veris gratia*. Stephen Varcoe and Clifford then performed Finzi's *Let Us Garlands Bring*: the silence that surrounded 'Fear no more the heat o' the sun' was a tribute to the matching of their artistry to the occasion. The music recalled the powerful, benign figure of its dedicatee, Vaughan Williams, so influential in the lives of Gerald and Joy. Each performer introduced his music with apt words to place it in context, written by Howard Ferguson, Gerald and Joy's oldest friend; this, together with the applause encouraged by a note in the programme, made for a friendly, intimate atmosphere. Paul Spicer conducted the Finzi Singers in four of the Bridges Part Songs, 'I praise the tender flower', 'My spirit sang all day', 'Clear and gentle stream', and 'Haste on, my joys', sending Joy's name ringing to the roof. Then Raphael and Clifford played the slow movement from Finzi's Cello Concerto, confirming one's gathering impression that never can his music have been performed with greater commitment and understanding than on this occasion.

Stephen returned to join Clifford in six songs, Gurney's 'Epitaph'—'Here lies a most beautiful lady | Light of heart and step was she'—and 'Sleep', the song that moved the young student Gerald, and Joy after him, to work for Gurney's reputation. 'When I set out for Lyonnesse' and 'Epeisodia' came from sets published during Gerald's life-time. 'I need not go' and 'In five-score summers' once again brought Joy's old friends to mind, for their first performance was by John Carol Case and Howard Ferguson at the Victoria and Albert Museum concert in

Finzi's memory. Indeed, without the spoken interludes it would have been puzzling whether this concert was a tribute to Joy or Gerald. Very possibly that is how she would have wanted it. But their sons Christopher and Nigel each spoke eloquently of her as wife and mother, as artist and organiser. Andrew Burn, too young to have known Gerald, read from her letters to him, stressing her love of the natural world of growth, and her role as someone who relished bringing together people who could work fruitfully with each other.

Finally, as L'envoi, Ian Partridge sang the last song Gerald composed, which can be heard as his glorious and poignant tribute:

> Since we loved,—(the earth that shook
> As we kissed, fresh beauty took)—
> Love hath been as poets paint,
> Life as heaven is to a saint;
>
> All my joys my hope excel,
> All my work hath prosper'd well,
> All my songs have happy been,
> O my love, my life, my queen.

So spellbinding was this that when Ian finished no-one moved or clapped, until finally Christopher walked down the aisle to lead everyone out into the sunshine, and then back to lunch at the hospitable house Joy and Gerald had built.

V

The poems of Joy Finzi

From 'A Point of Departure'

The piercéd side

Shelter me in this most dark night
Let me touch and feel the lily.

O dear heart
Throughout this bright world,
Immense mystery, our searchings,
The darkness and the light
And that end to which we go—
Imperishable eternity of love.

This stem, this roof, this sheltering tree.

Song

In so short a while
        I shall be gone
From the mead of sleep
Where the waters shone
        Soon, how soon.

In so short a while
        I must go
Through a cloister of quiet
Where no winds blow
        Soon, so soon.

In so short a while
        I will come
To that summons of joy
When all is done
        Soon, now soon.

Fallen tree with ivy bound

Farewell
In this quiet place
the winds fly over.
A song bird has flown
the nest outgrown.
Soft falling feather
into an upturned hand.

Here past is caught
and present held.
Great rooted trees swayed
by passing upper winds.

While all about and unaware
from turmoil far removed
shy purposeful stirrings
of a waking day
through leaf and frond
and trembling grass.

The flight

L'atmosphere de la Terre, opaque, agitée,
variable, un frein elans des astronomes.

From earth's dark sleeping shadow
we lifted into a wind cleared sky
and southward flew by Cassiopeia.

Jupiter a beacon bright between
incandescent cities pearled in flight,
spandrels of pulsing light, webbed jewels,
embedded in a velvet night.

Ocean and dark continents of strife
unseen merged
as steadfast we flew by Cassiopeia.

Below, the moon slim horned,
though trailing vapours rose from earth's
dim round curved to the dawn,
quenched man's opal lights
and laced the phosphorescent tidal edge
towards the imperial parapet of day.

Not upon any certainty do you stand
Nothing motionless is, but as night
And day must alter view.

Plumed imagination's flight
to higher, slower, ever further sight.
To chart uncharted lakes and seas
which ever change, reform to be
aerial certainties.

Artifice of air and sound,
clouds are now your solids.
A shadow becomes an inland sea,
the mountain peaks sharp reefs
that hide and pierce.

Beneath earth made variants. Mosaics.
Man's little mark in his uncertainty
a pattern sure to sun and wind adapted.
Ramparts to strengthen with their might withstand
plotting, ferments, ingeniously contrived
each within the limit of their cognisance.

While there upon the outer tidal reach
They jettisoned their birthright to earth's delight—
And ideas died helpless on a beach.

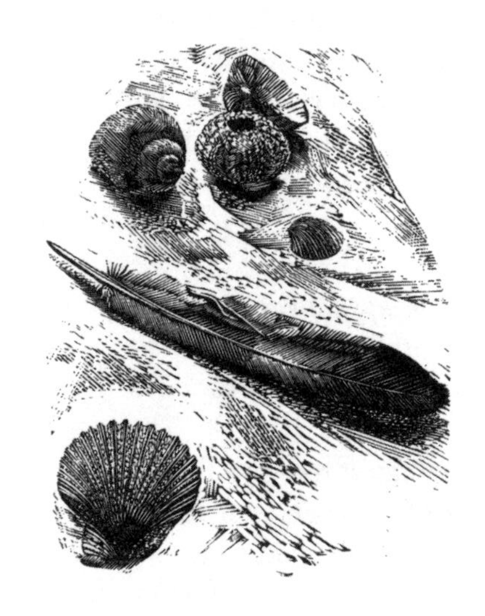

Sabine May Day

Haste, O haste, my honey throated dove
The day, silvered with a breeze,
shakes tremulous music from the trees.
A sparkling dancing tide
flows along the river side,
sounding a sea on a distant shore,
dappling the waving grasses
as it passes over the valley floor.

Unremembered rains have filled
the urgent streams
to channel deep the flowering tilth
in azure lines and seams
between the rows of coppered vines.

From mountain height
the sun pours down his gold
to deepen the shade
and sweeten in a secret glade
the nightingales cascade.

In this up-welling, all compelling,
Throng all the shining particles of May
to crown with song, this place
this hour—this day.

For Ivor Gurney

'Only envy hurts the heart
Only rust the steel.'
I Gurney

Now the last late song is gathered in—
Gleaned with love bright constancy
From that urgent scattered sowing
Before the fall of night

Forgotten now the anguish, hidden those deeds
Through love and hate, with wisdom and with folly.

Tempered in extremity they stand
Ardent battlements to times erosion —
In his beloved, most fair and watered land.

Come love

Come love
night hold eternity in her arms!

Moth dark the trees breathe quiet, and soft
airs lift a scented sigh along the river.
All day labourers sleeping lie moon beguiled,
the seeking Bat among the dream held eaves
while Swift wings scythe the upper sky.
Across the brindled stubble cobweb dewed,
in silence lie the corn cut swaithes,
stilled fountains the gilded sheaves.
A harvest gathered with Robin song and sun
warmth garnered under the quilted thatch.

Lightly pass the threshold, jasmine starred,
now hushed the gentle valley!

I come to keep my tryst
I come—
So silver shines the willow.
Unknown wonder in this night
Halts my heart across the stone
And all earths fragrance
Seems as snow.

Last lullaby

Peace now, sweet love, deep peace before you wake
into a world where truth holds clear the pattern
of our years. To move wide eyed amongst some
strange sweet flowering of all earthly strife.
Joy and sorrow pass as wind upon the grass
and that deep sown in darkness has a morning
in the light. Your gentle song is sung—
forever in eternity.
So sleep awhile, sweet love, before you wake.

From 'Twelve Months of a Year'

February encounter

Two cones of flame against an ivied wall
blaze up from whorls of fiery twisted thorn
into a lucent dusk.
Men resting pause
to gaze—while children awed in ruddy glow
amazed half-circle round this fierce delight:
sparks spiral upward and the snowdrops show
bright beneath a shadowed yew tree's night.
A blackbird singing through the woods of home
as daylight dies.
So, withered is that slow
green life and blackened now the naked stone.

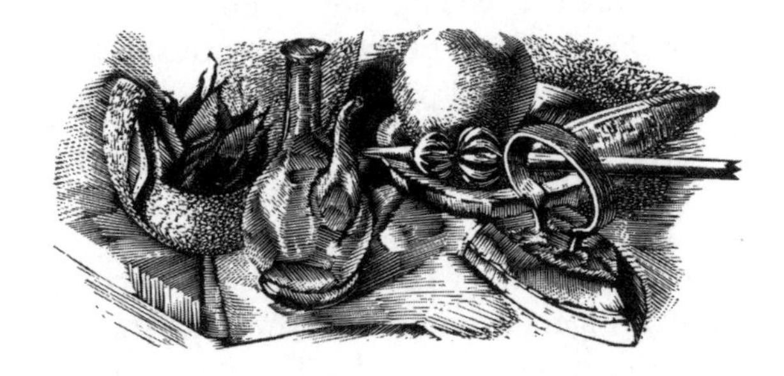

June granted

8.9.67
for Helen Thomas

On a downland summer day, the washing done,
I pegged the cobweb of her Shetland shawl,
a filigree compass with divided points,
upon the bright grass of a close cut lawn.

And she who spun
with flying fingers the long remembered
intricacy within a silent dusk
stopped to listen for a crisp footfall
to lay down a turf against the cold—
the deepening of unencompassed night.

And he who went
left the hearth that reared him, and the home,
to dissipate the seeping blood into the sand—
the broken betrayal of sunrise and the known
amidst the roar and passion of contested might.

And I, who lay
here a quiet hand upon a breast,
the singing of every bird beneath this sun,
slip my fingers through the flowering grass—
and know beneath the laden boughs of may
the hidden turmoil of a burning heart.
On such another summer day she came,
then nearly blind: smiled, and labouring wrote
of a remembered harvest, the gathering skills,
The petal fruit down avenues of green leaves—
joy and beauty vanished trackways
over these hills.

On hearing of the lightening Israeli attack
on Egyptian armoured forces in the desert.

New day

And then I saw the clouds
flowing endlessly
In light and darkness dissolving.

And I rose up and went, as they,
in purpose remade.

And I saw the sown lines of corn
Emerge from scattered swaithes of straw
to a far vanishing
Saffron shine over the dark earth
waiting the plough.

And the sun returned
While the wind soughing over the hill
summoned the day.

And I sung to my love, I am coming.

Time and the Comet

I saw Time gather his sickle and rake
his whetstone and his scythe
his long low shadow lay before him
in late October shine.
He gazed on the scene—then slowly moved
through rounded hillocks of green
his head down bent and bowed
with a life of steadfast toil.

The eastwind showered last leaves in the lane
a sound of a restless sea
eddying rooks as blown bonfire ash
sped on its strength to the west
tossing in strands of night—dark and clear.

The equinox stirred in the dormant sap
the last pear fell from the wall
while indifferent to the chimney's roar
the sparks last fugitive spin—
a Comet shone from stellar space.

A plume of smoke

I watched in a frozen morning of blue and gold—
again the ancient in a great-coat came
slow plodding through the hoar-frost woods
with his hayfork and sack of kindling sticks
                                        a ring of breath about his head.
He stooped to coax a little scarlet flame—
upon this blazing heart he lightly leased
his pile of growth and from the summit of his cone
                                        a plume of smoke rose to the sky
to swirl and seep through the white coral trees.

Two New Year poems

I

The moving moon went up the sky
and nowhere did abide
Softly she was going up
with a star or two beside

II

Where do the butterflies hide—
in what crevice do they bide
waiting for their aerial flight
in the warmth of summer light.

Where do the footsteps go
beyond the surface of the globe
when they set out alone
over the whiteness of the snow.

VI

Writings of Gerald Finzi

Absalom's Place

In July 1941, ever mindful of posterity and the increasingly unstable conditions of wartime Britain, Gerald Finzi put his affairs into order. He made a definitive Catalogue of Works, and as an introduction, he set out his own artistic creed in 'Absalom's Place'.[1] *That same month, July, he went to work in London at the Ministry of War Transport.*
Ten years later, in June 1951, he was diagnosed with non-Hodgkins lymphoma, and given between five and ten years to live. Finzi returned to 'Absalom's Place', and added a postscript. The full document is here reproduced in manuscript.

[1] In the Old Testament (Authorised Version), Absalom appears in 2 Samuel: 13-19. Absalom was the third son of King David. He was forgiven for murdering his half-brother Amnon, but later rebelled against his father. The passage Finzi quotes appears at 2 Samuel: 18: 18 after Absalom's death, when he is slain after being trapped in a tree.

Absaloms place.

It was Thomas Hardy who wrote
'Why do I go on doing these things?'
and, indeed, if appreciation were a measure of merit and cause for self-esteem, it wd long ago have been time for me to shut up shop, class myself as a failure, and turn to something of what the world is pleased to call a more 'useful' nature.

Yet some curious force compels us to preserve and project into the future the essence of our individuality, and, in doing so, to project something of our age and civilization. The artist is like the coral insect, building his reef out of the transitory world around him and making a solid structure to last long after his own fragile and uncertain life. It is one of the many proud points of his occupation that, great or small, there is, ultimately, little else but his work through which his country and civilization may be known & judged by posterity.

(As to stature, it is of no matter. The coral reef, like the mountain peaks, has its ups & downs.
"If he cannot bring a Ceder, let him bring a shrubbe.")

It was, then, in no mood of vanity that Henry Vaughan wrote
'Ad Posteros'

Diminuat ne sera dies praesentis honorem,
Quis, qualisque fui, percipe Posteritas.

(Englished by Blunden thus:

To After Ages.

Time soon forgets; and yet I would not have
The present wholly mouldering in the grave.
Hearken, posterity:)

Nor was Absalom guilty of mere self-aggrandizement when we read in the second book of Samuel:

> Now Absalom in his life time had taken and reared up for himself a pillar, which is in the Kings dale: For he said, I have no son to keep my name in remembrance: And he called the pillar after his own name, and it is called unto this day, Absaloms place."

And what of the main-spring of this curious force, this strange necessity?

There is no need here to go into the labyrinths of aesthetics & to discuss whether art is based on the need for communication or the need for organized expression.

For me, at any rate, the essence of art is order, completion & fulfilment. Something is created out of nothing, order out of chaos; and as we succeed in shaping our intractable material into coherence and form, a relief comes to the mind (akin to the relief experienced at the remembrance of some forgotten thing) as a new accretion is added to that projection of oneself which, in metaphor, has been called 'Absaloms place' or a coral reef or a "ceder or shrubbe"

It must be clear, particularly in the case of a slow worker, that only a long life can see the rounding-off and completion of this projection. Consequently, those few works of mine fit for publication can only be regarded as fragments of a building. The foundations have (perhaps) been laid, odd bricks are lying about, though comparatively little of the end which is envisaged is to be seen. Long may Absolom's pillar grow, but in the event of my death I am anxious for as much as is finished & fit for publication to be issued, preferably in as uniform an edition as possible. It would be unwise to give definite instructions; likely as not, with constantly changing conditions, they would soon be out of date or unpractical. I should like the whole question of revised publications, new publications & withdrawals to be dealt with systematically & I suggest that the advice of Howard Ferguson should be asked. Not only does he know my systematized marks of expression etc but his practical advice has always been of the greatest help. That, together with my dear Wife's judgment, sh.d be sufficient.

Gerald Finzi.
July 1941

Since the preceding pages were written, ten years ago, a good deal more work has been written. Performances, publication & some kindly & generous notice, have all taken place, which I hope my development has justified.

But a serious, & possibly fatal, illness has now been confirmed by the Doctors. At 49 I feel I have hardly begun my work "My thread is cut, and yet it is not spun;
And now I live, and now my life is done.

As usually happens, it is likely that new ideas, new fashions & the pressing forward of new generations, will soon obliterate my small contribution. Yet I like to think that in each generation may be found a few responsive minds, and for them I shd still like the work to be available. To shake hands with a good friend over the centuries is a pleasant thing, and the affection which an individual may retain after his departure is perhaps the only thing which guarantees an ultimate life to his work.

Gerald Finzi.
June 1951

Intimations of Immortality

Programme note for first performance, Gloucester Three Choirs Festival, 5 September 1950.

Although 1950 has been celebrated as the centenary of Wordsworth's death, it is quite fortuitous that this setting of his Ode now receives its first performance. Indeed, the work was conceived and much of it written, before 1939 when, owing to the war, it was of necessity abandoned, and it was only this year that the work was finished.

Perhaps one should say 'finished itself', if any justification is needed for the setting of a poem which, both in its philosophical content and poetic expression, is one of the greatest in the English language. It is sometimes argued that certain poems, complete and wonderful in themselves, are in no need of a musical setting, and that a composer should confine himself to words primarily intended for music. Such a view may express personal feelings but not necessarily the feelings of the composer, who is driven to composition by the impact of the words.

The poem is set complete except for two stanzas, Nos. 7 and 8, the omission of which in no way detracts from the train of thought. Wordsworth's repetition in stanza 10 of lines which appeared in stanza 3 helps to make for a natural musical 'reprise'.

Dies natalis

Programme note, Hereford Three Choirs Festival, 13 September 1946.

It is perhaps appropriate that these settings of Traherne's poems should be heard in Hereford, with which district the poet was so closely associated. The facts of Traherne's life are, as far as we know them, that he was born about 1638, probably in Hereford—though Ledbury, where there were Trahernes in the sixteenth century, has also been suggested as his birthplace. A shoemaker's son, he appears to have been connected with the old family of Traherne, who lived at Lugwardine for at least three centuries. In 1652 he was entered as a commoner of Brasenose, and in 1657 became Rector of Credenhill, a few miles outside of Hereford. In this quiet village he lived for ten years. From 1667 he was minister of Teddington near Hampton Court, and domestic chaplain to Sir Orlando Bridgman, Lord Keeper of the Great Seal. He died, aged thirty-six or thirty-seven, at Teddington on 10 October, 1674, and was buried there under the reading desk in the church. 'And so', to quote Sir Arthur Quiller-Couch, 'Thomas Traherne, B.D., with his manuscripts, stole out of men's regard of memory; no one in a noisy time missing a footfall that in life had passed so noiselessly.'

'But', continues Quiller-Couch, 'there are springs and streams which suddenly dive into chasms and are lost—to emerge into daylight at long distances, having pierced their own way through subterranean channels.' It was the discovery of Traherne's manuscripts by Bertram Dobell and their publication in 1903, followed by the publication of his unfinished prose work *Centuries of Meditation* in 1908, which first showed him to be of the company of Vaughan, Herbert and Crashaw. A further discovery by Dr H. I. Bell in the British Museum resulted in the publication of *Poems of Felicity* in 1910. This is a selection, mostly of the poems in the previous volume, but apparently edited and revised by the poet's brother Philip with a view to publication, which, unfortunately, never took place until two and a half centuries later. It is from this last volume, and from *Centuries of Meditation* that the text of *Dies natalis* is taken.

1. Intrada. This movement is for strings alone and sets the general mood of the work. It needs no discussion beyond saying that the form is of the simple A-B-A type. It leads directly into

2. Rhapsody (Recitative Stromentato). The text of this is selected

from Centuries of Meditation, and the music is based on the two main themes of the Intrada.

3. The Rapture (Danza). This is in the nature of an ecstatic dance. If analysis is necessary, the movement will be found to resemble the old Rondo type, where three contrasting sections are interspersed between appearances of the principal theme.

4. Wonder (Arioso). This, as Arioso implies, partakes of the character of both aria and recitative.

5. The Salutation (Aria). This is a more formal movement than the preceding, the structure being bound together by reappearances of the Ritornello with which it opens.

As guardian of genius

Talk given in tribute to Marion Scott for the Society of Women Musicians, London, 29 June 1954.[1]

When the full story of Ivor Gurney can ultimately be told, which will not be for many years, nothing more tragic in the history of music and verse will be found. That the time will come I have no doubt at all, for enough of Gurney's work has already been published for us to realise that it has enduring qualities and comes from an unique personality. That it has been published at all, and that the manuscripts, both music and verse, have so far survived, has been mainly due to some thirty-five years of care, wisdom, generosity and dedication, which Marion Scott gave to Ivor Gurney from his student days, through his few years of tribulation, and after his death, right up to the time of her own death. This, in itself, might have been work enough for a complete life, yet it was only a small part of the quietly unremitting work which she did throughout her life, the scope of which these tributes make clear.

Marion Scott's help and encouragement must have been given to many more young musicians than we shall ever know. Indeed, it was from a young composer, Ernest Farrar, my first teacher, who was killed in 1918, that I first heard of her. Before that war it was as a violinist that she was furthering his work and helping him with his concerts in the provinces. But it was to Ivor Gurney, more than any other musician, that this personal devotion was given.

[1] On the rear of the last page of the original typescript Finzi has pencilled in the times for his Paddington-Newbury trains.

But first a few words about Gurney. The bare facts of his life may be found in *Grove*, but the facts of his character, as seen by one who never knew him personally, must be mentioned if only to show that Marion Scott's care and sacrifice were even more remarkable than they would have been in the care of a normal person.

For there is no doubt that, according to the rules of the world, Gurney was a more than difficult person. He seems to have expected life entirely on his own terms. No-one was more unteachable or more difficult to befriend or to help, and even the best of his friends seem to have found his irresponsibility and arrogance, his unawareness of anything outside himself, to be more than they could accept for long. He was as near as anyone could be to the fictional idea of genius. But in this there was not the least trace of self-consciousness. The truth is that his mind was enflamed from his earliest days. That excitement, 'Rarely, rarely comest thou, Spirit of Delight', was with him at all times. Many of his early songs, such as the familiar 'Spring' and 'Sleep', which roused the enthusiasm of Stanford and Parry, already had that indefinable quality which marked all his characteristic work, something that took fire with fusion of words and music. On the purely instrumental side, or for work which called for more extended cerebration, his art was of less significance. His genius was of the incandescent type, and it burned too brightly to last. A fine intelligence and even a sound intuitive judgement, were at the mercy of a burning lyrical impulse which, within its limitations was, I am convinced, one of the most remarkable which we have possessed in this country. When, during the First World War, his music had to be partially silenced, his creative energies found an outlet in an easier, though no less intense, form of expression. The results were two books of mellifluous, individual, but immature verse. When, a few years later, he was in an asylum, and his mind again turned to verse, it was this time of a more rugged and powerful kind.

Gurney's creative life lasted only a few years: his student days before the war, then the war years, which included at least one breakdown, and, above all, a period of the most intense creative activity from 1918 till 1922, when he finally broke down. During this time he poured out songs which went, literally, into their hundreds and an enormous quantity of verse. Needless to say, only a small proportion of this was worthy of his best, but, even so, the residue ensures his permanence.

This, then, was the young composer whose worth was recognised by Marion Scott in his student days and whose artistic and personal life later became her full responsibility. What little could be done to ease his indigence was mainly due to her, for anyone less capable than Gurney of earning a living, or caring for his material wants, could not have been found.

We find her arranging for the first performance of his early work, writing round to ensure that a worthy audience would be present. We find her submitting his songs to publishers and dealing with the proofs of such as were published. We find her submitting his poems to the Poet Laureate (Robert Bridges) for advice and arranging for the publication of his verse, both in periodical and book form. Indeed, her correspondence on his behalf was endless and no paper or letter or manuscript relating to him was ever destroyed.

She clearly must have realised the devastating impact which the war was bound to have on a mind such as Gurney's, and a splendid series of letters written by him from France are a testimony to her continual correspondence with him, and her attempts to counter the horrors of war, and the squalor of army life, with some measure of civilisation.

Then with Gurney's breakdown, she was involved with army doctors and military hospitals, with specialists and with every possible attempt to restore him to health. That this was partially achieved can be seen by the output of the next few years, until that ultimate breakdown which saw him confined to an asylum for the remaining fifteen years of his life.

It was as a result of his final collapse that Marion Scott was enabled to take out Letters of Administration and make herself entirely responsible for him, constantly visiting him in the asylum and furthering the interests of his work. His manuscripts, scattered in every direction, were gathered together under her care, and even in the last year of her life she negotiated arrangements for the publication of a volume of his verse, selected by Edmund Blunden from the later unpublished manuscripts.

It might seem from such a brief and concentrated account of the endeavour of a lifetime that Marion Scott was a formidable character brushing all obstacles aside. Her energy seemed hardly consistent with her slightness and fragility, but one soon learned that beneath this exterior lay an iron will equal to a great heart.

Gurney himself left the best tribute to her that can be found, in one of the two early published poems to which he gave her initials. I do not think I can do better than to quote one of these, the dedication of his second volume, *War's Embers* which was published in 1919.

To M. M. S

O, if my wishes were my power,
You should be praised as were most fit,
Whose kindness cannot help but flower.

But since the fates have ordered it
Otherwise, then ere the hour
Of darkness deaden all my wit

I'll write: how all my art was poor,
My mind too thought-packed to acquit
My debt . . . And only, "Thanks once more."

Silhouette of Gerald Finzi made by Herbert Lambert (1881-1936), renowned photographer of musicians, instrument maker and dedicatee of Herbert Howells's *Lambert's Clavichord.*

VII

Writings on Finzi's music

Requiem da camera

Philip Thomas

It would appear that Mrs Finzi, Gerald's mother, was a charming woman but a defective map-reader. At the outbreak of World War One she removed herself and her children to Harrogate under the misguided impression that it was in the centre of England and therefore safe from aerial bombardment. In Harrogate young Gerald Finzi began taking lessons with the local church organist, Ernest Farrar, who had been a pupil of Stanford and was now attracting notice as a composer. There was a large element of hero-worship in Finzi's devotion to his teacher, and when Farrar was killed on active service in September 1918, Finzi was devastated.

After the war, he retreated to the Cotswolds and devoted all his energies to making himself into a composer. He became friendly with the group of utopian Arts and Crafts designers who had settled and were working in the area. He was attracted by their respect for the resonance of ancient things, the integrity of their craftsmanship and their love of art that, so to speak, smelled of the soil it grew in. I suspect their attitudes offered a bit of healthy balance to his deep identification with Hardy's bleak view of the human condition.

Finzi wrote his four-movement *Requiem da camera* in Painswick in 1924 and dedicated it to Farrar's memory. It is his earliest really substantial work. Into it he incorporated an even earlier setting of Hardy's 'In time of "The breaking of nations"', but not without entertaining doubts about its suitability; he consulted Vaughan Williams, who suggested adjusting the ending, and he even wrote out a neat full score where the setting is omitted altogether.

Finzi made no obvious attempts to get the *Requiem* published or performed—perhaps he was constrained by musical doubts, or by the painful memory of Farrar's death—but significantly he preserved all the manuscripts. Although highly self-critical, he was a man who couldn't easily destroy or abandon anything. The early deaths of his father, three brothers and his own serious illnesses made him unusually sensitive to the temporary and fragile nature of human achievements. The need to preserve and to cherish things ran deep in him—as the size and quality of his library (now dispersed) and his orchard (now much reduced) both testified.

At some later date, perhaps in the late 1920s, Finzi composed a new setting of 'In time of "The breaking of nations"', and there's plenty of circumstantial evidence that he considered this version definitive and intended to incorporate it into his *Requiem*. Perhaps the most affecting clue is that in his bound full score he has renumbered the pages to leave a twelve-page gap between the last two movements. Among his manuscripts in the Bodleian is a sketch for a full score of the new setting. It has been hastily written: in some places it's incomplete and in others virtually illegible, but if entire would run to exactly twelve pages. This is the score upon which I've based the completed orchestration of the song, retaining everything that could reasonably be salvaged and actually 'composing' only a single note.

The *Requiem da camera* is scored for solo wind (with a cor anglais but no bassoon), horn, harp, strings, a bass soloist and a small mixed chorus. The vocal and orchestral parts are kept scrupulously independent, as befits the chamber character of the piece; indeed Finzi even suggests replacing the chorus by four solo voices but at a serious cost in terms of balance and colour. The weakness of the *Requiem da camera* (it is surely an understandable weakness, even an interesting one at this distance in time) is its tone of one-paced, elegiac sweetness, but for all its stillness this *Requiem* is a protest—a desperate cry for some certainty in a faithless world. It is also a meditation on the achievement of all those musicians killed or blighted by the Great War, their works lovingly preserved in Finzi's library. In tribute to these yeomen of English music he chose texts in which stewardship of the landscape becomes a metaphor for everything lasting, secure and dependable, and it is a desperate irony that the last remnants of this Eden and the life it sustained were shot to pieces in the same carnage that robbed young Gerald Finzi of his heroes.

In 1981 Joy Finzi told me that 'Gerald was very critical of poets who cast out their early work. The early man is different from the later man isn't he? Listening now [to the early works] is interesting; like looking at an overgrown woodland path.' The bleak secular vision of the *Requiem da camera*—there is not a trace of divine retribution or heavenly expectation in it—might have led him to discover new possibilities in the deep-rooted English choral tradition, but he is prevented from carrying them through by the limitations of his inglenook and rush-matting musical language. It would be another six or seven years before his literary and musical tastes fell into step, and his style toughened and matured, but by then he had done his grieving and learnt that his special genius was for the solo song. Fortunately, he lived long enough to write some of the best by any British composer.

'Lo, the full, final sacrifice': an introduction

Philip Lancaster

In 1943 the Reverend Walter Hussey wrote in a letter to Benjamin Britten that he had a 'bee' in his bonnet about a 'closer association between the arts and the church', believing that they had become divorced from one another.

Throughout history the key to the growth and evolution of the arts has been patronage. It was under the auspices of the church that the principal developments in music were undertaken in order to transmit and transcend its teachings, from the monody of plainsong through the varying degrees of controlled polyphony, and thus harmony.

In 1937 Hussey had succeeded his father as vicar of St Matthew's Church in Northampton and in 1943 he saw the approaching fiftieth anniversary of the consecration of the church, and the annual patronal festival—St Matthew's Day, 21 September—as 'a good occasion to try to bring the arts into the celebrations'[1] to 'help re-forge the ancient link between the Church and the Arts.'[2]

For that year's patronal festival Hussey, having initially been turned

[1] *Hussey Patron of Art* (London, 1985)
[2] Letters from Hussey to Finzi 6 June and 7 July 1946.

down by William Walton, approached Benjamin Britten who replied that he had that same 'bee' about the association with the arts to provide a Festival Cantata, *Rejoice in the Lamb*. There was also a *Fanfare for Brass* by Michael Tippett and sculptor Henry Moore produced his initially controversial *Madonna and Child*—not actually unveiled until 19 February 1944.[3]

For the 1946 festival Graham Sutherland created his *Crucifixion*—a picture intended to hang opposite and complement Moore's 1943–4 sculpture, W. H. Auden wrote a Litany for St Matthew's Day (perhaps originally intended as an anthem to be set by Britten) and Alan Rawsthorne was approached to provide a festival anthem.

Rawsthorne failed to produce the work (for the second time, having also been asked to write one for the 1944 festival), and so Hussey wrote at rather short notice to Finzi on 6 June 1946. He wrote suggesting the works of the metaphysical poets: 'We have not so far had anything on the theme of the Eucharist . . . The sort of texts that pass through my mind are verses from Vaughan's "The Feast" or his "The Holy Communion", or Herbert's "Holy Communion", and many others of similar and other sorts.'[4]

Finzi turned to the seventeenth-century devotional poet Richard Crashaw, a near contemporary of George Herbert. Crashaw (1612–49) was the son of an anti-papist puritan preacher. He studied at Pembroke College Cambridge and, following the fall of the Royalists in the civil war, lost his fellowship to Peterhouse College and went into exile on the continent. During this time Crashaw turned to Catholicism and ended his days as holder of a minor office at the shrine of the Holy House in Loreto, south of Ancona on the Adriatic coast in Italy.

Finzi selected and amalgamated words from two adjacent poems in Crashaw's collected sacred poems, published in its most definitive version in the 1649 *Steps to the Temple*, and posthumously as *Carmen Deo Nostro* (1652). The two poems—'Hymn of St Thomas in Adoration of the Blessed Sacrament' and 'Hymn for the Blessed Sacrament: Lauda Sion Salvatorem' (reproduced in full below)—are very free translations of two Latin hymns by St Thomas Aquinas (1227–74): 'Adoro te devote' and 'Lauda Sion Salvatorem'.

[3] Moore had strayed from the conventional 'prettiness' of the Virgin and Child and there were initial claims that he had portrayed her with elephantiasis, was wearing jackboots and that it would have made a better doorstop.

[4] Letters from Hussey to Finzi 6 June and 7 July 1946.

In all probability Finzi turned directly to his extensive library of English poetry to find these, with his library containing three volumes of Crashaw's verse: an edition of the *Complete Works* edited by William Turnbull (John Russell Smith, 1858); *Steps to the Temple*, *Delights of the Muses and other poems* edited by A. R. Waller (Cambridge University Press, 1904) [incorporating a copy of the title page of the 1652 *Carmen Deo Nostro*]; and *Poems English, Latin and Greek* edited by L. C. Martin (Clarendon Press, 1927). None of the volumes appear to have any markings in so we cannot know when Finzi obtained them. It may be possible that Finzi could have been lead to Crashaw after stumbling on one of the translations used as a hymn in the 'Corpus Christi and the Holy Eucharist' section of Richard Runciman Terry's *Westminster Hymnal*, or similar.

Both poems are alike in language, imagery and ideas in their portrayal of the triumph of the Eucharist, allowing an easiness between Finzi's selected passages. The language and metaphor in places echo that of George Herbert, primarily in the addressing of the Lord and God as 'Love' (perhaps their most 'visible' manifestation). A distinct parallel can be found in the third stanza of Lauda Sion Salvatorem: Crashaw's '. . . and let us work a song | Loud and pleasant, sweet and long . . .' reflected in the third stanza of Herbert's 'Easter' (as set by Vaughan Williams in the *Five Mystical Songs*): '. . . and twist a song | Pleasant and long . . . ' —closer perhaps to Herbert than Aquinas:

Sit laus plena, sit sonora,
Sit jucunda, sit decora,
Mentis jubilatio

[With full praise, with noise
With pleasance, with grace,
And heartfelt shouts]

Crashaw most certainly knew George Herbert's verse (Crashaw's collection *Steps to the Temple* was named after Herbert's posthumously published collected poems *The Temple*) and it is most probable that Crashaw had met Herbert. Upon his deathbed George Herbert had entrusted the manuscript of his poems to Nicholas Ferrar (1592–1637) who, in 1625, had retired to Herbert's estate at Little Gidding in Huntingdonshire to found a 'Little Colledge'—a religious community to which Crashaw, due to his friendship with Ferrar, was a regular visitor.

One of the more poignant metaphors Aquinas, and thus Crashaw, uses

The Hymn Of Saint Thomas In Adoration Of The Blessed Sacrament

Lines in italics are those set by Finzi

WITH all the pow'rs my poor heart hath,
Of humble love and loyal faith,
Thus low, my hidden life! I bow to Thee,
Whom too much love hath bow'd more low for me.
Down, down, proud sense! discourses die,
Keep close, my soul's enquiring eye!
Nor touch nor taste must look for more,
But each sit still in his own door.

Your ports are all superfluous here,
Save that which lets in faith—the ear.
Faith is my skill, faith can believe
As fast as love new laws can give.
Faith is my force, faith strength affords
To keep pace with those pow'rful words:
And words more sure, more sweet than they
Love could not think, truth could not say.

O, let Thy wretch find that relief
Thou didst afford the faithful thief;
Plead for me, Love I allege and show
That faith has farther here to go,
And less to lean on; because then,
Though hid as God, wounds write Thee man;
Thomas might touch none but might see,
At least, the suff'ring side of Thee ;
And that, too, was Thyself which Thee did cover,
But here even that's hid, too, which hides the other.

So, consider then, that I,
Though allow'd not hand nor eye
To teach at Thy loved face, nor can
Taste Thee God, or touch Thee man,
Both yet believe and witness Thee,
My Lord, too, and my God, as loud as He.

Help, Lord, my hope increase,
And fill my portion in Thy peace,
Give love for life, nor let my days
Grow, but in new powers to name Thy praise.[1]

The receiving mouth here makes
Nor wound nor breach in what He takes.
Let one, or one thousand be
Here dividers, single he
Bears home no less, all they no more,
Nor leave they both less than before.

Though in itself this sovereign feast
Be all the same to every guest,
Yet on the same, life-meaning, bread
The child of death eats himself dead.
Nor is't Love's fault, but sin's dire skill
That thus from life can death distil.

When the blest signs thou broke shalt we,
Hold but thy faith entire as He,
Who, howsoe'er clad, cannot come
Less than whole Christ in every crumb.
In broken forms a stable faith
Untouch'd her precious total bath.

Lo, the life-food of angels then
Bow'd to the lowly mouths of men!
The childrens' bread, the bridegroom's wine,
Not to be cast to dogs or swine.

Lo, the full, final sacrifice
On which all figures fix'd their eyes,
The ransom'd Isaac and his ram,
The manna, and the Paschal Lamb!

Jesu, Master, just and true!
Our food, and faithful Shepherd too!
O, by Thyself vouchsafe to keep,
As with Thyself Thou feed'st Thy sheep.

O, let that love which thus makes Thee
Mix with our low mortality,
Lift our lean souls, and set us up
Convictors of Thine own full cup,
Co-heirs of saints, that so all may
Drink the same wine, and the same way;
Nor change the pasture, but the place,
To feed of Thee in Thine own face! Amen.

[1] Finzi sets 'to Thy name and praise'

The Hymn For The Blessed Sacrament

LAUDA SIGN SALVATOREM.
[Praise, O Sion, the Saviour]

RISE, royal Sion! rise and sing
Thy soul's kind shepherd, thy heart's King.
Stretch all thy powers, call, if you can,
Harps of heav'n to hands of man
This sovereign subject sits above
The best ambition of thy love.

Lo, the bread of life! this day's
Triumphant text provokes Thy praise—
The living and life-giving bread
To the great twelve distributed,
When Life Himself at point to die,
Of Love, was his own legacy.

Come, Love! and let us work a song
Loud and pleasant, sweet and long;
Let lips and hearts lift high the noise
Of so just and solemn joys,
Which on His white brows this bright day
Shall hence for ever bear away.

Lo, the new law of a new Lord,
With a new Lamb blesses the board!
The aged Pascha pleads not years,
But spies love's dawn, and disappears.
Types yield to truths, shades shrink away,
And their night dies into our day.

But, lest that die too, we are bid
Ever to do what he once did;
And, by a mindful, mystic breath,
That we may live, revive His death;
With a well-blest bread and wine
Transumed and taught to turn divine.

The heav'n-instructed house of faith
Here a holy dictate bath,
That they but lend their form and face,
Themselves with reverence leave their place,
Nature and name, to be made good
By nobler bread, more needful blood.

Where Nature's laws no leave will give,
Bold faith takes heart, and dares believe
In different species, name not things,
Himself to me my Saviour brings,
As meat in that, as drink in this;
But still in both one Christ He is.

O, dear memorial of that death
Which lives still, and allows us breath!
Rich, royal flood! bountiful bread!
Whose use denies us to the dead;
Whose vital gust alone can give
The same leave both to eat and live;
Live ever, bread of loves, and be
My life, my soul, my surer self to me!

O, soft self-wounding pelican,
Whose breast weeps balm for wounded man!
Ah, this way bend thy benign flood,
To a bleeding heart that gasps for blood;
That blood whose least drop sovereign be
To wash my worlds of sins from me!
Come, love! Come, Lord! and that long day
For which I languish, come away;
When this dry soul those eyes shall see,
And drink the unseal'd source of Thee;
When glory's sun faith's shade shall chase,
Then for Thy veil give me Thy face. Amen.

in the 'Hymn of Saint Thomas' (Adoro te), is a traditional Christian image of the 'Soft self-wounding pelican', plucking open her breast, feeding her young with her own flesh and blood. The parallel in Christ is obvious and is more explicit in Aquinas's original:

> Pie pellicane, Jesu Domine
> Me immundum munda tuo sanguine
>
> [Loyal pelican, Lord Jesus,
> Myself unclean, cleansed by your blood]

Finzi framed his text with two lines from towards the end of the second poem: 'Lo, the full, final sacrifice | On which all figures fix'd their eyes', guiding our 'eyes' to see the imagery within. That the text be constructed from two poems may be belied a little by the sometimes sectional nature of the work, although to some degree this is probably natural in such an extended work as this.

Towards the end of the work there appears a reference to Finzi's 1938 setting of Shakespeare's 'Come away, come away, death': the pleading to 'come away' to that final resting place, 'When this dry soul those eyes shall see, and drink the unseal'd source of Thee.'

Finzi's musical language suits the text and subject: the lines within the accompaniment and vocal parts moving naturally in themselves to create many coincident 'false relations': clashes of harmony which constantly tinge the seeming calm of the opening with a hint of pain and uneasiness that continues throughout. This uneasiness is increased with the disparate nature of some of the intervals used, (most disturbingly the use of a leap of a minor ninth, slightly adorned at 'Stretch all thy powers') perhaps word painting, 'stretching' beyond the octave, and used bare in unison at 'This sovereign subject'.

As is to be expected with Finzi's writing for voices, the word setting is very natural: almost all lines are set in speech rhythm with only occasional elongations. Likewise, as in all his songs except two (again, 'Come away, come away, death' and the 'Ode on the Rejection of St Cecilia'), there is only one note given to each syllable throughout (except for a brief slurring in the alto and tenor at 'thy heart's King' which he must have resented doing) until one reaches the Amen.

Finzi's Amen is arguably one of the finest ever set: it has even been deemed suitable for release on CD without the rest of the anthem.[5] The

[5]A very indulgent performance on Decca 'British Composers' disc 468 807-2.

long melismas give great contrast to the syllabic setting of the rest of the work and its simplicity of line and harmony, and rich texture (it is the only time in the work when all voices are divided) combine to form a most elegant and moving close to the work. The last few bars are a reminder of the pain in salvation: the key chord of E (translated from the Phrygian mode of the opening) being sustained while three voice parts move in parallel triads against it, the most strident and wrenching being the last F major against that sustained E major.

'Lo, the full, final sacrifice' became Finzi's most substantial work to date, and is one in which, as an agnostic, he seems to have been at his most open and inquisitive, even hopeful, of whatever greater being there may be, obviously feeling, and thus transmitting clearly, the power of the imagery evoked.

An Introduction to Finzi's Clarinet Concerto.

Philip Thomas

A talk by given at Worcester Three Choirs Festival, 23 August 1996.

Gerald Finzi is regarded, primarily, as composer of vocal music. For good or ill, his critical reputation rests on *Dies natalis* and his solo songs—particularly his fifty-odd settings of the poetry of Thomas Hardy. This is, of course, a distortion, for his concertante works—pieces in which the principal solo instrumentalist is heard in the context of an instrumental ensemble—are a significant part of his output. If these—published and unpublished—are added to Finzi's other music featuring instrumental soloists of some kind, they make up the largest proportion of his work other than vocal and choral music.

Why this emphasis on works featuring a principal voice? Superficially, both vocal and concertante works could be seen as springing from an interest in melody and in exploring the qualities of a solo 'line', but I think there are some less straightforward reasons. Firstly, Finzi's vocal works are prompted by his engagement with the text he is setting. Form, phrase structure and rhythmic expression are almost obsessively dictated by the form and content of the poem or prose text and by his response to them. In his concertante works he can explore line, form, phrase structure, tonality and other abstract musical matters divorced from the constraints imposed by poetic language or by his literary collaborator. Incidentally, the word 'constraint' carries no pejorative overtones in this context. When setting words, most composers see the formal implications of the text as challenging opportunities.

Secondly, the primary interest in Finzi's songs is not melodic, but lies in the balance between psychological and musical tension, in the drama, the expression of vision and the illumination of sub-text. Finzi uses the song medium to explore the inner life of the protagonist or of the poem; something at which the text may hint but which is often not explicitly stated. In his concertante music, however, he can fully explore melody and motif, and their abstract, structural possibilities without being tied to the narrative shape or psychological undertow of any text.

For example, what one might call Finzi's 'Songs Without Words', the Five Bagatelles for clarinet and piano, have a simple, lyrical charm which is absent from all but the most breezily two-dimensional of his songs. Of course his songs can be very lyrical indeed, though that may not be what we remember them for. This can be illustrated by his setting of, for example,

> Knowing that, though Love cease,
> Love's race shows no decrease;
> All find in dorp or dell
> An Amabel.
> ('Amabel')

Or again:

> Where in wild-winged crowds
> Blown birds show their whiteness
> Up against the lightness
> Of the clammy clouds;
> By the random river
> Pushing to the sea,
> Under bents that quiver
> There shall rest we.
> ('Epeisodia')

Thirdly, the solo instrument is an outsider. Finzi, who was himself an outsider in so many ways, may have found in his concertante works an opportunity to write his equivalent to Whitman's Song of Myself. I would offer for consideration the idea that Finzi's instrumental soloists are singing of his own inner life in unusually direct, often painful terms.

In many ways, Finzi is the ideal Three Choirs Festival composer. His music is clearly of the twentieth century yet it is tuneful, accessible and undaunting; it and he are profoundly English in musical idiom and lifestyle; many of his closest friends and many of the composers who influenced him most deeply were either connected with, championed by or had their music frequently performed at Three Choirs Festivals in the past—Parry, Elgar, Vaughan Williams, Howells, Sumsion and dozens of others. Tangentially, the Three Choirs Festival might even be said to have hastened his death.

For Finzi's Clarinet Concerto, today is a homecoming. The work was commissioned in 1948 for the 1949 Festival, at which the premiere was conducted by Finzi with Frederick Thurston as the distinguished soloist. It is a product of the most relaxed, untroubled and confident moment of his life, qualities that are apparent in the music itself.

The clarinet is one of that rarest category of instruments; those that did not evolve, but were consciously 'invented', yet which have survived in common use. It has become neither an historical curiosity nor obsolete, as have the baryton, glass harmonica, ophicleide and a great many more. The other notably successful survivor is the saxophone—closely enough related to the clarinet to suggest that instrument makers have identified a serious gap in the range of available timbres; single-reed wind instruments with a warm flexible sound. These are instruments overwhelmingly romantic in character, as you can hear triumphantly demonstrated in Finzi's Concerto.

The clarinet was invented very early in the eighteenth century, and it has not changed significantly since its fingering and key-work were perfected in the mid-nineteenth century. For complex physical/acoustical reasons it is unlike all other orchestral wind instruments in that it over-blows at the twelfth, rather than octave. This, and the fact that the inside bore of the instrument is distorted by the position of the sound holes, account for its unique tone-colour (particularly in extreme registers), its ability to slide suggestively between notes (like the celebrated glissando at the start of Gershwin's *Rhapsody in Blue*) and for its vulnerable, even unstable sound quality.

At its worst the clarinet can sound yelping and out-of-tune with other wind instruments—I know several good, professional players who half joke that the clarinet is never in tune. At its best it possesses a human warmth, an affecting vibrato and a persuasive, singing tone unrivalled except by the violin. With a wider compass than any similarly sized wind instrument, great flexibility and a capacity for extreme rapidity of execution, it is a great boon to composers. Its smooth, breathy, sensual sound has often been compared to the human voice—which might be expected to increase its Finzi-appeal. For similar reasons it has become the dominant instrument associated with jazz and the blues, where intense emotions lie half-exposed on the surface.

Perhaps more than any other instrument, its repertory and technical development have from the earliest days been consistently inspired by great performers. Mozart's Concerto, Weber's many clarinet pieces (sometimes it seems that there must be hundreds of them, all arpeggios!) and Brahms's wonderful chamber works were all inspired by, or created for particular virtuosi. No-one seems to have written a major clarinet work speculatively or just for the fun of it.

This tendency has continued and been reinforced in the twentieth century. Busoni's Concertino, the great concertos by Nielsen, Stravinsky, Copland and Hindemith, sonatas by Bernstein and Poulenc, Bartok's *Contrasts*, Peter Maxwell Davies's works featuring the instrument, Thea Musgrave's Concerto—all were inspired by great clarinettists. Virtuoso Artie Shaw even wrote a slight, but hilarious one-movement, jazz concerto for himself to play. The years 1949–1951 were particularly fruitful: the concertos by Finzi, Copland, Hindemith, Malcolm Arnold, and Joseph Horowitz—among others. Alun Hoddinott's came only shortly afterwards, written for Gervase de Peyer, and Finzi himself was not immune to the clarinet 'Cult of Personality'.

Finzi intended his Concerto for Pauline Juler who, with Howard Ferguson, had given the successful first performance of his Five Bagatelles in 1943, however she was not available, so the eminent clarinettist Frederick Thurston got the job and the honour.

He was Finzi's exact contemporary; both born in 1901 and both destined to die before realising their full capabilities, Thurston in 1953 and Finzi in 1956. Frederick Thurston received his initial training from his father and by the 1920s was playing with the Royal Philharmonic and Royal Opera House Orchestras. In 1930 he was appointed principal clarinet in the new BBC Symphony Orchestra, where he stayed until 1946 when he left to pursue a career as soloist and chamber music player.

His style was fastidious, elegant and extremely unshowy. Like his British counterparts, oboist Leon Goossens and viola player Lionel Tertis, his playing encouraged a generation of composers to write superb works for him. These include sonatas by Bax and Howells, Bliss's Clarinet Quintet, and Ireland's wonderful Fantasy Sonata with its fantastic, exposed opening phrase that can only have been composed with a particular player in mind, it is a gauntlet thrown down to all other clarinettists. Now, of course, he is also associated with the Finzi concerto, although it was not initially written with him in mind.

Gerald Finzi wrote four large-scale works which bore the title concerto at some time or other. Some part or parts of each have survived and made its way into print, though in some cases much revised as was his habit. They are:

1. Violin Concerto. (1925–7, quietly suppressed by the composer and revived in 2001.)
1b. Introit for small orchestra and solo violin—note the reversal of rôles in the title—is a revised version of the slow movement, published in 1935. It was reissued in 1943, further revised and shortened.
2. Piano Concerto. Finzi worked from the 1920s until the 1950s on many versions of something intended as a piano concerto, but never completed in that form. He took advice on the work from R. O. Morris and many drafts survive.
2b. Grand Fantasia and Toccata for piano and orchestra (1955) makes use of much material from sketches for the first movement of the concerto, to which is added a substantial toccata with the character of a brilliant finale.
2c. Eclogue for piano and strings is more-or-less the slow movement of the Piano Concerto. It was performed in Finzi's lifetime but published posthumously.
3. Clarinet Concerto (1948–9).
4. Cello Concerto (1955).

These works share a number of common characteristics. They have dark, deeply serious first movements; grand in character, tackling big musical issues, inclined to be rhetorical and incorporating occasional dramatic, not to say melodramatic gestures. The Grand Fantasia, Clarinet Concerto and Cello Concerto all conform to this pattern and all include some kind of cadenza. All include, or included at some stage in their gestation, a meditative, lyrical slow movement. These slow movements are studies in gentle, tender melancholy enclosing moments of great stillness and are based on musical material which tends toward the modal. They help to define a recognisable 'Finzi mood' which occurs instrumentally in the Interlude for oboe and string quartet (1936) and the posthumously published Elegy for violin and piano. Interestingly, both were at some stage intended as movements of much larger works, an Oboe Quartet or

Quintet and a Violin Sonata.

All four include a frolicsome rondo finale based on a long, gradually uncoiling theme. These final movements are essentially light-hearted though each includes a moment of deeper reflection or refers back to darker, more serious material from an earlier movement. This technique is heard at its most spectacular in the Grand Fantasia, at its most subtly convincing and unforced in the Clarinet Concerto.

None of this is revolutionary stuff, of course, but it is worked through consistently enough to suggest a thoughtful, personal vision of the concerto as a form; a consistent furrow being ploughed straight and deeply. Finzi's Songs of Myself begin by confronting and tackling demons (perhaps a little self-consciously, as if he thinks this is what's expected of him), are tender at the heart, and are hopeful at the end for a joy tinged with melancholy. Thus the echo of the composer's own life.

Finzi's three-movement Clarinet Concerto is scored for clarinet and strings, a combination designed to offer a smooth, homogenous background against which to hear the soloist. A string orchestra has its own distinct character and integrity as an ensemble and is capable of the quietest, most subtle effects yet even at its grandest will neither compete with nor entirely cover the sound of the clarinet. It is also a medium of which Finzi had proved himself a master in *Dies natalis*—mastery gained as conductor of the Newbury String Players, and as eager student of the works of Parry, Elgar and Vaughan Williams. His string scoring—a virtuosic compendium of thoroughly practical effects, unsuspected doublings, daring divisi—is an entertaining study in itself.

The first movement is as we might have predicted noble and melancholic, serious and occasionally spectacularly dramatic. Running through it is a handsome string ritornello, a rhetorical flourish that frames each section of the movement and which excludes the soloist—though motivically it gives rise to important solo material. Between varied restatements of this ritornello, the clarinet explores and develops more introspective material, loosely following the outline of classical sonata structure. There is even a minute solo cadenza just before the end (apparently inserted on the advice of Vaughan Williams), a tiny essay in controlled passion which artfully, achingly, avoids landing on the tonic note C.

After an atmospheric introduction—an evocation of that intense, rapt stillness of which Finzi is so particularly the musical master—the second movement is a ternary meditation based on a surprisingly bleak little three-note cell, turned by the composer to wonderful melodic account.

However, the brusque introduction to the third movement pushes contemplation aside. The finale is to be a cheerful rondo with a stunningly memorable theme, heard three times in three different keys—an effect as likely to be the product of obduracy as of calculation. These complete, though varied, statements of the rondo theme enclose two tripartite episodes in contrasting moods—rather surprisingly, the first one includes a waltz. A nostalgic reference back to the sobriety of the first movement is developed and allowed to shimmer into ravishing near-silence, only to be brushed aside by a loud, romping coda. Finzi was largely self-taught as a composer, as in most things, and felt himself hampered by lack of technique, whilst despising technique as an end in itself. His painstaking, intuitive method of invention meant that some works were written intermittently over as long a period as thirty years! Consequently he found composing fast music difficult; there were so many more notes to set down, yet the music would easily become dry and stilted if laboured over. The Clarinet Concerto was, of necessity, written quickly so it is not surprising to find him falling back on ideas from old sketchbooks. Its memorable rondo theme derives from a fragment drafted in the 1930s and intended for an Oboe Quintet—presumably the work from which the published Interlude was eventually drawn. His original sketch began strongly, but each of Finzi's three attempts to develop it ran into the sand. Fifteen years later, it found fertile soil, flowered and bore fruit in the finale of the Clarinet Concerto.

More surprising is what seems to me to be the fairly naked, yet until now unremarked, adaptation of material from an admired work by one of his English contemporaries. We know that Finzi admired Walton's music, indeed there are occasional moments of near-imitation—and I remember Joy Finzi telling me that Gerald thought the Viola Concerto particularly fine. Knowing he had only a short time to compose his own Clarinet Concerto, I suspect that Finzi cast about for a stimulus outside himself. He found one in Walton's Violin Concerto, premiered and well received only a few years earlier.

The Walton opens with the soloist playing a hauntingly bittersweet theme, characterised by the upward leap of an octave which has contracted to an astringent major seventh within the space of a few bars (Ex.1):

Ex.1

If the repeated note at the start is removed, it sounds like this (Ex. 2):

If we then remove the little triadic ornament at x and adjust the final interval, we get (Ex. 3):

Transposed into C minor, with the major seventh filled-out as shown at z and a falling octave placed at the end to echo the rising octave at the start we have arrived at Finzi's opening clarinet phrase (Ex. 4):

It would be quite wrong to hear Finzi's work merely as some sort of copy of Walton's, or to think it in any way diminished by what seems to be the clear relationship between them. They are entirely different in their working out and in their effect. Finzi has taken the material and reinvented it in his own terms. Moreover, he has used it not as an opening gambit but as the clarinet's soft answer to an assertive tutti also based on the upward leap of an octave. This gives the material a quite different mood and personality.

Buried in this new tune is a motif, a tiny pattern of intervals (marked z above) which runs through the entire work, giving it a degree of motivic unity perhaps unexpected in a composer as intuitive as Finzi. This shape—a tiny interval followed by a much larger one, or vice versa—permeates every aspect of the concerto, melodically, harmonically and structurally. This is not the place for detailed analysis, but if I might give some idea of how all-pervading and cleverly varied this three-note motif is, it is implied in the vigorous, leaping octaves at the start (Ex. 5):

Ex. 5

which has buried within it a shape like (Ex. 6):

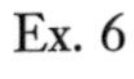

Ex. 6

which appears in the opening solo statement, much compressed, as z. Finzi even uses a version of this shape to spell out the harmonic relationship between the first two movements, the first ending with a curious D flat to C cadence and the second settling eventually into F, which might be perceived thus (Ex. 7):

Ex. 7

But before it settles, the second movement's atmospheric introduction is entirely based on versions of the motif (Ex. 8):

Ex. 8

Which, arriving at the comfort of F major, sweetens into (Ex. 9):

Ex. 9

Even the last movement rondo theme, based on material conceived so many years earlier, joins in. Here are the opening few notes (Ex. 10):

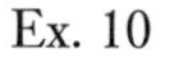

Ex. 10

which, if we remove the ornamental turn, become (Ex. 11):

Ex. 11

Of course, laying bare selective aspects of the composition process as crudely as this can make the whole business seem terribly calculating. Undoubtedly some of these connections are deliberate, but others will be accidental—or at least subliminal. Some will be there simply because many of the ideas invented and developed by an intelligent artist working within an established tradition will share a 'family likeness'.

There was a time when one felt almost obliged to apologise for admiring any aspect of Finzi's art. Fortunately, that is no longer the case. We have matured sufficiently to be suspicious of critical zeitgeist and to realise that fashion is the least important quality of art. Sooner or later, time will render it meaningless and 'good work' can be relished on its own terms.

In many ways, Finzi's Clarinet Concerto is one of his most satisfying, elegant and personal works—certainly the most immediately approachable of his concertante works. It manages to be thoughtful and well-crafted whilst retaining its freshness and spontaneity. It has warmth, gentle humour, a touch of drama (even melodrama in the first movement), and an immense charm and direct appeal that has earned it a place at the heart of the twentieth-century wind repertoire.

Finzi and Wordsworth

Stephen Banfield

A talk given at the tenth birthday gathering of the Finzi Friends in Gloucester on 25 August 1992.

'Finzi and Wordsworth': what a curiously unequal yoking! Imagine, say, a cultured German or Frenchwoman passing through Gloucester—or even dropping in on us—and seeing the title. She would be puzzled that a name ranked inferior only to Shakespeare and Milton by Matthew Arnold, in other words one of the world's greatest poets, should be linked in this quintessentially English context with one which was so foreign-sounding and, for her, so unknown. She would, in my opinion, be right to expect a reasoned explanation of both concerns from any Finzi Friend she happened to waylay.

Let us consider for a moment Finzi's stature. He was by most yard-sticks a fairly minor composer. He lived exclusively in a country generally felt to be short on Olympic medallist musicians. Indeed, he lived mostly in the country, showing a limited desire to become involved in the metropolitan doings of the musical academy or other aspects of public life. He almost never travelled abroad. He wrote relatively little: no symphony, no solo keyboard music, little chamber music, no opera, not even any film music. What he did write was, by and large, self-consciously isolated from the dominant trends in his art, conservative in style and not so much nationalist as parochial, or maybe vernacular, in ways such as its avoidance, in the vocal music, of foreign-language texts, even Latin, and of technical virtuosity.

Many of his British musical contemporaries went about things in a similar way, of course, and we have become used to the idea of the small, exquisite English talent, particularly in song. Gurney, Quilter, Warlock, Milford, Harry Gill . . . indeed, the idea of 'Finzi and his friends' has become a bit of a joke. The model comes partly from the tradition of minor lyrical poets, stretching back through William Barnes, John Clare and the eighteenth-century folk revival to Gray's concept of the 'mute inglorious Milton'; and to recall that the phrase 'far from the madding crowd' also stems from Gray's Elegy brings us full circle back to Finzi via Hardy. Perhaps the concept of repose in obscurity is virtually innate in lyrical poetry, to the extent of its origins in the epitaph. The model is also partly that of the gentleman scholar, the antiquarian clergyman constructing his little world of knowledge in whatever remote parish he has been banished to after his cosmopolitan classical education. (The two models often went together, of course, as with Barnes and with Finzi's 'own' poet Traherne.) There was certainly a good deal of the pastoral antiquarian in Finzi, impressive where it concerned his reclamation of eighteenth-century English music, less so where it was merely a hobby (as it was with his books and apples, resources which he preferred to share largely with friends rather than develop into published research), and sometimes close to self-parody, as in his correspondence with the curator of the Newbury Museum after he had dug up bits of a prehistoric pot in his garden at Ashmansworth.

Wordsworth himself fostered the philosophy of the poetic recluse, retreating to Grasmere and conservatism after France and the Revolution. He has attracted a good deal of censure for it as well as admiration, and it has a direct bearing on the Immortality Ode, whose argument, to simplify cruelly, suggests that life's pattern is to settle down at the cost of losing the ecstatic tumult of youth. To read the poem or to listen to a musical setting of it is therefore to be made to ask the question: is this true? One may also ask what the poem does not, namely whether there is any choice in the matter. Wordsworth, particularly by comparison with his friend Coleridge, may not have wanted to be reminded that he had opted for a life of self-preservation rather than risk.

We are talking about two different things here, artistic lifestyle and artistic destiny. We also need to consider the differences between music and poetry, music as a professional performance art being far less amenable to creative reclusion than poetry. But taking all things together, I would argue that, unlike the subjects of Gray's Elegy, Finzi chose to be a minor composer: I think there is a lot of evidence to suggest that he knew exactly what he was doing, though not without uneasiness and an enduring capacity to surprise himself which I consider to have been one of the great strengths of his creative personality.

However, he also chose to be one of the few composers to set Wordsworth, and to go straight to one of the greatest poems in the English language. This was such an apparent contradiction, an affront to some, that across the road in the Cathedral forty-two years ago the critics were inclined to echo that famous reviewer of Wordsworth himself and say, 'This will never do'. Yet the paradox of the smaller talent fixing on the larger is not something that can ever be dismissed. It is a most curious form of power relations, for the larger talent, even when alive, is impotent to shake off the smaller, and the smaller can get more or less whatever he or she wants out of it purely by persistence and willpower. One of the things I have to say to PhD students is, 'You do realise that you will become a world expert on this subject whether you want to or not?' It is the relation of Boswell to Johnson, of Robert Craft to Stravinsky, of Jerrold Northrop Moore to Elgar. Setting literature to music is a comparably public act of research and criticism, and thus in a real sense Finzi chose to add his name to the list of Wordsworth's critical biographers by interpreting his Ode. However, since he was already seen as having an authorised relationship with Hardy, some felt that he would have done best to remain monogamous. 'What Finzi has to say he seems to have said once and for all in the Hardy songs', wrote Wilfrid Mellers in *Music Survey*.

Posterity plays some strange games in this field. The smaller talent can very swiftly turn out to be the larger, as countless operatic adaptations of popular plays and novels have proved (take *Carmen*, for instance); or our view of the larger may be irrevocably altered by the smaller—no-one who has seen *Kiss Me, Kate* can ever find *The Taming of the Shrew* quite as funny again, as W. H. Auden recognised. And while I am not suggesting that Finzi's Immortality Ode, the one that is sung or listened to, will ever overtake the one that is read or read about as the primary object of artistic consumption, I do believe that we should not underestimate the number of people, proportionately more, one presumes, as the years pass, who will come to the poem indirectly through Finzi the composer rather than directly through Wordsworth the poet. Thus by sponsoring information, recordings and performances the Finzi Trust, indeed the present audience, becomes surprisingly deeply implicated in the processes of history. I well remember, as an undergraduate twenty or more years ago, picking the Finzi vocal score off the shelves of the Pendlebury Library in Cambridge and playing it through on the piano, wondering if I should ever have a chance to hear it properly; and a friend's mother who had been in the audience in 1950 remembered it as a work she assumed would not enter the repertoire. Finzi assumed this too, writing to Robin Milford in September 1953:

> It's too much to think that it will become part of our choral repertoire. One has seen too many better things passed over to be able to have much faith in a possible welcome by the future, but a few friendly souls in a century or two may find something likeable in you and me, and that is pleasant enough to think about.

He was wrong: the work has found more than 'a few friendly souls', in considerably less than a century or two, and he was not to know that the hi-fi boom would add a whole new dimension to the musical marketplace. Between 1950 and 1980, twenty-six UK performances of *Intimations* are registered, about one per annum if we allow for evident gaps in the record (e.g. Leeds 1953, Birmingham 1954). Then in 1981 the number suddenly began to shoot up—there were six performances that year alone and a total of thirty-five over the ensuing decade; by 1987 the work had even percolated to such remote outposts of civilisation as Leighton Buzzard. This rising fortune may be partly due to the rapid reversals of taste and shifts of perspective of our post-modern times; nevertheless, I feel sure that without the Trust, Finzi's *Intimations* might still be as neglected as Somervell's, the 1907 Leeds Festival setting which made no impact and which Finzi may not even have known. Nor am I prepared to say that Finzi's setting has risen to the surface over the course of time simply because it is better, since we are not to know that in another twenty years' time there may not also be two recordings of Somervell's. The judgments of posterity are never fixed, for the addition of every atom of knowledge changes them, however slightly and often massively.

Enough of this talk of minor stature and rising reputation. What matters equally is that mixed in with the modesty and the sense of limitation there was a splendid creative arrogance about Finzi, especially as a young man, and it leaves us in little doubt that at the bottom of his heart he felt all along that he was the person to set the Ode to music. His comment in the well-known December 1936 letter to Howard Ferguson—about the difference between choosing a text and being chosen by one—suggests as much, though its apparently rather Mosaical tone was not, I think, intended, for Finzi was quoting something Herbert Sumsion had said to him and his preceding statement in the letter was the blander humanistic credo (albeit one which still begs the big questions) 'that a composer is (presumably) moved by a poem and wishes to identify himself with it and share it.' In fact it is difficult to imagine anyone else having made an 'authorised' setting of the poem. It had to be someone English, with impeccable word-setting and a musical idiom warm or conservative enough to suit the romantic verse and metaphysical enough to sustain the argument. Perhaps the young Tippett could have matched most of these requirements; but Finzi's Traherne settings already made him the more obvious person by the late 1930s. He himself must have sensed where he stood and gained resolution from it.

Finzi certainly knew his Wordsworth and would have been familiar with the Ode from a relatively early age. His library contained twenty-six volumes of Wordsworth's and his sister's writings and twenty books about him. Many of these were purchased in the 1940s, when he was expanding his collection at a phenomenal rate, but one of the books on Wordsworth was bought in 1926 and an *Observer* cutting from December 1922 is interleaved in another. His 1919 edition of Dorothy Wordsworth's journals contains a pencil mark which may indicate that it was purchased as early as the year of publication. His copy of one of the chief exegeses of Wordsworth's poetic thought and particularly of the Ode, Garrod's *Lectures and Essays* of 1923, is comprehensively marked in pencil, not just in the 'Ode' chapter—or rather it was until he or someone else took rather extraordinary pains to rub out or, in the case of the inside back cover opening, to paste the markings over. Whether this was an attempt to cover his tracks we can only guess. Unfortunately at the time of writing Hutchinson's 1917 edition of Wordsworth's poems is out of the Finzi Book Room on loan to an exhibition; it would have been interesting to see whether it is marked with any clues about a particular early interest in the poet or the Ode. So we cannot know when he decided to compose his setting or when he actually began it. Joy, when launching the Finzi Friends, talked of *Intimations* being 'conceived some twenty-five years before' and testified that it 'was certainly with us all our married days', i.e. from 1933. Finzi himself told the poet Ian Davie in a letter of 1955 that it had 'simmered for about sixteen years'; yet he already seems to have been well into the composition of it by September 1931, when he wrote to Ivor Gurney's friend, the poet Jack Haines, asking him if he thought Wordsworth intended the accentuation '*shout* round me' or 'shout *round* me' in Stanza III. We cannot be sure that this was vis-à-vis the actual musical setting which we now have, but if it was, it rather scuppers my conviction that *Intimations*, this section above all, could never have been written without the example of *Belshazzar's Feast*—the first performance of *Belshazzar* was not for another three weeks. In February 1938 Finzi wrote to William Busch saying that he was half way through, exaggerating somewhat if we are to believe what he wrote to Robin Milford in 1945, that it 'was left more than a third done before the war.' The rest of it seems to have come in a rush in 1949–50, presumably when he received the Gloucester commission.

It was his biggest work, and an ambitious one not just in the sense discussed earlier. Wordsworth, despite having pioneered the romantic lyrical ballad, has generally not been found an easy poet to set to music, for his stream of thought characteristically has a flux and an intonation, not to mention a vocabulary, all of its own, and they are not the flux and intonation of music. One engages a distinctive 'inner ear' when reading Wordsworth, no less a part of his essence than the inner eye he so often called upon. This is particularly true of his iambic pentameters, and the very first line of Intimations is a case in point:

> There was a time when meadow, grove, and stream,

Wordsworth goes straight into his 'narrative-as-ramble' mode: indeed, at the end of the first line he is not even at the end of his list: the earth and every common sight are still to come. And for all the rich and attractive-looking metrical fluctuation that immediately and, since it is an ode, habitually ensues, the first five lines remain one indivisible thought and one extended grammatical clause, personal and leisurely in their stamp:

> There was a time when meadow, grove, and stream,
> The earth, and every common sight,
>   To me did seem
>   Apparelled in celestial light,
> The glory and the freshness of a dream.

What these lines do is set the stance and suggest something of the scale of the philosophical thought, they establish the poet's viewpoint; and Finzi accordingly must above all provide them with a theme—a structural motive—and the right pace. This he does satisfactorily enough, but with all respect it is not his best word-setting, as Hans Redlich quite rightly pointed out in a severe review of the score in 1952. He is on easier ground with the short-lined, corybantic apostrophes that make up the ecstasy-evoking portions of the poem; but Wordsworth continually abandons these for introspection—and indeed mixes the two up metrically—and when Finzi develops his equivalent types and mixtures, moving and mediating between the immediacy and 'innocence' of choral homophony or solo melody and the self-consciousness of imitative writing, the effect is not always happy. The clumsy gear-change at figure twelve ('To me alone there came a thought of grief') is an acute instance, and I well remember Philip Brunelle in Minneapolis telling his basses that they sounded as though they were at the dentist at this point; I don't think it was entirely their fault. Nor do I think it has been adequately pointed out what a problem Finzi was inviting in taking on such an extended piece of rhapsodic philosophy all in the first person singular. Wordsworth's 'we', as well as his apostrophes, are still spoken by his 'I', and unlike, say, Gerontius, he offers no opportunity for other characters to speak for themselves. This mode of address is fine for *Dies natalis* but can no longer play on its own innocence when a chorus is involved. One is never entirely sure who the chorus are in his setting.

This is all the more so because Finzi was making a statement with it. To point this out may seem so obvious as to be crass; but the history of composers doing so in large-scale choral music, of giving, as it were, public readings not of narrative poetry as enactment, nor of liturgical or ceremonial texts as vehicles for corporate affirmation of belief, but of major, pre-existing literary works as testimonies of personal identification (Goethe's 'elective affinities'), which, as we have seen, Finzi acknowledged to be what he was attempting in *Intimations*, is a relatively recent phenomenon in the history of western music. As such, we can nowadays see that it operates in a specifically romantic context of artistic communication, one within which Finzi might not have been pleased to be told that he was still instinctively working. Beethoven setting Schiller's 'Ode to Joy', Schumann, Liszt and Mahler setting part eleven of Goethe's *Faust*, Parry setting Shelley's *Prometheus Unbound*, Elgar setting Newman's *The Dream of Gerontius*, Delius (and Strauss) setting Nietzsche's *Also Sprach Zarathustra*—these are aspiring and presumptive partnerships one and all; every one of the composers is saying, 'Look, I can partake of this greatness; and through me you can'. Once this is recognised as the way these pieces function, Elgar's 'This is the best of me' inscribed at the end of the manuscript of *Gerontius* becomes tautological.

Understandably, in our unhappy twentieth century this role has come rather literally to grief. Even before the First World War it appears doomed, as in the spate of Whitman settings climaxing with Vaughan Williams's *Sea Symphony*, or even somewhat repellent, as in Elgar's *The Music Makers*. Later composers, when they choose to sustain a metaphysical tone, are more likely to ask us to share in penitence or protest, psychoanalysis or confession. Yet I believe Finzi manages to uphold the tradition of romantic heroism—which at root is what it is—with courage, integrity and ultimately success in *Intimations*. I should like to devote the remaining time to two or three suggestions as to how and why he is able to do so.

First, I think he was more closely and pervasively connected with Wordsworth than we realise, maybe more closely than he realised. Here may I recommend a stimulating little book, Jonathan Bate's *Romantic Ecology: Wordsworth and the environmental tradition*, published in 1991 by Routledge. Bate shows how a great deal of the ecological, conservationist way of thinking and the holistic values that go with it—things for which we admire Finzi the more as the years pass and our planet reels from ill-health—stems from Wordsworth. The key figure in their development and transmission was Ruskin. He too revelled in the Wordsworthian vision of personal empowerment through nature, as the following passage makes clear:

> although there was no definite religious sentiment mingled with it, there

> was a continual perception of Sanctity in the whole of nature, from the slightest thing to the vastest; —an instinctive awe, mixed with delight; an indefinable thrill, such as we sometimes imagine to indicate the presence of a disembodied spirit. I could only feel this perfectly when I was alone; and then it would often make me shiver from head to foot with the joy and fear of it . . . and this joy in nature seemed to me to come of a sort of heart-hunger, satisfied with the presence of a Great and Holy Spirit. These feelings remained in their full intensity till I was eighteen or twenty, and then, as the reflective and practical power increased, and the 'cares of this world' gained upon me, faded gradually away, in the manner described by Wordsworth in his Intimations of Immortality.

This passage reminds us also, of course, of Traherne and *Dies natalis*, and of Finzi's comment about many a dead poet inhabiting a live stockbroker. But this was only Ruskin's starting-point. He recognised the threat to nature from the industrial revolution and developmental economics and, unlike Wordsworth, made it his lifetime's job to preach and warn and try to do something to change a whole civilisation's cast of thinking. Some accordingly blame him for initiating the decline of the industrial spirit in Britain. No-one reads him now, though maybe we shall once we realise how his influence has survived until again it seems needed.

Finzi probably didn't read him either—he possessed only five books by him and one about him (not many by his standards) and they show no signs of his use; Ruskin was too Victorian to remain current reading in, say, the 1920s. But he was undoubtedly influenced by him. In 1888 Ruskin, 'then in his declining years and suffering from intermittent bouts of madness' as Clive Aslet puts it in *The Last Country Houses*, acquired a companion on a trip around Europe, a young architect whom he had found sketching in Abbeville Cathedral. His name was Detmar Blow. Blow, harnessing Ruskin's advocacy of craftsmanship and organic creativity, went on to play a prominent role in the Arts and Crafts movement in Britain.

Finzi latched on to this movement and its values when he was still very young and may even have persuaded his mother to move with him to Gloucestershire from Harrogate in 1922 specifically so as to live in the movement's emblematic place of habitation, the Cotswolds. He soon met Blow, whose recently-built house on the escarpment, Hilles, became a place of hospitality and intimacy to him and who with his wife and children offered Finzi a surrogate family, the one he would have chosen to be born into if he could. Blow, who was agent for the Duke of Westminster, also found him his subsequent lodgings in London, the little house behind Sloane Square, and must also have been the ultimate inspiration behind Finzi's decision to build his own house (Blow died the year Finzi moved into Ashmansworth).

The links and continuity in cast of mind can be demonstrated by continuity in turn of phrase. Bate quotes a passage from Wordsworth's best-selling book *A Guide to the Lakes*, in which he describes Lakeland cottages, which may be said rather 'to have grown than to have been erected; —to have risen, by an instinct of their own, out of the native rock'. This organicist vision was the foundation of Ruskin's beliefs, beliefs which when put into practice by the Arts and Crafts architects were demonstrated with the same illustration: an early locus classicus was Ernest Gimson's Stoneywell Cottage in the Charnwood Forest, an extraordinary stone building of 1899 with enormously thick walls and, as Pevsner notes, a main chimney 'built into the rock'. Detmar Blow was Gimson's foreman and builder for the cottage. Finally there is Joy Finzi's description—for which, alas, I don't have a source—of the sexton's cottage on the top of Chosen Hill (the one where Finzi caught his death) 'looking like something that had come up through the ground.'

Second, I think Finzi, as in his Hardy settings, had a happy and perhaps unconscious ability not so much to illuminate the tone or imagery of the poet's thought, but to mirror, or simply to follow, its structure. What Wordsworth's Ode says and does is described very simply by Garrod, in a passage which Finzi—if it was Finzi—carefully marked:

> The first four stanzas of the Ode put the fact: 'There hath passed a glory from the earth'; and in the last two lines of them, ask the explanation of it. Stanzas v-viii give the explanation in the form of the doctrine of anamnesis or Reminiscence. Stanzas ix-xi are an attempt to vindicate the value of a life from which 'vision' has fled.

Finzi, like Somervell, omitted stanzas vii and viii, but otherwise he kept with the argument. This has an effect on the music different from the effect it has on the poetry. The poetry can expound its doctrine of consolation—its view of life as a kind of 'double decrescendo', as I have described it elsewhere, from the glory of pre-existence to the vestigial glory of early childhood and from the ecstasy of childhood to the ordinariness of adulthood—without the form of the verse necessarily being affected by this structural view of life (though in fact the metre does become incrementally more philosophical, in terms of longer lines and more abstract address, after stanza iv, where Wordsworth broke off composition for at least two years). With music, however, thought is form, and thus Finzi, if he wanted to avoid falsifying Wordsworth's intentions, had to 'accept a structure pivoted about an ecstatic Before and a disappointing After' (forgive my repeating myself from a sleeve note here). But this suited him in any case, not least because of his long preference for oblique neo-baroque pairings such as recitative and aria and prelude and fugue. (He even virtually ignored one of the two points of motivic recurrence which the poet had helpfully offered. See if you can hear [in the evening performance] any element of musical recapitulation at the moment near the end when Wordsworth recalls his first line with its 'Meadows . . . and groves'; it is very slight and subtle.) Thus he was happy that the work, although it begins and ends in D minor, should depict Wordsworth's philosophy in terms which at bottom are those of a big symphonic allegro followed by a funeral march, the moment of pivot between the two—the silent bar before figure twenty, for those who like to know—suggesting a corresponding large-scale fall from B minor to Bb minor. This may sound like the cobbling together of scraps (Finzi tended to work that way rather than to a conscious tonal plan), but we should not underestimate the skill with which he manages his overall shape. For instance, he takes care that the various climaxes are differentiated by pitch in the first half, the soprano line rising successively at rhetorical moments to G, A, Bb and finally the B natural which articulates the pivot. Likewise, in the second half the line rises only as high as the structural Bb.

Intimations therefore reverses the more usual trajectory of climax and catharsis, and I suspect that the assertively humanistic Finzi rather enjoyed the iconoclasm of writing a cathedral piece which does away with the whole eschatological bag of tricks by placing the numinous behind rather than in front of us—though he doesn't quite manage to avoid the conventionally anticipatory choral hush at the thought of God, any more than Wordsworth avoids the mention of his name. As Tony Waiter, taking a cue from Bayan Northcott, put it in a recent *Musical Times* article entitled 'Angelic choirs': 'Think of all those requiems, with little musical equivalent celebrating birth.' Why, he asks, do paintings depict the Madonna and Child while music prefers to career towards death? Finzi bucks the trend.

This leads to the final thought as to why Finzi had cause to identify with Wordsworth's feelings and experience. The most immediate answer is already before us, in the shape of his liberal humanism. He believed that in our civilisation 'Shades of the prison-house begin to close | Upon the

Gerald Finzi on St Catherine's Hill, Winchester, in 1926. The photograph was taken by his mother (note her hat behind him), apparently the first time she had used a camera, which perhaps accounts for Gerald's anxious expression.

Joy and Kiffer Finzi on the roof during the construction of Church Farm in 1938. Photographs by Gerald Finzi.

Nigel Finzi in April 1941 (see p. 28).

Photograph owned by Herbert Howells which he has titled 'Finzi's two sons': Nigel (left) and Kiffer at Church Farm in the 1940s.

Gerald Finzi and Ursula Howells in 1925. Photograph by Herbert Howells.

Photo-Russell

Ralph Vaughan Williams and Ursula Wood (later Ursula Vaughan Williams) with Gerald, Nigel and Joy Finzi in 1948, at Worcester Three Choirs Festival.

(Facing page) Ralph Vaughan Williams in the early 1940s.

Gerald Finzi, Ursula Wood and Ralph Vaughan Williams outside Hereford Cathedral, Three Choirs Festival, 1949.

The Finzi and Rubbra families, Worcester Three Choirs in 1948 (Edmund Rubbra in beret). Note the programme seller in the foreground.

THREE CHOIRS FESTIVAL
HEREFORD
Sept. 4th, 6th, 7th, 8th and 9th, 1949

FRIDAY
(SEPT. 9TH)
(MORNING AND AFTERNOON)
11.15 2.30

CREATION (PART I) . *Haydn*
PIANOFORTE CONCERTO *Beethoven*
CONCERTO FOR CLARINET AND STRINGS . *Finzi*
MESSIAH (SELECTION) . *Handel*

Division 1
Block FF
Row 5
Seat 3

25/-

ENTRANCE - NORTH PORCH (IN THE CLOSE)

Ticket for the first performance of Finzi's Clarinet Concerto in 1949, Hereford Three Choirs Festival.

Gerald Finzi dressed in conductor's tails, with soloist Frederick Thurston (centre), prior to the concert.

Ashmansworth
June 22nd. nr Newbury
Berks.

Dear Mollie

We were most entertained by your account of the screech owl audition! I had actually noted the 7th July & fully meant to be there, but since then I've promised to do a work for the St Cecilia Chorus & Orchestra for the Festival & I can see that I'm going to have a pretty tough job & must stick here for a while. I'm already rather cursing that I've been given tickets & hospitality for Glyndebourne next week! Being a choral work

Letter to Mollie Sands, 1947. Sands was singing the first performance of four songs from *Love's Labour's Lost* on 7 July at the Wigmore Hall, accompanied by Ruth Dyson.

work it must be done at least
a month or six weeks before the
concert a being in the Albert Hall
it will need some rather heavy
scoring. So St Cecilia come
to my aid, and forgive me if I
dont turn up. I sh^d have enjoyed
the concert quite apart from my
own things, as I'm very curious
about the Stoke!! W^d you
care to let me have half a dozen
hand bills. I know one or two
people who might like to go, but
I feel that they ought to pay for
their tickets. If you are having
programmes (other than the bills)
c^d I have one, later on?

Toy sends greetings

Gerald.

Perhaps just a couple of
tickets.

House party at Gloucester Three Choirs Festival, 1956. Joy and Gerald Finzi are on the left, Howard Ferguson and Ursula Vaughan Williams on the right, Ralph Vaughan Williams at the front. Nigel Finzi and Richard Shirley Smith are in front of the window at the back, Meredith Davies in front of them, Kiffer Finzi to his right, and David Willcocks to Kiffer's right.

Nigel, Joy and Kiffer with cellist Christopher Bunting, Worcester Three Choirs Festival, 1957.

Howard Ferguson in South Africa, 1957.

Robert Gower, Michael Salmon, Joy and Nigel Finzi at the Twenty-Fifth Anniversary Celebration, Ellesmere, 1981.

Raphael Wallfisch, Joy Finzi and Vernon Handley at the recording of Finzi's Cello Concerto, Liverpool 1986.

Kenneth Leighton at Ullapool, 1987

Composers at the Summer Weekend of English Music, Oxford 1984. Left to right: Alan Ridout, Howard Ferguson, Paul Patterson, Stephen Pratt and Kenneth Leighton.

Joy Finzi and Diana McVeagh, Oxford 1984.

(Facing page) Philip Leech in an *Earth and Air and Rain* masterclass with John Carol Case, Ellesmere, 1981.

Clifford Benson and Stephen Varcoe in rehearsal, Radley College, 1986.

Joy Finzi and Howard Ferguson, May 1990.

Kiffer and Nigel Finzi with baritone Howard Wong, Hereford Three Choirs Festival, 2006

Paul Spicer at Ludlow, Weekend of English Song, 2004.

Susan Bickley, Roderick Williams, James Gilchrist and Iain Burnside recieve flowers from Martin Lee-Browne, Ludlow, 2004.

Roderick Williams and Iain Burnside in rehearsal with composer Hugh Wood at St Laurence's Parish Church, Ludlow, during the Weekend of English Song, 2007.

growing Boy' because we build the prisons—hence his refusal to follow his family into commerce, his rejection of school, his avoidance of music college, his dislike of creeds and dogmas and the intellectual establishment, his short-lived academic connection and his relatively brief residence in London, his country living and organic lifestyle, his conservationist mentality and so on. This is all true and well known. But we need to look a little further. It is not so easy to identify him with Wordsworth's own childhood self, for their backgrounds and experiences were so utterly different. Certainly, as has been pointed out, Finzi's childhood became more quickly and more heavily overcast than most, with the death of his father when he was eight, in circumstances (cancer of the roof of the mouth) which would have been extremely distressing to a young boy, followed by the deaths of his three brothers and his first composition teacher, Ernest Farrar. But had heaven ever lain about him in his infancy? According to Joy, he was 'an unwanted addition to a bursting upper-floor nursery', and he himself could not remember, only 'suppose that there was a time when "every common sight . . . did seem apparelled in celestial light".' I believe that a profounder source of his feeling for precognition must be sought elsewhere, in a place it would never have occurred to him to locate it, namely in his Jewish ancestry. This was a birthright, a whole heritage, that was utterly lost to him. It could be argued that for any non-Zionist, non-Messianic Jew the Wordsworthian model, of a divine home to which access can never be regained, of a cultural pivoted for all time on the diaspora, is applicable. But in Finzi's case there was much more to it than this. It is difficult to be certain whether he himself made a conscious decision to reject his Jewish heritage as he became aware of it, whether perhaps the rejection represented deeply sublimated and lifelong anger at his father's having taken it away from him by dying when he did, or whether the loss had occurred in his father's generation, the generation in which the most obvious degree of assimilation into English society seems to have occurred. Whatever the truth, loss it certainly was, for Finzi's father's family was of an extraordinarily distinguished Sephardic pedigree, tracing its Italian lineage back to the second half of the thirteenth century and including notable rabbis, physicians and scholars, astronomers, mathematicians, bankers, grammarians, poets and a nineteenth-century member of the Italian Parliament, Giuseppe Finzi, who was a confidant of Mazzini, Garibaldi and Cavour and fought in the wars of liberation. Thus the star which rose with English music in the twentieth century had indeed had elsewhere its setting, and although Gerald Finzi would never for a moment have accepted that all this had anything whatever to do with his setting of Intimations, it surely behoves us, more than a generation after his death, to take a longer and ultimately more understanding look at where he and his Ode came from.

Reflections on the Rejection of Cecilia

Philip Lancaster

Rise, underground sleepers, rise from the grave
Under a broken hearted sky,
And hear the swan singing nightmare grieve
For this deserted anniversary
Where horned a heart sobs in the wilderness
By the thunderbolt of the day.

Echoing footstep in the ruins of midnight
Knock like a clock in a catacomb
Through the toothless house and the derelict skull
Where once Cecilia shook her veils,
Echo and mourn.
Footstepping word, attend her
Here, where, in echoes, she prevails.

Sleep, worm eaten weepers.
Silence is her altar.
To the drum of the head, muffled
In a black time, the sigh is a hecatomb.
Tender Cecilia silence,
Now, silence is tender
As never a voice was.
Here, dumbstruck she mourns in long abandoned grandeur.

O stop the calling killer in the skull
Like beasts we turn towards!
For was the caterwauling siren beautiful
Chanting warlong until her bed was full of the uxorious dead?
Let the great moaners of the Seven Seas
Let only the seas mourn,
With the shipwrecked harp of creation on their knees
Till Cecilia turns to a stone.

George Barker (1913–91)

Finzi's setting of George Barker's 'Ode, on the rejection of St Cecilia (Arioso)' has been very much at the forefront of Friends' events this last year [2003], principally due to the efforts of baritone Howard Wong. Howard first performed Finzi's posthumous set *To a Poet*, from which the song comes, at the Association of English Singers and Speakers (AESS) event in February, following which he was invited to give a performance at the Friends' AGM at Ashmansworth in June. But what does this song mean, and what attracted Finzi to the text? Stephen Banfield in his biography of Finzi describes it as 'the idea of silence being preferable to music in a "black time"'; Trevor Hold in his song survey *Parry to Finzi* corroborates this, although suggesting that this idea is not quite in keeping with Finzi's philosophy, and goes on to describe the song's 'histrionic, almost snorting posturings'. Do these comments really sum up the song?

The stories about the life of Cecilia vary somewhat, the most well known account in English literature probably being Chaucer's 'Seconde Nonnes Tale of the lyf of Seinte Cecile'. It seems that Cecilia was a woman of noble Roman descent who was firm in her devotion to Christ but was forced to marry against her wishes. With the help of a man by the name of Urban—later to become Pope Urban I—she converted her husband to the faith and they lived together in chastity. In the persecution against Christians by Emperor Marco Aurelio, Cecilia's husband was martyred, and Cecilia was to follow. However, because of her noble descent it was more difficult for the Emperor to order her execution, so she was shut in the caldarium (the hottest room in a Roman baths) of her house at Trastevere to suffocate with hot steam (in some accounts this gets transformed into a bath of flames). She was left there for three days but survived; she was ordered to be beheaded. Cecilia was struck three times with a sword but survived for a further three days, reputedly dying on 22 November c.230 AD.

The church of St Cecilia in Trastevere was apparently built in the third or fifth century on the site of the house in which Cecilia lived. During the reign of Pope Paschal I (817–824) Cecilia's body was discovered in the Catacomb of St Callistus, and Paschal rebuilt the original church, burying Cecilia under the high altar. During restoration work in 1599 the tomb was opened and the body of the saint discovered intact. Pope Clement VIII summoned the sculptor Stefano Maderna (c.1576–1636) to make an exact reproduction of the figure. In Stefano's words, sculpted around the base of the tomb, 'Behold the body of the most holy virgin Cecilia whom I myself saw lying incorrupt in her tomb. I have in this marble expressed for thee the same saint in the very same posture of body.'

According to Robert Fraser's biography of George Barker, early in 1949 some members of Barker's circle were obsessed by Vasari's *Lives of the Painters*, and especially that of the 'Life of Michelangelo' with its 'suggestions of homoeroticism and heroism of struggle.'[1] They undertook to produce illustrated book about Italy, being a pilgrimage in the footsteps of Michelangelo and taking as its principal focus the tomb of Pope Julius II which it took Michelangelo forty years to complete. When they reached Rome Barker sought out the Basilica of St Cecilia at Trastevere to see the sculpture by Maderna, only to find that the church was locked. Barker had known a reproduction of the effigy since childhood at the Brompton Oratory, where much of his education took place. Having been unable to see the sculpture in Rome, on his return to England he paid a visit to St Wilfrid's Chapel at the Oratory to see the reproduction. It was 22 November and Barker had hoped to attend a Mass in Cecilia's honour. There was none. Instead he wrote his 'Anthem Against St Cecilia's Day', which Fraser appends to the long tradition of odes for Cecilia in the footsteps of Dryden, Pope and, latterly, Auden.

The dates don't add up: the above claim of the Ode being written in 1949 is quite impossible considering Finzi had already set the poem in 1948. This date of 1949 could be a result of George Barker's claim about the probable difficulties of someone writing his biography, telling Robert Fraser 'I've stirred the facts around too much . . . it simply can't be done'. More likely, the 1949 episode brought a revisitation to the poem, the earlier version as set by Finzi probably dating from 1947 as a response to the BBC commission that was to bring the Barker text and Finzi together in the early part of 1948. The published version of the poem certainly has some significant differences compared with the version as set by Finzi. The visit to the Oratory on St Cecilia's day was certainly a return visit, given his close associations with the place, and it is likely that it was this chapel and effigy of Cecilia that brought the initial version of the Ode to fruition. Barker's personal mission in Rome to see the original Maderna could have stemmed from a close association with the Oratory copy brought about as a result of his focusing on Cecilia in the writing of the Ode.

In the Ode itself George Barker's occasional predilection for the

[1] Robert Fraser: *The Chameleon Poet: A Life of George Barker* (Jonathan Cape, London, 2001) p.283.

surreal in his poetry may pass as an excuse for some of what we may not understand in the text, but hopefully in the light of the above background we may find some illumination.

For Robert Fraser the poem begins by 'imagining the fallen of the recent war rising from their graves to witness the blasted hopes of the Cold War'. Barker's highly evocative 'Under a broken hearted sky' in the second line seems to recall 'Octologue of the Emotions' written in 1932, the opening of which evokes the devastation of the First War, albeit from second-hand knowledge and his poet's 'inner eye', given that he was born in 1913 and would not be old enough to have seen it at first hand. It nonetheless portrays the inherited impact on the next generation:

> After all the tears that fell
> Into patriotic mud;
> The Historical patrimonial tears,
> And the first tears of God—
>
> It appears
> That the years
> Must be two thousand of God's tears for us—
> All that you have to do (must do, will do)
> Will expedite your tears, for which,
> Encasing the earth, observe
> Our bright cosmic and cosmetic handkerchief
> Bespread over all.

God's tears manifested in the 'broken hearted sky' once again show themselves in Barker's post-second-war thoughts in the Ode. Diana McVeagh, in her talk in February at the AESS event, found further reflection of this in the 'hecatomb' of the third verse—a great public sacrifice such as that of the second war which had ended only two years prior to the probable composition of the poem.

In the first stanza we find our first recollection of Barker's visit to the copy of Maderna's Cecilia in the Oratory: the 'deserted anniversary', no Mass being held in her honour that day, later epitomised at the end of the third stanza: 'Here, dumbstruck she mourns in long abandoned grandeur.' A sense of distance exaggerated in the first stanza with a lone, 'horned heart' (perhaps an idea of a full heart, as in 'horn of plenty', or a pierced heart?), sobbing in the wilderness. The sense of isolation is recurrent, seen again earlier in the third stanza at 'silence is her altar', 'Here, where in echoes she prevails', following a request to the 'worm-eaten weepers' to sleep—perhaps those same dead who were awoken in the opening of the Ode, or perhaps a reference to a fact that only the dead remember and mourn for her. The silence is so deep that all one can hear is the 'muffled drum' of your own heartbeat as the blood is pumped through your head, and any slight noise such as a sigh is likened to the dark dramaticism of the 'hecatomb'. This significance is certainly not lost on Finzi who gives it one of his rare melismas—one of perhaps only two in his solo song output.

Another reference to silence later in the third stanza found comment in Diana McVeagh's talk. She drew attention to parts of an entry for George Barker in Margaret Drabble's *Oxford Companion to English Literature*, which says his 'earlier work is rhetorical, Dionysiac, and surreal though some critics have suggested that he achieves disorder more by accident than by intent.' Drabble goes on to speak of 'puns, distortion and abrupt changes of tone.' In the light of Barker's 'puns' Diana considered the lines 'Tender Cecilia silence, | Now, silence is tender | As never a voice was'. She questioned whether the first 'Tender' is an adjective describing the gentle saint, or the imperative of a verb: to make tender, in other words, offer Cecilia silence. Perhaps it could even be construed as the original order for Cecilia's execution, the sword marks from which are clearly seen on the neck of Maderna's sculpture, although this doesn't work grammatically. The year following Barker's attempted visit to Trastevere and the supposed writing of the Ode, David Wright brought a great irony to this silence in his own ode for Cecilia written after a successful visit to the Basilica, declaring, 'Cecilia there is none: No silence anywhere.' [2]

Robert Fraser describes Barker's Cecilia as representing 'the cost of principles too tenaciously held; she is thus the cause of war as well as its victim. It is because of her supposed obduracy that this anthem for the patron saint of music is directed "against" her feast day.' [3] The use of war imagery is undoubted. Maybe it is the Blitz of Second World War London, Barker's home, that is recalled in that 'thunderbolt of the day'. The great question in the Ode, posed by Barker in the final stanza, is perhaps the crux of Fraser's point: 'For was the caterwauling siren beautiful, chanting warlong until her bed was full of the uxorious dead?' In likening her to a siren—Greek sea nymphs whose song was so

[2] 'Verses to St. Cecilia', from *To the Gods in the Shades* (Carcanet, 1976), p.49 (quoted in Fraser).

[3] Fraser, p.288.

beautiful that they distracted sailors to their deaths—Barker perhaps draws a simile with the call to war, so contemporary in the 1940s and from which relatively few who followed that call returned. From the point of view of Cecilia as patron saint of music it is possibly a jibe at the power of music, used powerfully both in war and peace, a power that draws the adoring man to Cecilia's 'bed'. 'Like beasts we turn towards' earlier in the stanza could imply that music is something 'bestial' and innate in the human spirit and impossible to avoid. Surely this rhetoric actually draws us to a conclusion that, despite her memorial rejection by the living, Cecilia is all the more present and revered through her 'blessed art'?

Finzi's association with Barker's Ode, as touched on briefly above, came in the early part of 1948 when he was approached with a commission from the BBC. They had commissioned six poems, especially for musical setting, and sent them anonymously to six composers with a questionnaire for the composer to fill in about their choice of poem and the setting of it. Edmund Rubbra, who had also been approached with the commission, wrote to Finzi in April 1948: 'I'm almost inhibited when I even think about it: God knows what the result will be. In my desperation I've even thought of making a collage from bits of all the poems.' [4] In the event, Finzi was the only one to complete his setting—although refusing to fill in the questionnaire, thinking the subject of words for music too serious to be dealt with in such a trivial manner.

Finzi decided to set the Ode, describing it as having 'something of the magnificence and fury which one associates with, say, Dylan Thomas.' [5] He was not far off. George Barker had certainly been influenced by Dylan Thomas, and had even been classified as part of the same 'school' of poetical thought; in c.1937 Barker wrote an 'Epistle to D. T.', stressing, not their differences, but a shared alienation and undistinguished social beginnings.[6] The timing of the commission in relation to Finzi's work couldn't have been more ironic: he was just completing his setting for tenor, chorus and orchestra of Edmund Blunden's ceremonial ode *For St Cecilia*. The great irony of Blunden's 'But where in all the saintly company | Is one beloved beyond melodious Cecily?' compared with the silence surrounding the forgotten Cecilia in the Rejection Ode must

[4] Quoted in Stephen Banfield: *Gerald Finzi: An English Composer* (Faber, London,1997) p.353.

[5] Quoted in Diana McVeagh, sleeve note for the recording *Finzi and his Friends* (Hyperion CDA66015, 1981/Hyperion Helios CDH55084, 2003)

[6] Fraser, p.94.

surely have been one of the key reasons for Finzi's choice. Barker's war imagery could have attracted Finzi, the idea of stopping 'the calling killer in the skull' attempting to bring peace as opposed to war, a notion that would have appealed to Finzi's pacifist sensibilities, and hence the desperate cry at the top of the baritone register in his setting.

It could also be that in the counterpoint of the two works we find a questioning of an agnostic, at once celebrating Cecilia, as well as Saints Valentine, George, Dunstan and Swithin, in the Blunden, and at once denouncing them, perhaps questioning the human—or indeed extra-human—sanctification of such figures as Cecilia, and the human need to look towards such figures as exemplars in life.

The music of the settings themselves are quite different—as may be expected for such contrasting works. *For St Cecilia* is full of fanfares, and much regal pomp and ceremony, with lyrical interludes; the Rejection Ode on the other hand is full of Finzi's 'magnificence and fury', with much dramatic and bitter music. Having said that, the quieter moments of the Barker setting, when Finzi is depicting the 'echoing footsteps' in the catacomb where first she was laid to rest, and in the chapel where Barker found her, have a recurring footstepping theme in the bass of the piano (Ex.1)—a quintessentially timpanic figure which could reflect the now distant celebration of Cecilia with trumpets and drums in the Blunden setting; this perhaps brings us to the reality of Cecilia's existence.

Ex.1

Towards the end of both works appears a moment which could be a conscious effort from Finzi to link the two works, the similarity being significant. Halfway through the last section of the Blunden setting Finzi depicts 'music's strife' with a *Belshazzar*-like cascading figure of semi-tones, fourths and augmented fourths almost identical to that used in the Barker setting (Ex.2) after 'the uxorious dead'. Both are highly accented, and both end sharply in silence. The Blunden ode continues in an appeased unaccompanied pianissimo 'and music's calm', the Barker setting continuing into a brutal setting of the last four lines of the Ode:

> Let the great moaners of the Seven Seas
> Let only the seas mourn,
> With the shipwrecked harp of creation on their knees
> Till Cecilia turns to a stone.

These last four lines of the Ode could take us to a point where that call to war has overtaken and the human race has been self-consumed; without her human lyres—the 'harps of creation'—Cecilia and her art have grown cold and voiceless like the stone of her effigy; only the seas, the great pools of 'God's tears', wept for the human race, are left to mourn. Perhaps the Romans' attempt to 'stop the calling killer in the skull' would be justified.

Ex.2

Finzi's Serenade

Edward Venn

Finzi began work on a Serenade for string orchestra some time in the 1940s, but unfortunately the work never progressed beyond sketches. (These are now collected together as folios 18–6 in the Bodleian Library MSMus.c398.) There were at least two working titles for the Serenade, the first being Serenade: Light-music for String Orchestra, whereas the second, barely visible on brown paper, reads: Serenade/Victoriana or A Casket of Melody (Gems) for strings. In his biography of Finzi, Stephen Banfield said of the sketches:

> Finzi's Serenade sketches . . . deserve further comment. Two of them are unusually sustained: neat and fluent (though not very good) ink

> continuity drafts for fast movements, an opening one with an introduction in D major, 4/4 time, and a third or fourth one in A minor/major, 6/8 time . . . Both drafts break off, the former at some point prior to a middle section, the latter, after as many as 150 bars, before a return, and both are supplemented by a good many shorter workings, including some labelled alternatives for recapitulation purposes, as well as for preferential choice, mostly in pencil . . . In terms of quality they would unfortunately not make satisfactory end-products even if the return could be completed in the 6/8 movement (one of whose pencil workings does get to the end).

Of the various abortive attempts at movements for the Serenade, three are long enough to warrant close attention. Two of these three were described in the above quote, and form the first and third movements. There is also a two-page sketch of a possible second movement, which contains a lyrical melody in F major related in spirit to a passage in the Romance for strings. This sketch proved to be crucial for understanding the Serenade as a whole, for the melody recurs in an epilogue at the end of the third movement, demonstrating that Finzi envisaged some cross-references between the movements.

The sketches for the third movement make up over half of the total sketches in the Bodleian Library collection. Of the thirty-four sides containing material relevant to the third movement, around a quarter belong to two extended continuity drafts. The first of these accounted for about two-thirds of the completed movement, whereas the second provided the remaining sixth. These drafts proved invaluable in assessing the nature and relevance of the other sketches, and gave pointers as to how to fill in the missing sixth of the work. Although much of the material is presented on two staves in piano reduction, there are also fragments hinting at how Finzi might have scored the work for string orchestra.

The material presented in these drafts, and indeed the other sketches relating to the movement, is characterized by attractive (and extended) lyrical passages, which frequently remain wholly diatonic. This can be best heard in the lengthy first subject, which dominates the movement (Ex.1).

Stylistically, the third movement has Finzi's fingerprints all over it. There are many textural resemblances between the Serenade and other works composed in the 1940s and in particular the song cycle *Before and After Summer*. The pianistic idiom of songs such as 'Childhood among the ferns' can clearly be seen to influence certain passages of the Serenade such as the frequent use of thin textures. Indeed, the use of such textures is another characteristic trait, and one need look no further than the string writing for the earlier *Dies natalis* to imagine how easily the continuity drafts would adapt to string orchestra.

Ex.1

There is a great deal of charm about the work, which makes it all the more regrettable that Finzi did not complete it. This is perhaps due to the fact that, even by Finzi's standards, it is tonally meandering and vague, an issue he sought to rectify in his many reworkings. Unfortunately, as far as the history of the Serenade goes, and also as far as reconstructing the movement goes, Finzi ultimately failed to hit upon a satisfactory solution that would unify the entire work, or even draw the two continuity drafts together, and hence it remained unfinished. In the completion presented at the University of Birmingham [6 March 1999, with Stephen Banfield on piano], it was decided that to try and 'improve' the tonal plan of the work would result in losing much of its charm (a fact Finzi appeared to realise) and so no attempt was made to rationalise the key structures. The join between the two continuity drafts was made as inconspicuous as possible by means of using material from the first draft although in a different key. In the event, only about a bar and a half was actually 'recomposed'; the rest was all Finzi.

There was much to be gained through the completion of the movement. Working through the various sketches, seeing how Finzi altered the material, trying out new ideas and combinations in order to link together the different sections, gave a fascinating insight into his compositional processes. And yet there were ultimately more questions raised than answers given. The chronology of the sketches can never be certain and so any ordering is based on informed guesses rather than solid facts. This in itself means that one can never know which of the many attempts at a solution Finzi preferred, if any. Thus the recomposition process became a fascinating piece of detective work, trying to draw conclusions based on fifty-year-old sketches, and, at best, interpreting them in one way rather than presenting a definitive solution.

Whilst completing the movement, the validity of such an endeavour was called into question. Did the movement truly deserve to be completed, or was it a case of scrabbling around in a composer's wastebasket, looking for discarded fragments that could be woven together, exploiting the post-Elgar's Third climate? As with Elgar's Third, I truly believe that there is a piece of music here that ought to be heard, and that would also complement Finzi's other works in this medium. For example, the Prelude for strings, the Romance for strings, and the completed third movement of the Serenade would make an attractive and well-balanced suite. Indeed, the similarity noted between the melody quoted at the end of the Serenade and the theme from the middle section of the Romance, demands that the Serenade is paired with the Romance, so that the passage makes some (intellectual) sense. This relationship justifies the completion of the movement on artistic and not just academic grounds, and I look forward to a day when perhaps the three movements can be heard together.

IIX

An improbable partnership

Hardy and Finzi

Christopher Stunt

An adaptation of his BA Special Hons dissertation, University of Bristol, 1996.

1. Hardy and Finzi: an improbable partnership

Gerald Finzi was only twenty-six when Thomas Hardy died at the age of eighty-seven. The poet was thus by sixty-one years the composer's senior: old enough to have been his grandfather. Yet even in his teens Finzi found himself irresistibly drawn to Hardy's verse, and spent much of his short life setting it to music. He completed settings of more than fifty Hardy poems, and had designs on many more which he did not live to fulfil.

In many ways, the two men were so utterly different that it is difficult at first to see what could have united them in such a marriage of words and music. Hardy's life was unusually long, and his total output, of novels and verse, enormous. Much of the poetry that Finzi admired dates from the last third of Hardy's life, and represents the thoughts and attitudes of an old man. Finzi, by contrast, was only fifty-five when he died and his list of completed works is decidedly short. Most of his Hardy settings were written, or at least started, before he was thirty-five.

Thomas Hardy was born to parents who were unmarried when he was conceived. His father was a stonemason, and later what we would now call a jobbing builder; his mother came from a family brought up on parish relief. He was the oldest of four children, two of them very much younger than his loved and trusted sister Mary and himself. His education at local schools, good by the standards of rural Dorset of the period, was nevertheless severely limited, and he had to work at his own basic self-education well into his twenties. It was many years before his success as a writer brought him much financial reward.

Gerald Finzi, on the other hand, was born into the security of a well-established family, with all the trappings of middle-class comfort. He was the youngest in a family of five, and educated privately. Notwithstanding his father's early death, he never had to work for a living.

Hardy grew up in a conventional church-going family. Losing his Christian faith in his mid twenties[1] deeply affected his personal view of the world and the image of it projected in his novels and poetry. Finzi's Jewish background did not prevent him from growing up from an early age as an agnostic, spared in this respect much of the trauma and embitterment of a first generation unbeliever like Hardy.

Their experiences in marriage were very different. Hardy's long and unhappy marriage to Emma Gifford was followed, when he was nearly seventy-four, by a far from easy union with Florence Dugdale. Over the years before and during his marriages, he enjoyed, or suffered, many unconsummated 'affairs' with younger women. He left no children. Finzi, however, lived a rather solitary and celibate life until his happy and fulfilling marriage to Joyce Black at the age of thirty-two, which yielded two sons.

Their approaches to their respective arts also differed considerably. Hardy passed scarcely a day without writing something, whereas for Finzi composing was only one of many interests. Hardy's poetry is almost always provocative and technically innovative; Finzi's musical language is generally conservative and undemanding. The older man stands out as one of the giants of English literature of his, or perhaps any, generation; the younger is still regarded by many as not much more than an interesting minor composer of his day.

Yet Finzi felt a rapport with Hardy which profoundly affected his whole life. In 1938, he wrote: 'I have . . . from [my] earliest days

[1] His widow quotes one of his typically sweeping statements on the subject in his old age: 'I have been looking for God for fifty years, and I think that if he had existed I should have discovered him.' F. E. Hardy: *The Life of Thomas Hardy 1840–1928* (in one volume, Macmillan, London, 1962), p. 293. [Hardy described himself, however, as an agnostic, not an atheist: see footnote 5.]

responded, not so much to an influence as to a kinship with him (I don't mean kinship with his genius, alas, but with his mental make-up).' [2] In 1949, he wrote to Edmund Blunden: 'Alas, I never knew Thomas Hardy except through his work, and that has been to me what the Bible must have been to Bunyan.' [3]

The following chapters may shed some light on what drew two such different men together. They both distrusted religious dogma, grieved over suffering, detested war, and believed that creativity was more important than fame or wealth. Especially relevant to Finzi's urge to set Hardy to music were the obsessions they shared about the fragility of human existence and the inescapable tyranny of time. They were also united in an acute sensitivity to words, to their rhythms and inflections in poetry, and especially to the ways in which simple and accessible images (or in Finzi's case music) can convey and illuminate subtle and profound thoughts. Without such common concerns, such an improbable partnership could never have borne lasting fruit.

2. Thomas Hardy: novelist, poet and would-be musician

Thomas Hardy's popularity and reputation in the world at large is still probably based more on his novels than his poetry. The most widely read half dozen or so of his fifteen novels span the years from 1872, when *Under the Greenwood Tree* was first published, to 1895, when *Jude the Obscure* appeared. By then, Hardy was fifty-five, and, notwithstanding his humble and impecunious start in life, a famous, successful and comparatively wealthy man.

Within a few months thereafter, however, he chose to turn his back on the fashionable literati of Dorset, where for a further thirty years he led a largely reclusive existence, writing nothing but verse. His biographers have speculated about whether this dramatic decision was triggered by the damning critical reception accorded to *Jude*, or by his increasing estrangement from Emma, or by anxiety that with increasingly rheumatic fingers, and without Emma's aid, he could no longer cope with the physical labour of novel-writing.[4] There is probably some truth in

[2] Stephen Banfield: *Sensibility and English Song: Critical Studies of the early Twentieth Century* (Cambridge University Press, Cambridge, 1985), p. 276, quoting from Joy Finzi's journal.
[3] Quoted by Andrew Burn, in an article about Finzi's home at Ashmansworth for *Country Life*, 16 July 1987.
[4] See, for instance, Robert Gittings: *The Older Hardy* (Heinemann, London, 1978, Penguin Books, 1980), p. 121.

each of these possible explanations, but it seems likely that he also felt an urge to immerse himself again in the childhood habitat which had been the well-spring of his creativity.[5]

Hardy began writing poetry at about the age of seventeen. Some forty dated poems belong to the 1860s, the decade of his twenties, but few of these give the reader much idea of what he was later to achieve. The flow of verse more or less ceased during his years as a novelist, but an astonishing 900 and more poems were written after 1895. Many of his greatest achievements in verse date from after Emma's death in 1912, by which time he was already seventy-two. It seems that he needed to wait until he was in his sixties and seventies in order to write so challengingly about the great universal themes of Life and Death, the unreasonableness of Love, the irrationality of Nature, and the ruthless domination of Time.[6] His twenty-five years as a novelist may also have been a necessary preparation for his subsequent work as a poet.[7]

Given his age and background, it comes as no great surprise to find that Hardy's mature poetry frequently reveals the philosophy of an old and disillusioned man: a deeply felt stoicism, dour and fatalistic, even if not quite pessimistic or cynical, borne out of the loss of his Christian faith and a multitude of unhappy personal experiences. However, few of his best poems are overtly philosophical; his deepest thoughts are not expressed in generalized abstractions, but allowed to emerge as by-products of the description of everyday incidents and scenes. He

[5] His own notebook suggests yet another reason for the switch from prose to verse, if not for his decision to leave London for good, though the two can hardly have been unrelated. Florence Hardy quotes an entry dated 17 October 1896: 'Poetry. Perhaps I can express more fully in verse ideas and emotions which run counter to the inert crystallized opinion—hard as a rock—which the vast body of men have vested interests in supporting. To cry out in a passionate poem that . . . the Supreme Mover or Movers . . . must be either limited in power, unknowing, or cruel which is obvious enough and has been for centuries—will cause them merely a shake of the head; but to put it in argumentative prose will make them sneer, or foam, and set all the literary contortionists jumping upon me, a harmless agnostic, as if I were a clamorous atheist, which in their crass illiteracy they seem to think is the same thing . . . If Galileo had said in verse that the world moved, the Inquisition might have let him alone.' F. E. Hardy, op. cit., p. 386.

[6] 'It also seems clear that to be a great poet he had to be an old poet. He needed time, for time would be his central subject; and he needed the retrospective vision of age.' Samuel Hynes (ed.): *Thomas Hardy–A Critical Selection of his Finest Poetry* (Oxford University Press, Oxford, 1984), p. xxiv.

[7] In a letter dated April 1937, Ezra Pound describes Hardy's *Collected Poems* as 'a harvest of having written twenty novels first': D. D. Paige (ed): *Letters of Ezra Pound 1907–1941* Faber and Faber, London, 1951), p. 386.

addresses the most profound aspects of the human predicament by building up vivid images of the commonplace. Trees and leaves, streams and riverbanks, birds, sheep and cattle, apples and cider-making, gates and hedges, features of the human face, windows and doors, clocks, mirrors, clothes, fire and frost, wind and rain, sun, moon and stars; all these and many other humdrum elements of the simple rural lifestyle of Hardy's youth, are sharply and purposefully recalled.[8]

Hardy's poetry has been aptly described by Trevor Hold as 'craggy and rugged'.[9] The texture is often dense and complex, making use of unusual, even invented, words to leaven and sharpen the mixture of everyday language and the sometimes almost conversational tone of voice which give his verses their directness. Archaisms and Dorset dialect words do not merely extend and colour his vocabulary; they also by association or allusion recall visions and experiences from older worlds and different social milieux. The same is true of his frequent references to the Bible, especially to Old Testament passages which had impressed him in his youth. In a poem, these things can, and should, be relished and pondered, and the words can if necessary be re-read. In a song setting, however, it is different: the words go by only once, and all too quickly.[10]

Illustrating Hardy's style would require large chunks of poetry, to set archaisms and other unusual features in a meaningful context. From among the poems set by Finzi,[11] however, it is worth mentioning 'The Clock of the Years' where Hardy uses the word 'smalled' as the aorist of the archaic verb 'to small', meaning to make or become small, and 'The Sigh' and 'Waiting both' where he refers in one case to abiding 'till my appointed change' and in the other to waiting 'till my change come'. These are references to the Book of Job, chapter 14, verse 14, which in the Authorized Version reads: 'all the days of my appointed time will I wait, till my change come.' A sermon on this text made a great impression on the twenty-year-old Hardy.[12] Clearly the 'change' to which such poems refer is death.

[8] Illustrations here would be otiose. However, every one of the elements listed in this sentence is mentioned at least once in the tiny percentage of Hardy's vast output which Finzi set to music.

[9] Trevor Hold: '"Checkless Griff" or Thomas Hardy and the Songwriters' in *Musical Times* volume 131 (June 1990), pp. 309–10, p. 309.

[10] Some indications of Finzi's response to this challenge will be found in Chapter 4.

[11] Illustrative quotations in this dissertation have been taken only from poems which Finzi set, even when better examples might be found elsewhere.

[12] In a letter to the Bishop of Durham (a member of the Moule family) dated 29 June 1919, Hardy wrote in reference to this verse: 'That was the text of the Vicar of Fordington

Hardy's verse also reflects his lifelong interest in music. His grandfather and father (both called Thomas Hardy) and his uncle had been prime movers in the musical life of the parish church at Stinsford, usually playing cello, tenor and treble viol respectively. His father was seemingly 'more enthusiastic about playing the fiddle than about his work as a builder, and a great one for jigs, hornpipes and other dances which he performed with all the old movements of leg-crossing and hop.' [13] The third Thomas Hardy was as a small boy 'wildly fond of dancing'. He continued practising the fiddle when he was studying architecture in London in the 1860s and he could still play old dance tunes on his violin when he was seventy-eight.[14] It seems that, secretly, he always yearned to be a musician.[15]

His novels and poetry are rich with musical incident and imagery. More than a quarter of the poems refer to music, to singing, dancing or playing, or to an instrument or a performer. Many more reflect music in their metrical schemes: hymn tune metres or country dance rhythms, or variations on such sources. Hardy sometimes uses the structure of a hymn as an ironic comment on his own agnostic stance.[16] An example is 'I look into my glass':

> I look into my glass,
> And view my wasting skin,
> And say, 'Would God it came to pass
> My heart had shrunk as thin!'

one Sunday evening in about 1860. And I can hear his voice repeating the text as the sermon went on—as was the way they used to repeat it in those days—just as if it were yesterday.' F. E. Hardy, op. cit., pp. 390–1.

[13] Eric Crozier: 'O bygone whirls!' in *Early Music* volume 8, no. 3 (1980), pp. 291–7, p. 293.

[14] Vilma Raskin Potter: 'Poetry and the Fiddler's Foot: Meters in Thomas Hardy's Work' in *The Musical Quarterly* volume LXV, no. 1 (1979), pp. 48–71, pp. 48–49.

[15] 'Mrs Florence Hardy told the writer of her husband's secret longing, which never quite left him even in his later years, to be a musician.' Elna Sherman: 'Music in Thomas Hardy's Life and Work' in *The Musical Quarterly* volume XXVI (1940), pp. 419–427, p. 423.

[16] In *A Journey into Thomas Hardy's Poetry* (Allison & Busby, London, 1990) Joanna Cullen Brown declares (p. 273) that ' . . . [M]any of [Hardy's] most agnostic poems are ironically cast in the Common Measure of hymns of faith' but she gives no examples. Common Measure (8.6.8.6) is by far the commonest format for hymns in late Victorian hymnals, usually accounting for more than 20% of the total. The writer has, however, found very few examples of it in *The Complete Poems* and many agnostic sentiments expressed in other metres. Only three Common Measure poems were set by Finzi: 'Paying calls', 'So I have fared' and 'The Comet at Yell'ham'. At least two of these are characteristically depressing, but none is explicitly agnostic.

For then, I, undistrest
By hearts grown cold to me,
Could lonely wait my endless rest
With equanimity.

But Time, to make me grieve,
Part steals, lets part abide;
And shakes this fragile frame at eve
With throbbings of noontide.

One wonders whether both metre and language are not meant to remind the reader of the very different sentiment of George Herbert's devotional hymn, which includes this verse:

A man that looks on glass,
On it may stay his eye;
Or if he pleaseth, through it pass,
And then the heaven espy.[17]

Hardy devoted much time to experimenting with rhythm and metre.[18] Dennis Taylor has reckoned that in 1,093 poems he uses over 790 different metrical forms, of which he invented well over 620.[19] In theory, setting overly simple, hymn-like, metres could lead to too much potentially boring symmetry, but in practice the challenge for the composer lies rather in coping with Hardy's more elaborate metrical and rhyming schemes, and the way he has, even in the simplest of stanza forms, of setting up expectations of regularity in order to bring his point more forcefully home to the reader when the expectation is frustrated.[20]

Much of Hardy's later verse looks back to events and scenes of thirty or forty years earlier, but the images are usually as clear and vivid as if

[17] Both Herbert and Hardy here use Short Measure (6.6.8.6.), usually the third most frequent metre in Victorian hymnals.

[18] 'Among his papers [at his death] were quantities of notes on rhythm and metre: with outlines and experiments in innumerable original measures, some of which he adopted from time to time. These verse skeletons were mostly blank, and only designated by the usual marks for long and short syllables, accentuations, etc . . .' F. E. Hardy, op. cit., pp. 301–2.

[19] Dennis Taylor: *Hardy's Metres and Victorian Prosody* (Oxford University Press, Oxford, 1988), p. 71. 'As far as I can see, Hardy invented more verse forms than any other poet in the accentual-syllabic tradition . . .'

[20] The almost throwaway line 'With equanimity' in 'I look into my glass' is an example. See also the line 'Where the dead feet walked in' in 'The Self-Unseeing' discussed below.

they were only yesterday's. This is partly because he had an exceptional ability to recall the distant past [21] as well as the technique with which to describe it; but it is also because so much of the poetry is based upon his personal experiences, which he very often recounts bluntly and directly in the first person. In more than a quarter of his poems, the very first word is a personal pronoun or a possessive adjective and in well over half there is a personal pronoun or possessive adjective in the first line.[22]

One further example must suffice to illustrate the matters touched upon in this short chapter. 'The Self-unseeing' recalls a visit by Hardy to his childhood home.

Here is the ancient floor,
Footworn and hollowed and thin,
Here was the former door
Where the dead feet walked in.

She sat here in her chair,
Smiling into the fire;
He who played stood there,
Bowing it higher and higher.

Childlike, I danced in a dream;
Blessings emblazoned that day;
Everything glowed with a gleam;
Yet we were looking away!

In twelve short lines, Hardy evokes the old floor, the loss of the door, the death of both parents, his mother's chair, the fire, his father's violin playing and his dancing to the music. Typically, he interrupts the triplet rhythms of the opening lines with four plodding stressed syllables at 'Where the dead feet walked in'. The first long word is the unexpected 'emblazoned', strictly concerned with heraldic adornment, but here

[21] An example is 'In Time of "The Breaking of Nations."' The verses date from 1915, but hark back to an incident of August 1870. 'I believe it would be said by people who knew me well that I have a faculty . . . for burying an emotion in my heart or brain for forty years, and exhuming it at the end of that time as fresh as when interred.' Quoted by F. E. Hardy, op. cit., p. 378.

[22] Of the 947 poems in *The Complete Poems of Thomas Hardy* edited by James Gibson (Macmillan, London, 1976, Papermac, 1981), as many as 256 start with a personal pronoun or possessive adjective, which in 153 cases is the word 'I', and in 29 'We'. The word 'I' appears somewhere else in the first line in a further 101 poems, and 75 more have 'me', 'my' or 'mine' in the first line.

carrying overtones of a blazing fire. From the bleak picture of the at first unrecognizable remnants of the family home, Hardy conjures up the glow and gleam of his childhood. He acknowledges the scene as personal to himself only in the last stanza, and then abruptly shatters the nostalgic image with a cryptic last line. Death and decay, the march of Time, familiar everyday things, music and dancing, the simple blessings of family life and the realization that they were not then perceived as such: the whole picture is built up and broken down again in a mere sixty words, forty-six of them monosyllables.

3. 'The too short time': a shared obsession with mortality

Gerald Finzi's early years were repeatedly overshadowed by the premature deaths of those closest to him. His father died shortly before Gerald's eighth birthday and his three older brothers all died before he was eighteen. His tutor and mentor in his early teenage years, Ernest Farrar, was called up in 1916 and was killed after only two days at the Front in September 1918, less than a month before the effective ending of hostilities. The shock of losing his hero in this way, following the deaths of his father and all his brothers, marked the seventeen-year-old Finzi for life.

It is therefore perhaps not surprising to find that a great many of the texts which he later set reveal his concerns about human mortality, the inexorable passing of the years, and the urgent personal question of whether he would have time to complete the music he felt he had it in him to write. The Milton sonnets he chose to set in 1928, for instance, were 'On his Blindness', which begins:

> When I consider how my light is spent,
> Ere half my days, in this dark world and wide,
> And that one talent which is death to hide
> Lodged with me useless . . .

and 'On his being arrived to the Age of Twenty-Three', where the first few lines are:

> How soon hath Time, the subtle thief of youth,
> Stolen on his wing my three-and-twentieth year!
> My hasting days fly on with full career,
> But my late spring no bud or blossom shew'th.

Even before his worrying brush with tuberculosis in 1928, Finzi had in 1925 set a poem by W. H. Davies ominously entitled 'Days too short'. Death is the theme of his three Drummond Elegies of 1926 and of all save one of the six Hardy poems in *By Footpath and Stile*, completed in 1922, when Finzi was only twenty-one. War and death were the subject of all three songs in the *Requiem da camera* of 1924, in which John Masefield's poem 'August 1914' includes these despairing lines:

> The breaking off of ties, the loss of friends,
> Death, like a miser getting in his rent,
> And no new stones laid where the trackway ends,
>
> The harvest not yet won . . .

The Requiem was understandably Finzi's outworking of his grief and anger at the death of Ernest Farrar. Even so, of the seventeen poems which as a young man in his early twenties he set between 1921 and 1926, twelve were directly and primarily concerned with human mortality.[23]

The Aria in *Farewell to Arms*, also dating from the 1920s, is a setting of George Peele's poem which climaxes with the line:

> O time too swift, O swiftness never ceasing . . .

The innocently pastoral poems of Robert Bridges in the Seven Part Songs were composed during Finzi's first, and one presumes happiest, years of marriage. The third song, a poem of twenty-four brief lines, aptly spells out Finzi's wife's name 'joy' twelve times. But although the sequence as a whole is basically happy, it contain many lines about the ephemeral nature of life's pleasures, and it ends with the telling words:

> I praise my days for all they bring,
> Yet are they only not enough.

Two of the five Shakespeare songs in *Let Us Garlands Bring* are directly about death. 'Come away, come away, death' may concern the mock death of a slighted lover, but Finzi treats the words seriously enough.[24] 'Fear no

[23] And a thirteenth comes close: the last quarter of the tiny 'Only the wanderer' (Gurney) (1925) concerns the lines 'And who loves joy as he | That dwells in shadows?', where the last word is pointedly reflected in sombre added flats.

more the heat o' the sun' (1929) is of course a classic statement about the inevitability of death. But the second stanza of the less serious 'O mistress mine' is permeated with the same idea, and its final line, though far from morbid, is quite plain:

> Youth's a stuff will not endure.

Two points emerge from these examples. First, Finzi's constant awareness of the remorseless passage of time is evidenced not only by his choice of texts from Hardy, but also by his settings of poems by other authors which emphasize similar themes. That so many of his songs are about the impact of time and death cannot therefore be explained away as merely a by-product of his passion for Hardy's verse. These were issues which exercised him deeply throughout his life.

Secondly, Finzi's sensitivity to the passing of time and the fragility of human life is not a wholly negative, pessimistic affair, any more than was Hardy's. Both the Milton sonnets conclude with a philosophical view of the poet's predicament, and many other songs at least hint at a positive attitude to the problem of fleeting time. Indeed, the climax to 'O mistress mine', is in both words and music:

> In delay there lies no plenty,
> Then come kiss me, sweet and twenty

where the piano has its loudest and crunchiest chords, and the voice leaps a minor ninth, its largest interval, on the words 'come kiss' (Ex.1).

Ex.1

[24] Highlighting the penultimate word 'weep' with an extended melisma, the longest by far in any of Finzi's songs. Stephen Liley has remarked upon the similarity of its angular line and chromatic neighbour notes to the agonised melisma on the word 'weinete' (wept) in *Bach's Passion according to St. John*. See Stephen J. Liley: *Gerald Finzi 1901–1956 Musical Poet: a critical study of his songs for solo voice and piano* (Liverpool, 1988), p. 40.

This positivism and realism is underlined in Finzi's choice of his own setting of James Elroy Flecker's poem 'To a Poet a Thousand Years Hence' as one of the artefacts which he and Joy set in a time-capsule under the porch of their new house at Ashmansworth in 1939. The poem recognizes that some good things, and specifically good poetry, can last much longer than the lives of the humans who create them.

> I who am dead a thousand years,
> And wrote this sweet archaic song,
> Send you my words for messengers
> The way I shall not pass along.
>
> . . .
>
> Since I can never see your face,
> And never shake you by the hand,
> I send my soul through time and space
> To greet you. You will understand.

There are indications that, like Flecker, Finzi wanted to believe that as an artist he could cheat death and achieve something approaching immortality for his creations if not for himself. In his preface to 'Absalom's Place', his catalogue of his own works, he wrote:

> Yet some curious force compels us to preserve and project into the future the essence of our individuality . . . The artist is like the coral insect, building his reef out of the transitory world around him and making a solid structure to last long after his own fragile and uncertain life . . . the pressing forward of new generations, will soon obliterate my small contribution. Yet I like to think that in each generation may be found a few responsive minds, and for them I sh[oul]d still like the work to be available . . . the affection which an individual may retain after his departure is perhaps the only thing which guarantees an ultimate life to his work.

It is against this background that one has to view Finzi's powerful urge to set so many of Thomas Hardy's poems. Most serious poets sooner or later grapple with basic questions about human existence, and many other composers than Finzi have naturally also felt an urge to set poems on such subjects. It is nevertheless remarkable that something like two-thirds of all Hardy's poems, and nine-tenths of all Finzi's songs, directly or indirectly concern the implications of the relentless march of Time.

Of his sixty-four completed songs for solo voice and piano, forty-four are settings of Hardy.[25] Eighteen of these were written between 1926 and his marriage in 1933 (though bearing in mind his slow and piecemeal way of composing, it seems likely that at least several more were already started by 1933). In all save three of these eighteen, the damage wrought or disillusion brought by the passage of time is either the main theme of the poem or an essential part of its argument. When he assembled ten of them for publication in 1933 as *A Young Man's Exhortation*, Finzi recognized the fleeting character of human life as his underlying theme by using some words from Psalm 89 [26] as headings for its two groups of five [27] songs: 'Mane floreat, et transeat' for Part I, and 'Vespere decidat, induret, et arescat' for Part II. These words comprise verses 4 to 6 which together say (in the King James Version) that:

> For a thousand years in thy sight are but as yesterday when it is past, and as a watch in the night.
> Thou carriest them away as with a flood; they are as a sleep: in the morning they are like grass which groweth up.
> In the morning it flourisheth, and groweth up; in the evening it is cut down, and withereth.

The message which Finzi, like Hardy, wished to convey is illustrated by the following extracts, each from a different song in the set:

> For what do we know best?
> That a fresh love-leaf crumpled soon will dry,
> And that men moment after moment die,
> Of all scope dispossest.

[25] Excluded from these figures is 'The temporary the all' which is a complete working of Hardy's poem, but one which Stephen Banfield says that 'Howard Ferguson rightly decided not to publish . . . posthumously, since Finzi regarded it as unsatisfactory'. See Banfield, op. cit., p. 288.

[26] Finzi refers to these texts as taken from Psalm 89, but all the major English translations after Coverdale's of 1535 place them in Psalm 90. Finzi probably took his Latin words directly from the Vulgate, in which Psalms 9 and 10 are treated as a single Psalm, and all the subsequent Psalms are numbered accordingly. Some Hebrew manuscripts, however, also combine Psalms 9 and 10, so it is conceivable that he was influenced by a Hebrew version of the Psalms inherited from his mother.

[27] It seems that by 1929, only a few months after Hardy's death and four years before the set was published, Finzi had completed a cycle of 15 Hardy songs, divided into two parts 'the first dealing with various moods of youth and love, and the second with philosophical retrospect, under the shadow of age': see Edmund Rubbra (then known as Duncan-Rubbra): 'Gerald Finzi' in *The Monthly Musical Record* LIX (1929) P 194. By 1933, however, the cycle had lost five of its songs. Several of them probably reappear in the two Hardy songsets published posthumously: see Banfield, op. cit., p. 291.

These market-dames, mid-aged, with lips thin-drawn,
And tissues sere,
Are they the ones we loved in years agone,
And courted here?

And mourn not me
Beneath the yellowing tree,
For I shall mind not, slumbering peacefully.

Notwithstanding his evidently happy and fulfilling marriage, Finzi continued after 1933 to set poems of Hardy's in which 'Time the tyrant fell' is the dominant character. Indeed, of all the other twenty-six completed Hardy songs, only two say nothing whatever, either directly or by ineluctable implication, about Time's impact on human affairs,[28] and no less than twenty of the twenty-six unfinished Hardy sketches and fragments are about Time or Death or both.

Typical in its utterly truthful bluntness is 'I look into my glass', set out in Chapter 2. Finzi saves his fiercest dissonances for the penultimate line, with doubled major sevenths on 'shakes', and a wry false relation on 'fragile' (Ex.2):

Ex.2

Many more harshly realistic lines could be quoted, but there is always a leavening of verses in which a more positive note is struck. In these

[28] One of these is the rumbustiously cynical 'Rollicum-rorum', and the other the ostensibly dewy-eyed romance of 'When I set out for Lyonnesse'. By the time he set the latter, Finzi could hardly have been unaware of the damage time had done to Hardy's relationship with Emma long before the poem was first published in 1914, by which time Emma was already dead. Indeed, while Hardy's text is, on the surface, all magically romantic nostalgia, Finzi's setting reveals the underlying truth, with its ghostly accompaniment marked 'misterioso', the piano's marching, staccato, bass lines (mostly moving downwards by step: see Chapter 4), and at both ends of the song a bleak, thinly harmonised, E minor.

poems, admittedly only six or seven out of the thirty-nine where Time is the principal theme, there is an acceptance of the naturalness of death, a recognition that change, sometimes change for the better, grows out of decay, and that the future may bring hope. A good example is 'Proud songsters', with which Finzi chose to end his set *Earth and Air and Rain*. The first of two verses describes the birds singing in the April evening 'as if all time were theirs', and the second declares:

> These are brand-new birds of twelve-months' growing,
> Which a year ago, or less than twain,
> No finches were, nor nightingales,
> Nor thrushes,
> But only particles of grain,
> And earth, and air, and rain.

The setting of these words (Ex.3) suggests, for a few moments at least, that Finzi is going to be able to share Hardy's calm acceptance of the implications of the cycle of Nature, as he allows the music to settle peacefully into D major, the key in which the set began. The piano's postlude, however, like many of Schumann's, stirs again the unease of the song's opening, and brings the whole set wistfully to a close in B minor.

Ex.3

An interesting sidelight is thrown on Finzi's obsession with the march of Time by the way he changes the titles of some of Hardy's poems.

Unlike many other songwriters, Finzi was utterly faithful to Hardy's texts, never changing or re-ordering words or phrases, nor even repeating a single word unless Hardy had repeated it first. It is rather strange, therefore, that he should have felt free frequently to tamper with Hardy's titles.[29]

Some changes are readily explained by external factors. It is, for instance, not very surprising that Finzi felt that 'The Sergeant's Song' was no longer a meaningful title for 'Rollicum-rorum' after it had been wholly divorced from Hardy's novel *The Trumpet Major* in which it had first appeared in 1880. Likewise, there is nothing very remarkable in his abbreviation of the title of 'Overlooking the River Stour' by omitting the river's name. The decision to retitle '1967', written by Hardy in 1867, by using its first line 'In five-score summers' is also intelligible on purely practical grounds: Finzi was setting it in 1956, by which time the poet's imagined century was already nearly over.

But why did Finzi call 'Shortening Days at the Homestead', first published by Hardy as late as 1925, just 'Shortening days' when he set it in 1928, only a few months after Hardy's death? Was this just to make the title shorter, or did he perhaps want to emphasize the thought, only implicit in the poem itself, that the days get shorter, not only as winter approaches, but also as the years go by, and that the strange figure of 'the cider-maker, and apple-tree shaker' may be a disguise for the Grim Reaper himself? The relentless march of the bass line in the second stanza and the exultant conclusion in A major may perhaps be a celebration of the joys of harvest, but they are also at the same time unmistakably sinister (Ex.4).

In the 1870s, when he was still in his thirties, Hardy wrote a sad little piece of macaronic verse, looking back on what he saw as the failure of his career to date, which he entitled 'After reading Psalms XXXIX, XL, etc.' Finzi set this poem in 1928, when he was only twenty-seven. His footnote to the song says: 'This recitative should be sung with the flexibility and freedom of ordinary speech, and the crotchet should approximate to the reciting note of Anglican chant'. It may therefore be relevant to note that Psalm 39 figures prominently in the Anglican Burial Service.

[29] This is an issue to which no-one seems to have previously drawn attention. None of the title changes is mentioned by Banfield or Liley in their detailed studies of Finzi's Hardy settings. In addition to those mentioned in the next few paragraphs, other songs to which Finzi gave new titles (with Hardy's titles in brackets) are: 'In years defaced'('A Spot'); 'The Dance Continued' ('Regret not Me'); 'The Phantom' ('The Phantom Horsewoman'); and 'In a Churchyard (Song of the Yew Tree)' ('While Drawing in a Churchyard').

Ex.4

It is perhaps understandable that Finzi should have thought Hardy's title cumbersome. But he did not replace it with the first line of the poem. He chose to call his song 'So I have fared' drawing attention to the penultimate verse, and the concern about the passing years he already shared with Hardy:

> So I have fared through many suns;
> Sadly little grist I
> Bring my mill, or any one's,
> *Domine, Tu scisti!*

At these words the flexible recitative is replaced by 'A tempo giusto (un poco con moto)' and a steady crotchet pacing appears for the first time in the bass line. It is not difficult once again to discern the inexorable march of Time.

Perhaps the most remarkable title change is to a poem which the eighty-three year old Hardy wrote in November 1923 and which he called 'The Best She Could'. This is another autumnal poem, philosophizing over the limitations of summer. Hardy takes his title from his closing lines, describing Dame Summer's garb as:

> Alas, not much! And yet the best
> She could, within the too short time
> Granted her prime.

Finzi, however, setting the poem in 1949, chooses as his title for the song a blunter phrase from the same sentence, calling it simply 'The too short time', a phrase which seems to sum up his lifelong attitude to his own creativity. The erratic motion of a falling leaf is mimicked by the haphazard descent of the introductory piano line, and yet again an ominously regular pacing appears in the bass line at the start of the second stanza, as the words describe the stealthy onset of winter.

Following the diagnosis of Finzi's leukaemia in 1951, there appear a few compositions which suggest a rather more sympathetic attitude towards a broadly Christian view of the world, including the setting of several specifically Christian texts.[30] Some of these works were commissions, a factor which no doubt influenced the choice of text, and all of the words he chose were poetic, not dogmatic, statements about aspects of Christianity. Even so, given Finzi's instinct to set only words with which he felt an urge to identify himself personally,[31] one wonders whether in his later years he experienced at least some nostalgia for the church music with which he had become familiar during his five years of study, mainly as an impressionable teenager, with Edward Bairstow at York Minster.

There is, however, no evidence to suggest that his illness led him to modify in the slightest his firmly agnostic stance. No completed songs can

[30] Though 'Lo, the full, final sacrifice' (1946) and 'My lovely one' (1948) comfortably pre-date the prognosis of 1951 that he had at most ten years to live.

[31] In a letter to Howard Ferguson in December 1936, Finzi wrote: '[T]he first and last thing is that a composer is (presumably) moved by a poem and wishes to identify himself with it and share it . . . I don't think everyone realizes the difference between choosing a text and being chosen by one.' Howard Ferguson: 'Gerald Finzi (1901–1956)' in *Music and Letters* XXXVIII (1957), p. 131. And in his second Crees Lecture (see Chapter 4), Finzi refers twice to the composer as wishing to identify himself with the subject matter of the poem he sets.

be dated to the period between 1950 and March 1955, when Finzi's last surge of songwriting seems to have begun, but the five late Hardy settings contain very much the same mixture as before, some of them grieving over the loss of the past whilst others reveal a resigned, stoical, acceptance of the inevitability of decay and the natural renewing cycle of death and rebirth.

'Life laughs onward', for instance, dates from March 1955.[32] In this poem, as in so many, the poet revisits former haunts, presumably Emma's and his own, and is saddened to find no trace of what he vividly remembers. In the last verse, however, he comes to terms with the loss of his past and the need for change:

> Life laughed and moved on unsubdued,
> I saw that Old succumbed to Young
> 'Twas well. My too regretful mood
> Died on my tongue.

As the song progresses, the changed appearances of the places visited are tellingly paralleled by key changes, but, just as Hardy's closing words only reluctantly accept the need for change, so the music returns at the close to its initial G major, and to a nostalgic echo of its opening phrases.

'It never looks like summer here', set in February 1956, displays another typical mood of Hardy's, looking back in 1913 to what he saw as the halcyon early days of his relationship with Emma.[33] Words and music are in two matching stanzas, the first ending with only the merest hint of a major key at the words 'Summer it seemed to me', and the second drooping to end with a wistful echo of the piano's opening phrase a major third lower than at the start.

Finzi's last Hardy setting is the dramatic and far from typical 'I said to Love', composed on 12 July 1956,[34] just ten weeks before his death. After three stanzas in which the poet sternly refuses to tolerate any further domination by Love, comes an impassioned cadenza-like outburst from the piano in response to the words 'Depart then, Love!' (Ex.5).

This piano passage is unique among Finzi's solo songs.[35] The finality

[32] Banfield, op. cit., p. 447.
[33] The title is a remark made by Emma which Hardy wrote on a drawing of her which he made at Beeny Cliff in Cornwall in 1870: Hynes, op. cit., p. 512.
[34] Banfield, op. cit., p. 447.
[35] Though at the start of the Grand Fantasia there is a remarkable cadenza for the piano, lasting for some five minutes, before the orchestra plays a single note.

of Hardy's renunciation must have struck Finzi very forcibly to have provoked it. The dissonant setting of the last two verses matches the bitterness of Hardy's thought.

Ex.5

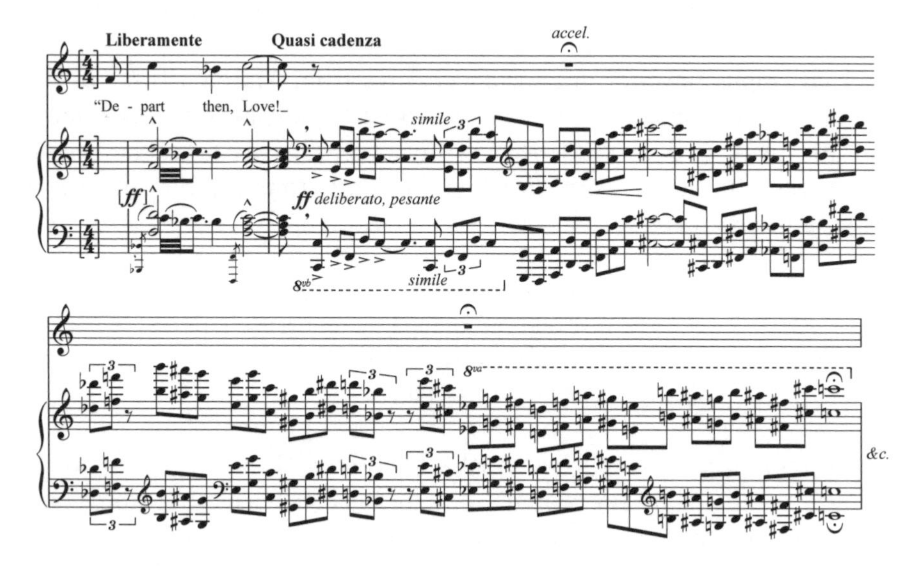

But by no means all Finzi's Hardy settings are morbid or introspective. A few, such as 'Ditty', 'Rollicum-rorum', and 'The Market-girl' are, in their different ways, positively cheerful, and scarcely touched by the obsession with Time which united poet and composer. Others, such as 'Budmouth dears' and 'When I set out for Lyonnesse' are superficially neutral or even upbeat, in spite of their minor keys, and only by implication troubled by the contrasts between past and present. In several others, Time is merely a subtheme to a poem about Nature or Love, presented, in both words and music, as at least potentially happy and satisfactory: examples are 'Childhood among the ferns', 'Summer schemes' and 'Epeisodia'. Though few, these more outgoing songs are sufficient to vary and lighten the overall mood of the songsets a little, even if in the context they inevitably come across as of a piece with Hardy's generally gloomy world view.

Finzi's last two songs were not settings of Hardy. In 'Harvest', Finzi identifies himself with Edmund Blunden, recognizing that his time is up and that he has not achieved all that he hoped:

I see some shrivelled fruits upon my tree,
And gladly would self-kindness feign them sweet;
The bloom smelled heavenly, can these stragglers be
The fruit of that bright birth? and this wry wheat,
Can this be from those spires
Which I, or fancy, saw leap to the spring sun's fires?

I peer, I count, but anxious is not rich,
My harvest is not come, the weeds run high

At the end, however, like Blunden, he is reconciled to the Earth's indifference to human notions of success or achievement:

The Sun's eye laughing looks.
And Earth accuses none that goes among her stooks.

For what was to be his very last composition, a month before he died,[36] Finzi returned to Robert Bridges. 'Since we loved' may not be one of his best songs, but in a determined effort to take a positive view of his own 'too short time' he sets these words:

Love hath been as poets paint,
Life as heaven is to a saint;

All my joys my hopes excel,
All my work hath prosper'd well,
All my songs have happy been,
O my love, my life, my queen.

As he saw his time running out, Finzi must have known that Bridges' lines about 'my work' and 'my songs' were for him demonstrably untrue. His compositions were not yet being widely performed or appreciated, and many of the Hardy poems he had chosen to set were far from 'happy'. It seems right, therefore, to conclude that the song was primarily intended as a retrospective tribute to his happy marriage. It was first sung at Ashmansworth by Wilfred Brown with Herbert Sumsion at the piano, shortly after Finzi's death.

[36] But, according to Christopher Finzi, at a time when he still had no inkling how near his end was to be. His ill-fated visit to Chosen Hill was still a week away.

4. 'Who is this coming with pondering pace?': Word-painting and hidden messages.

In May 1955, little more than a year before his untimely death, Gerald Finzi gave three Crees Lectures at the Royal College of Music under the title 'The Composer's Use of Words'.[37] These lectures reveal not only his truly encyclopaedic knowledge of English poetry and vocal music but also his acute sensitivity to how a poem can move a composer and how that emotional response can be reflected at various levels in its musical setting. He never once mentions his own compositions in this extended discussion of the craft of song writing, but what comes across is that he always found himself passionately involved with the text he was working with, not just 'setting words' but rather as he put it 'being enflamed by them'. He must have been speaking for himself as well as others when he went on:

> Some composers have never written a song or a choral work without at least one line being instantaneously matched with a musical equivalent on the very first reading of the words. That does not make it a work of art, but it is the initial excitement which brings the intellect into play to carry the emotion to its end.

In his Hardy songs, Finzi repeatedly makes skilful use of music both to encapsulate an image and to convey a mood. Pieces of effective word-painting can be found in almost every song. One example, already mentioned above, is the delicate way in which the piano imitates a falling leaf at the start of 'The too short time'. Another is the unmistakable sound of birdsong in 'Summer schemes', at the end of the first stanza and of bubbling streams in the second. Birdsong reappears in the plaintive piano phrases which open and close 'Proud songsters', with the minor key resonance of a thrush's song. Water is again evoked in 'Childhood among the ferns', first as raindrops and later as trickles and 'slow-creeping rivulets'. After the rain of an English summer, the music pauses, just as our English weather usually does, before the sun bursts through at the return to Tempo I. In 'Before and after summer', February's 'later shafts of sleet | Sharper pointed than the first' are indeed sharply pointed in the piano's detached quavers in the first half of the song, and the dreary blankness of October is all too evident in the second.

'The comet at Yell'ham' provides a very different example of Finzi's

[37] I am indebted to Christopher Finzi for kindly supplying me with a slightly abbreviated typescript of these lectures.

ability to enhance Hardy's depiction of a natural phenomenon. The comet's slow and silent motion and its other-worldly strangeness are symbolized by the piano's tiptoeing bitonality. Its apparently parabolic path through the night sky, as it seems first to approach the earth and then to return to the heavens, is reflected first in an introduction which slowly descends from the piano's highest register and then in a postlude which equally slowly returns to the top of the keyboard.

Human characteristics are pointed up in the music as well as features and forces of Nature. The marching soldiers are obvious in 'Budmouth dears' as are the echoes of 6/8 dances in 'the gay tunes we trod' of 'Former beauties' and the 'triple-timed romance' of 'The Dance continued'. The 'great guns' reverberate at both ends of 'Channel firing', while at the close high thirdless chords reveal the cold starlight over Stonehenge. The piano's drooping phrases at both ends of, and between verses in, 'The sigh' must surely represent the sigh itself.

Some pieces of vivid imagery, visual or emotional, are extremely brief. False relations intensify momentary pangs at 'a fresh love-leaf crumpled' in 'A young man's exhortation', at 'for all I know' in 'Waiting both', at the word 'fragile' in 'I look into my glass' (Ex.2) and, with a single unexpected D#, on 'smart' in 'Ditty'.

Finzi captures moods as well as images. In 'Waiting Both', the movement of the voice from tonic to dominant via a flattened seventh at the words 'So mean I' aptly expresses the star's patient and resigned acceptance of an exceedingly long wait for extinction. There is something here of the mood conveyed by the bugle's repeated tonic to dominant progression at the end of the Last Post. By contrast, in 'To Lizbie Browne', the first and only semi quavers in the whole long song arise at the words 'You disappeared' and seem to capture exactly Hardy's sudden recollection of his almost indignant surprise at the loss of one of his earliest loves.

On a larger scale, of course, Finzi uses a range of styles to convey the overall mood of a Hardy poem. At one extreme, we have the cynical cheerfulness of 'Rollicum-rorum'; at another, the confessional repentance of 'So I have fared'. But he can also express changing moods within the same song. A straightforward example is 'A young man's exhortation', where the music mirrors the varying moods from verse to verse. The determined Ab major cheerfulness of verse 1 is followed by an almost ecstatic 'poco piu mosso' for verse 2, with the voice's highest notes set against busy semiquavers in F major. Tempo I returns for verse 3, 'dolce' and pianissimo, an echo of verse 1, but sounding quite different now that it is in A major. The sadder and more philosophical mood of verse 4 is marked 'poco meno mosso' and wavers musingly between D major and B minor, with a 'molto rit. e dim.' on the words 'Of all scope dispossest'. The last verse is unbarred and 'a piacere', the poet reconciled to 'the passing preciousness of dreams' in a calm D major, as far removed as possible from the original Ab major. The music turns on the very last chord to a wonderful, wholly unexpected and open-ended E major.

Key changes like these are in Finzi's songs often important as pointers to shifts of mood. In 'Life laughs onward', for instance, as noted in Chapter 3, the changed appearances of the places revisited by Hardy in his old age are matched by shifts of key. But there are more complex and subtle inflections of mood and key in 'In the mind's eye'. The ghost of his mistress haunts the poet as he looks up at what used to be her window. The opening phrases of the music (Ex.6a) ambiguous as to key, uncertain in rhythm, reflect his blurring of reality and recollection. When the voice enters, C minor becomes G minor. The second verse, with sharper dissonances, begins in D minor and progresses quickly to Eb minor, with an anguished conflict at the word 'Ah' between the pianist's hands (Ex.6b), one seeming momentarily to be in B minor[38], the other in Bb major, as he realizes that it is 'but her phantom | Borne within my brain.' Verse 3 opens with ghostly mezzo-staccato footsteps, even paced, in G# minor (Ex.6b), which give way to legato quavers and an even more rapid sequence of minor chords at the words 'Change dissolves the landscapes' (Ex.6c), with a characteristic false relation on the climactic word 'abide': the poet seems more distraught by the persistence of the vision than by the realization that it is only a ghost that he sees. The piano interlude echoes the poignant thrush's call from 'Proud songsters' which is followed by a despairing descent to a dominant D. The last verse attempts more calmly to face the future as it starts in a resigned and mournful diatonic G minor, but it reveals the truth that nothing has been resolved as it drifts questioningly back to an insecure D minor in the last few bars.

Ex.6a

[38] Though this clash is not the 'compound' false relation that it appears to be at first sight. The B natural in the bass is really a Cbb.

Ex.6b

In Hardy's poetry, mood and message are often closely bound up with imagery. Finzi frequently achieves the same coherence. In 'At Middle-Field Gate in February' (Ex.7a), the depressed mood merges with the atmospheric description. The tonally uncertain piano part in the first verse and for part of the second seems both to peer through the clammy fog and to amble dejectedly across the landscape. The piano imitates the dewdrop's fall 'at the feeblest jog' in bars 8–9 (Ex.7b), and the plodding of mud-clogged boots can be heard at the end of verse 2 (Ex.7c). As the poet recalls ‘How dry it was on a far-back day’, the fog seems to clear a little, but only to reveal a pensively nostalgic G# minor for the last verse. The voice descends as low as a B for the last word ‘underground’, and once again ends indecisively on the dominant D#.

Ex.7a

Not every feature or mood change is musically signposted moment by moment as the song proceeds. Sometimes the piano merely sets the general tone, leaving the shape of the vocal line to bring out the meaning of the words. In ‘Ditty’, for instance, the rambling accompaniment creates and sustains a contented rural atmosphere in a sunny G major, accidental-free apart from the one unexpected D# on ‘smart’ mentioned above. In ‘At a lunar eclipse’, the piano maintains a slow and steady pace, the bass moving mainly downwards and almost entirely in crotchets, like the Earth’s shadow moving imperceptibly across the Moon’s face, leaving the voice space and time to soliloquize philosophically.

There is a serious question to be addressed here, already hinted at in chapter 3, about the long sequences of stepwise movement, sometimes ascending but more often descending, in Finzi's bass lines. An explanation is needed for such a conspicuous compositional practice which would have been unthinkable to any of the composers who might have influenced Finzi (with the possible exception of Holst) and even to those of a similarly contrapuntal turn of mind. We all know that sixteenth-century vocal lines[39] move mainly by step, of course, but rarely in the same direction for more than four or five steps in a row, whereas Finzi's bass lines sometimes go on marching in the same direction for two or more octaves.

Ex.7c

So far as I am aware, published commentaries on Finzi's music do not really grapple with this question. In her article about Finzi for what was then the *New Grove*,[40] Diana McVeagh merely remarks that 'the limited idiom and the regularity of his harmonic pace can become monotonous.' Another unpublished commentator rather condescendingly attributes his perambulating bass lines to Finzi's habit of composing at the piano:

> His bass lines habitually move by step because that was how his left hand moved up and down the keyboard as he composed. He used, in fact, a sophisticated version of the technique of the village organist who moves his left foot stepwise over the pedals while extemporising, and operates the swell pedal with his right. It is one of the intriguing features of Finzi's music that even some of the best of it was produced using simple, even amateurish technical procedures.

Now it is clear that Finzi was neither amateur nor dilettante. There must

[39] Finzi had studied sixteenth-century counterpoint with R. O. Morris in 1925.
[40] *The New Grove Dictionary of Music and Musicians*, edited by Stanley Sadie (Macmillan, London. 1980)

be a better reason for so painstaking a composer to write such bass lines than that 'his left hand moved up and down the keyboard.' Let us review the evidence.

First there is 'Budmouth dears', where the regular crotchet beating in the bass surely has something to do with the soldiers marching. Then there are the four songs mentioned in Chapter 3 in which a relentless pacing, whether stepwise or no, seems to signify the march of Time. In much the same way, 'At a lunar eclipse' suggests a link between a steadily moving bass line and Finzi's obsession with the passing of time.

Next, there are cases where the piano's ascents and descents are part of the word-painting: the falling leaf in 'The too short time', for instance, the dewdrop in 'At Middle-Field gate in February', the piano's sighs in 'The sigh', the journey of the comet in 'The comet at Yell'ham.' There are also descents such as the one at the words 'So down we lay again' in 'Channel firing'. Expressing images in music has been part of vocal writing for many generations.

But ascents and descents in the word-painting often mesh closely with the underlying mood or message. The falling leaf, for example, is already dead and doomed to decay, and as it lands the dewdrop ceases to exist. As they die, both move downwards, as does the piano line, and earthwards. The boots in 'At Middle-Field Gate on February' similarly plod downwards in heavy mud and deep depression. By contrast, the comet is not earthbound: it comes from, and returns to, another unearthly realm, symbolized by the highest notes on the piano that Finzi uses in any Hardy song.

In 'Summer schemes' the link between image and message is slightly less obvious. In the first stanza, the piano does not only mimic the summer birdsong: the bass line, and with it the whole accompaniment, expresses the eager anticipation of spring as it rises through more than two octaves to the tessitura the birdsong demands and the higher air they occupy. But the last part of the verse casts a cloud of doubt on the whole project:

> '—We'll go,' I sing; but who shall say
> What may not chance before that day!

And the piano line descends, step by step, as the enthusiasm subsides into uncertainty.

The imagery is different in the second verse. Water can only flow downhill, as does the bass line. But this does not contradict the underlying message, because although the verse structure is the same, the mood is not. The eager uprising of the first verse cannot be repeated: the singer already knows too much about possible disappointment.

In 'Waiting both', the piano describes the star as high above the Earth, but looking down at the poet in the descending figuration of bars 3–5 (Ex.8):

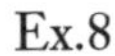

It would not be over-fanciful likewise to see the poet as looking up at the star in the rising chromatic bass line of the opening bars. The star's music reappears, a fourth lower than before, in the pianist's right hand at 'Tempo I'. In the left hand at this point the poet seems to look up again, but now from three or even four octaves lower than before. Why does the accompaniment settle for such low registers in the last part of the song, when the star gives its reply? The answer seems to be that the piano is no longer merely describing an image, but also conveying a mood and a message. Even the star is a little more subdued than before, but the poet has sunk into the depths of a fatalistic gloom. When Hardy writes 'Till my change come' he is quoting from the Book of Job (see Chapter 2). So both star and poet know that what they are waiting for is death.

From these examples—and many others might be cited—the symbolism seems clear enough. A steady pacing movement in the bass, upwards or downwards, and whether or not stepwise, stands for the irresistible march of Time. A downward sequence, whether or not in steady pacing, represents a downward, earthbound movement, dying, ending, gloom and depression. The less common upward sequences signify movement towards the ethereal or heavenly, new life, spring, renewal and optimism. When a bass line moves by step with a steady pace the two metaphors coalesce: the progression, whether towards death and decay, or less often towards renewal and hope, is rigorously ruled by 'Time the tyrant fell.'

Indeed, it is possible to portray movement in both directions at once.

In 'Transformations', Hardy expresses his own grim view of resurrection as he describes how those long ago buried continue to exist in the trees and flowers of the graveyard, and he concludes:

> So, they are not underground,
> But as nerves and veins abound
> In the growths of upper air,
> And they feel the sun and rain,
> And the energy again
> That made them what they were!

In the closing bars of Finzi's setting, the pianist encapsulates Hardy's paradoxical vision. The left hand marches downwards into the earth while the right surges upwards, ultimately to the same high D as the comet.

Once this fairly elementary symbolism has been grasped, it can be seen at work throughout the songsets. A particularly powerful example, with a remorselessly continuous descent of more than three octaves, comes at the end of 'Amabel', as the poet, more in sorrow than in anger, finally and emphatically turns his back on his time-worn former love.

Hardy's dour stoicism and regretful nostalgia permeate almost all his poetry, even when it is no more than implicit in the images and experiences he describes. Much the same can now be said of Finzi's music: even when the words do not appear to call for music containing statements about Time and Death, Hardy's underlying message can nevertheless be conveyed symbolically. Not every descending sequence can be mapped on to a directly parallel thought, but there is no reason to expect such precise matching when the message pervades the whole. In 'He abjures Love', for instance, Hardy's bitter recrimination is in breathtakingly powerful terms directed not against Life, or Death, or Fate, but against Love. He knows, however, what the end of it all will be:

> —I speak as one who plumbs
>   Life's dim profound,
> One who at length can sound
>   Clear views and certain.
> But—after love what comes?
>   A scene that lours,
> A few sad vacant hours,
>   And then, the Curtain.

Finzi, in one of his most dramatic settings, anticipates the message of the final stanza almost from the start. There are long, vigorous, descending lines in verses 1 and 3, and the longest of all, again resigned rather than angry, stretches across the piano's interlude between verses 4 and 5. By the time the last verse arrives, the piano's rage, like the poet's, is long spent: there is a descending bass line at the close, but the stronger metaphors are the piano's relentless seconds-pendulum pulse at 'Ancor meno mosso' and the singer's low register.

Such symbolic movements of the bass line can be discerned in virtually every Finzi song. Of the seven Hardy settings which do not have bass sequences as long as an octave or more, six have one or more substantial but shorter sequences. Only the very early 'Two lips' (1928) has none at all. There is no way of knowing whether Finzi was aware that he was working these symbols of Hardy's deeper thinking so thoroughly into his compositions. But it does not matter whether he did it deliberately. If by any chance the commentator who compared him to a village organist should be proved right about the movement of Finzi's left hand, the musical effect would still be the same. If the degree to which the music is saturated with extended stepwise movements persuades the reader that it was no more than a habit, the result at worst would only be to discount the less effective passages. The associations of pitch level with mood and of a regular pulse with Time's march are too strong to be disregarded.

And whether he chose it consciously or not, it is apt that Finzi's principal messenger should be the bass line. Time and Death and their implications are, after all, deep and basic issues. Like a bass line, they usually lie beneath the surface features of daily life, which, like the upper parts of a musical texture, often obscure or disguise them.

Of many other instances worthy of analysis, it seems appropriate to end by returning to 'Proud songsters'. The shortness of life is first signalled by the descending bass at the words 'As if all Time were theirs', both Hardy and Finzi knowing full well that, especially for the birds, it is not. Then as Time is unwound in verse 2, and the young birds are seen as 'only particles of grain, | And earth, and air, and rain', Finzi seems to hesitate (Ex. 3). The music is running down, the songset is ending: is the birds' life-cycle to be construed finally as a hopeful symbol of renewal and resurrection or as yet another metaphor of our fragility and transience? The descending bass line wavers: perhaps the single steps up and down around A show how pitifully short the birds' life is anyway, or how frequent and rapid for them is the cycling between death and renewal.

The postlude maintains an exquisite balance with a heart-rending internal contradiction. The harmony opts, narrowly, not for the expected D major but for B minor. The bass line, however, no longer descends or dithers: hoping against hope, it rises, stepwise, from D to B. And the thrush sings on as the twilight fades.

IX

Friends and influences

Ernest Bristow Farrar 1885–1918

Donald Webster

Lecture given in Harrogate, 3 August 1996.

Many of us made our first acquaintance with Wilfred Owen's poems within the pages of Britten's *War Requiem*; I have tended to maintain a somewhat equivocal attitude towards that composition—as much for biographical as for artistic reasons, I will readily admit. Such greatness as it has rests, in my view, more on the brilliance of its conception, and the placing of vehemently anti-war poetry alongside the traditional Latin text of the Requiem, rather than on the quality of its musical ideas. This view can, I think, be upheld whether one looks upon the *War Requiem* as a cynical juxtaposition reminiscent of *Oh! What a Lovely War*—or as an expression of how mankind has failed to carry out God's will.

The most affecting part of the work for me is the Offertorium. Here a boys' choir sings the text pleading for God's deliverance from the pains of Hell, in accordance with the promise made to Abraham and his seed. Then comes Owen's poem, 'The parable of the old man and the young', which alludes to the story in Genesis where God, as a test of Abraham's faith, instructs him to offer his son as a sacrifice. Because Abraham showed his obedience he was further told to lay no hold on Isaac. Owen's poem reads: 'But the old man would not so, but slew his son, | And half the seed of Europe, one by one.'

In addition to the immense distress in individual families caused by the carnage of war in all countries, there has to be taken into account the loss of an enormous amount of talent, the flower of our so-called civilisation, whom no nation could afford to lose. Among the musicians we have lost, I think most immediately of George Butterworth, who spent much of his boyhood in York, where his father was manager of the North Eastern Railway. Butterworth, composer of *A Shropshire Lad*, was killed on the Somme in 1916, aged only thirty-one. From the Second World War we remember Jehan Alain aged twenty-nine, Anton Webern, and Walter Leigh among many others.

It took two years' preparation for Ernest Bristow Farrar to lead his men bravely into battle, and just two days out at the Front to kill him. Farrar's tragic death took place only six weeks before the signing of the Armistice. To begin my talk on Farrar with references to Britten and others may seem rather odd, but as my words unfold, I hope to establish a connection between them. My contemplation of musicians killed in their prime is shared by many others when thinking of their contemporaries. A frequent theme in Harold MacMillan's speeches and writings was a questioning of why so many of his more gifted friends and colleagues were vanquished, and he was left. In making this observation, MacMillan commented—as a Christian—on the strange workings of Providence.

Farrar's father, the Reverend Charles Druce Farrar married Rose Alice, daughter of a retired Colonel, William Handyside, on 10 May 1882. The Reverend Farrar was at that time curate of St Mary's South Lewisham, London. Their first child Ethel Rose was born a year later, and Ernest two years after that. When Ernest was two, the family moved to Micklefield, a village almost equidistant between Leeds and Selby. The church had recently been rebuilt, and they were the first occupants of the new vicarage. Ernest became a pupil at Leeds Grammar School on 14 November 1895. This was a place where John Ireland had attended for a short time some years previously. Farrar probably had his first organ lessons on the instrument in the school chapel. Herbert Austin Fricker, Leeds City organist, promoter of orchestral concerts in the city and chorus master of the Leeds Festival, had tenuous links with the school, and may have taught Farrar; though it is not firmly established that this was so. Farrar obtained his ARCO at the age of eighteen, certainly an achievement of merit.

Like the rest of his family he was rather reserved, tall and well built, well-liked and noted for his twinkling blue eyes. He wished to see functional and undreamlike commonsense attend the celebration of the Holy Mysteries, with austerity and dignity, and without anything sentimental or profane. His life in the country at Micklefield must have inspired the *Vagabond Songs*, whose first performance by the Halifax Choral Society was directed by Fricker in 1911. Fricker was the dedicatee of the choral suite *Out of Doors*; friendship and indebtedness must have characterised the relationship between the two men.

Ernest Farrar had a younger brother, Cecil, born 1889, who worked for a time in a bank in Pontefract, but studied for the Anglican ministry, obtaining a Durham degree, as his father had done. Cecil was ordained deacon at Ripon Cathedral in 1913. After a short spell as priest at St Saviour's Church in Leeds, known then, as now, for its extreme Anglo-Catholic tendencies, he joined the Church of Rome. His priestly appointments were mostly in the North Riding or Yorkshire, ending at St Wilfrid's Church, York—within a stone's throw of the Minster—where he was an immensely respected (but much feared) canon.

Ernest Farrar was organist for his father at Micklefield from 1903–5, entering the University of Durham in 1904—following the family tradition—as an unattached member, passing the first part of the B.Mus examination during his first term. There is no evidence that he proceeded with the degree requirements.

Mrs Amy Jewill, who worked at the Vicarage in 1906, remembered that the lid of the baby grand piano was never opened when Ernest was away, and that Ernest shared his father's ruddy complexion. 'Big Mick', as Charles Farrar was known locally, was not well liked by the Wesleyans, but he would bring back from Leeds market parcels of fish for distribution among the sick of the parish, regardless of denomination. Kippers were eaten on Fridays as part of the ritual in the Farrar household, and Charles loved to extract every morsel of fish from between the bones, leaving his table napkin in a frightful mess, much to the consternation of the servants.

Ernest Bullock remembered him as an exemplary parish priest, devoted to his family and to his people, kindly, wise and loveable, a man of large stature, with a large heart and a great sense of humour.

As befitted his Anglo-Catholicism, he loved ceremonials. Mrs Farrar was a quiet, gentle lady, tall and stately, immensely dedicated in helping her husband in the parish, and a kind mother. Her daughter, Ethel, qualified in domestic science at the 'Pudding School'—as it was called—in Leeds, and returned home as a paid housekeeper.

The Ernest Bullock to whom I referred later became Sir Ernest Bullock. How did he enter the Farrar's life, you may ask? As a child, he became a pupil of Edward Bairstow, who was at that time organist of Wigan Parish Church. In 1906 Bairstow was appointed to Leeds Parish Church. I'll let Bairstow take up the story:

> In Wigan, a worthy man, an ardent Freemason, who kept a small music shop, died leaving a large family of sons, one of who became a much respected precentor at Leeds Parish Church in the 1920s. The youngest, Ernest, was very gifted musically. He came to me as a choirboy of nine years. The Masons articled him to me just as I left Wigan for Leeds. The only thing to do was to take him into our house. My wife became a second mother to him. We never regretted the decision. On the contrary we were thankful for it. Ernest and I played together on the few evenings I was at liberty.

Their playing was not confined to piano duets; they could frequently be seen in the Bairstow sitting room playing with a large train set, with many wagons and points. There was only sixteen years difference in their ages: at the time of their arrival in Leeds, Bairstow was thirty-two and Bullock sixteen. Bullock became Bairstow's deputy at Leeds in 1908, alongside positions as organist at Micklefield in 1908, and Adel (near Leeds), in 1910. He obtained his B.Mus degree from Durham in 1908, at the age of eighteen, and his doctorate in 1914. He was five years younger than Farrar, but far exceeded him in academic achievement—not that this necessarily denoted superior musical ability. After war service, Bullock became organist at St Michael's College, Tenbury, for a few months, followed by similar appointments at Exeter Cathedral in 1919, and Westminster Abbey in 1927. In 1941 he was appointed principal of the Royal Scottish Academy of Music and Professor at Glasgow University, and eleven years later director of the Royal College of Music in London.

Curiously, during the time that Bullock was organist at Micklefield, there was no contact between him and Ernest Farrar. Bullock used to cycle from Leeds for a midweek choir practice, and on Sundays spent the day at the Farrar vicarage. The college vacation times may have been the very times when Bullock's services were needed at Leeds. Farrar no doubt was only too happy to assist at his father's services. There was an interregnum between Farrar's leaving his Micklefield post and Bullock's arrival. On taking up the post, Bullock found (then modern) settings by Stanford and others in the repertory, which he deemed to be beyond the choir's capability. Does this suggest that Farrar was a little over ambitious in his choice of music for the choir, or was it that standards had fallen between Farrar's departure and Bullock's arrival? At all events, the two Ernests didn't meet until 1909, but from the very beginning a warm friendship developed that ended only in Farrar's death.

The vicar suggested a massive injection of plainsong into the services as a means of overcoming the choral problem, and to this Bullock agreed. It accorded with the reverend's ritualistic churchmanship, and Bullock's austere temperament (his RCM students years later frequently referred to him as 'Deadly Ernest') and most of the choir left, not returning till some time later.

During Farrar's time as a student at the RCM, his principal study was Composition; Piano was his second study. He was awarded the Sullivan Prize in 1906, and was Grove Scholar from 1907–9. His teachers were Sir Charles Stanford for Composition; Sir Walter Parratt, a native of Huddersfield, for Organ; Sir Frederick Bridge of Westminster Abbey for Counterpoint; and Jack Dykes for Piano. The latter had been a pupil of Clara Schumann, and his brother was vicar of Holy Trinity Church in Boar Lane, Leeds. They were the sons of John Bacchus Dykes, the famous hymn tune composer. Farrar obtained no college diploma, but the Leodensian, the magazine of Leeds Grammar School, reported, 'We hear that E. B. Farrar, who has been composing love songs for Sir Charles Stanford with considerable success, has now begun to play the big drum in his College orchestra.' During his time at the RCM, he had joined the 'Beloved Vagabonds', a club founded by Audrey Alston, Benjamin Britten's viola teacher in East Anglia. Other members included Marion Scott, Harold Samuel, Felix Salmond, Clive Carey, Frank Bridge and Ivor Gurney, all of whom achieved distinction in later life.

His scholarship had two terms to run when he was offered, through the college, the post of organist at All Saints' English Church in Dresden for six months from February to July 1909, whilst the regular holder of the post, Albert Mallinson and his Danish singer wife went to Australia, partly for health reasons and partly to give recitals. Mallinson, born Leeds 1870, had been a chorister and deputy organist at Leeds Parish Church, and was a prolific and very accomplished songwriter, whose compositions attracted much favourable comment. At this time Dresden was second only to Vienna as a musical Mecca, and it attracted musicians from all over the world, including Delius, Elgar, George Dyson and Basil Harwood. Though earlier in the nineteenth century both Weber and Wagner had directed the Dresden Opera, it is generally agreed that the time of Ernst von Schuch, 1879–1914, were Dresden's golden years. The organist at Dresden's American Church was Willoughby Williams, répétiteur at the Royal Opera. He succeeded Edward Bairstow when the latter left Leeds to become organist at York Minster. A fascinating Yorkshire web was spun around Farrar throughout his life.

The Dresden church magazine said, 'Latterly under Mr Farrar's able and inspiring leadership the music has improved, and the services have been brighter and more tuneful.' Farrar had been recommended for the post by Parratt and Sir Hubert Parry, Director of the RCM, and he hadn't let them down.

Farrar was back in Micklefield to give an organ recital on 1 August 1909, and for a recital on 19 August with violinist and musicologist Marion Scott, the eminent Haydn and Beethoven scholar, to whom the first movement of his *Celtic Suite* was dedicated two years later. Some years later, in a Harrogate recital, they played the César Franck Violin Sonata, which showed Farrar's pianistic ability to be of a very high order. This is reflected too in the idiomatic piano writing to be found in his compositions.

Stanford conducted Farrar's *The Blessed Damozel* in Leeds, and his *Orchestral Rhapsody* was also premiered there by the Municipal Orchestra, conducted by Fricker.

Dr (later Sir) Henry Hadow selected Farrar from more than seventy applicants for the post of Choirmaster at St Hilda's Church, South Shields in 1910. In his application, Farrar had received strong support from Parry, Stanford and Parratt. During his time at St Hilda's, he formed a friendship with John Pullein, Organist of St Peter's Church, Harrogate, who had given a recital there.

Farrar moved to Harrogate at the start of September 1912, as organist of Christ Church, returning to South Shields in order to marry Olive Mason (to whom he had become engaged in 1911), on 8 January 1913, with Ernest Bullock as best man. He became conductor of the Harrogate Orchestral Society, and may have taught at Queen Ethelburga's School, since there is a photograph of him seated at the chapel organ. A correspondent in the *Harrogate Advertiser* toward the end of 1913 praised the great improvement in the standard of the music that Ernest had wrought at Christ Church. The friendship that Julian Clifford, conductor of the Harrogate Municipal Orchestra, extended towards him had profound artistic consequences, as he was given the opportunity to conduct several of his compositions.

In 1914, Gerald Finzi, then aged thirteen, went to Farrar for lessons, and an immediate rapport was established. At this time Finzi was living at

22 Duchy Road, quite close to St Wilfrid's Church and the Farrar home in Hollins Road. Even though Finzi became a pupil of Dr Bairstow at York after Ernest joined the forces, it was to Farrar that Finzi turned when confronted with a musical problem. There is little doubt that the spiritual intimacy between the two men is reflected in a certain idiomatic similarity in their compositions.

Although there was no direct link between Farrar and Bairstow (other than young Finzi), the former's anthems were sung regularly at York Minster. By way of contrast, we read:

> More than once Bairstow included compositions by Finzi in his choral concerts. After a few years, Finzi left ECB to study with R. O. Morris. It appears that he could have been disenchanted with the strict methods employed by Bairstow, or at any rate felt the need of some sort of change. He was scarcely even mentioned by ECB and none of his works were in the repertoire of the Minster Choir. [1]

Finzi's lessons with Bairstow had continued for five years, from 1917–22, and he became a pupil of Morris in 1925. Despite Bairstow's great reputation as a teacher, it says much that Finzi derived more from Farrar.

On 11 December 1915 Farrar joined the Grenadier Guards, and some months later he wrote to Finzi saying that his hands were getting 'knocked about' and stiff from rifle work. Around the beginning of 1917, he said that he'd been to some concerts, and how nice it was to see something of his old life, and meet some London friends again.

Stanford and Vaughan Williams persuaded him to take up a commission, and he was made 2nd Lieutenant, 3rd Battalion, Royal North Devon Yeomanry on 27 February 1918. He returned to France on 6 September, and twelve days later he was killed in action by machine gun fire, leading his men over the top at Epéhy Ronssoy. [2]

Whilst waiting to embark, he formed a brief friendship with J. B. Priestley, who was with him in the same dugout, and gassed in the same battle. Ernest Bullock, who had reached the rank of Captain, was also serving in France, and was given permission to visit his friend at base camp, but Farrar had already left for the Front when he arrived.

Olive was heartbroken. They had no children and she never remarried, dying sixty-one years to the day after her husband. Stanford wrote:

[1] Francis Jackson: *Blessed City, the life and works of Edward C. Bairstow*, (York, 1996) p. 128.

[2] He is buried in Ronssoy Communal Cemetery, grave B.27.

> Farrar was one of my most loyal and devoted pupils. He was very shy but full of poetry. I always thought very high things of him as a composer, and lament his loss both personally and artistically.

In adjacent columns of the local newspaper there was mention of a posthumous performance in Harrogate of the Variations for Piano and Orchestra and a letter from Farrar's commanding officer, Major General Eric S. Gridwood:

> Please forgive my intruding on your great sorrow at the loss of your husband. I want you to know how much I personally feel the death of this gallant officer. He was a magnificent example to all in courage and devotion to duty, and was beloved by all ranks in his battalion. Please accept my heartfelt sympathy in your bereavement.

Marion Scott also paid tribute to the Celtic poetry and sturdy Anglo-Saxon fibre in his music—an unusual combination. J. B. Priestley, writing from hospital said, 'Your husband was one of the finest types of humanity . . . It was a privilege to know him'.

A scholarship at the Royal College of Music was founded in his memory and there have been many distinguished recipients. A significant memorial is Frank Bridge's Piano Sonata (1921–4). It is an agonised and far-reaching reaction to the tragedy of war, and a genuine sense of inconsolable personal loss seems to emerge in this violent and radical work. Anger at his friend's death is demonstrated in the immense emotional power; it is no doubt the new Bridge idiom that so attracted Benjamin Britten in the late 1920s and contributed to his uncompromising pacifism.

If we listen to Farrar's beautiful setting of Herrick's 'To Daffodils', we can wonder whether he had had some premonition of his untimely end:

> We have short time to stay, as you,
> We have as short a Spring;
> As quick a growth to meet Decay,
> As you, or any thing,
> We die,
> As your hours doe, and drie
> Away,
> Like to the Summers raine;
> Or as the pearles of Mornings dew
> Ne'r to be found againe.

There are some who believe his setting of 'Silent noon' is better than Vaughan Williams's; his *Margaritae Sorori*, a setting of W. E. Henley's 'A Late Lark', invites comparison with Delius's orchestral song. In all his music, contrapuntal resource, an essential element in all musical workmanship, is virtually beyond reproach.

An inevitable but ultimately fruitless question is 'how may Farrar's career have developed had he lived?' Compared with others of his near contemporaries who died tragically young—Hurlstone, Butterworth and Warlock—the verdict cannot be more favourable than promising. Yet the most crucial verdict of all is surely that of his teachers and contemporaries. Granted that he was a much loved person, could this alone explain the impact that he made on them? Men of the discernment of Stanford, Vaughan Williams, Frank Bridge, Ernest Bullock and many more were aware of a profound and developing musicality; as they must surely have reflected on how the world lost a rich treasure and still fairer hopes on that September day in 1918.

Harrogate and Ernest Farrar

Adrian Officer

From 1906–7 Julian Clifford had taken charge of the Harrogate Municipal Orchestra, which gave concerts at 3.15p.m. on Wednesdays in the Kursaal (later the Royal Hall) from April through to October. One wartime press cutting remarks, 'Mr Julian Clifford will be receiving the Iron Cross soon if he does not change the title for the building.' Ernest Farrar would have known the set up and he certainly knew John Pullein, the organist at St Peter's Church who had given a recital at South Shields at Ernest's church in 1911. Julian Clifford being rather flamboyant and Ernest Farrar being somewhat reserved, it would have been interesting to see them working together.

Farrar came to Christ Church in 1912, in the autumn. He gave an organ recital after Evensong on Sunday 22 September, and a recital with a singer on 27 October when he played St Ann's Fugue (so styled) by Bach, Cantabile by César Franck and Toccata by D'Evry (from Brompton Oratory). On 11 June 1913 there would have been a flutter when Dr Ethel Smyth was billed to conduct her own compositions. Sometimes Farrar would conduct (Clifford liking to perform a piano concerto), and sometimes he could be seen in the orchestra—playing the celesta for instance, in his own composition *The Forsaken Merman* in 1914. The next year, on his thirtieth birthday he conducted his new piece Variations for Piano and Orchestra. Back in 1913 *Lavengro*, after George Borrow, became 'Lavengio' in the press (this piece is still lost) and his own name frequently appeared as Farrer or Farrah (as in toffee).

From the summer of 1913 until the spring of 1916, Harry Gill and Horace Dixon went to 15 Hollins Road for their music lessons. Gerald Finzi started in 1914, but did not know the other two until Olive Farrar introduced them in about 1920. Harry Gill joined up through the (Lord) Derby Scheme for the under-aged and wore an armband until he was called up in 1916 and joined the Royal Fusiliers. Later he became a signaller in the Machine Gun Corps. In 1918 he was with the British troops in Italy and in 1919 he rejoined the Civil Service from which he retired in 1962.

Horace Dixon was in France when Ernest was killed. He worked for the *Yorkshire Evening Press* in Leeds and later went to live in York. He was apparently writing a novel which concerned Ernest Farrar but to conceal his identity, at Olive's request, the main character was named Julian Bossall—Bossall being the name of the village near Malton where Dixon played the organ.

Amongst Farrar's papers there is a talk on Church Music in two slightly differing versions, one better spoken and the other better read. In it he said there are two kinds of music: sacred and secular. 'Hymns are for the people, voluntaries should be listened to, special settings are suggested once a month.' He said 'rubbish was to be got rid of, and a little austerity does no harm if it encourages dignity and strength.' Harry Gill remembered him dismissing 'our favourite tune for 'The Day Thou Gavest' as "that damned waltz"! '

When he left home for the last time Ernest wrote every day to his wife, up to and including two letters on 15 September, three days before his death. He usually wound up with 'take the greatest care of your small self' and 'you are all the world to me' followed by three rows of seven kisses. Poor Olive had no address to write to him.

This sketch ends with three letters to Olive from friends: the first, from J. B. Priestley, is dated 6 October 1918; the second, from Horace Dixon, is dated 27 March 1953; and the third, dated 16 May 1953, is from Gerald Finzi, who had written to Maurice Miles, the conductor of the Yorkshire Symphony Orchestra, about the possibility of performing music by Farrar, and enclosing Mr Miles's reply.

Dear Mrs Farrar,
From the casualty list in Monday's *Continental Daily Mail* I have just learned to my great sorrow of the death of your husband. Will you please accept my deepest sympathy. The short term of friendship I enjoyed with him has made the news a great blow to me so I can imagine what it means to you. He and I were at the 3rd Battalion together and soon discovered common interests and ideals in music and literature so that we became good friends in a very short time. We came to France together and to our mutual satisfaction were posted to the same Battalion. Up to the morning of the 18th September we were together sharing the same dugout but as soon as we moved forward in the fog I lost sight of him and shortly afterwards was knocked out and sent down gassed. I am still in hospital, still confined to bed, in fact I have been wondering this last two weeks how he was faring. Your husband was to me a representative of one of the finest types of humanity, a creative artist free from all meannesses and jealousies. It was a privilege to know him, and for myself I know that what was destined to be a lasting friendship has been severed, and that is why I have taken the liberty of writing to you. Like all sincere artists he was an idealist and you have the consolation of knowing that he died fighting for a great ideal which shines above all petty ideas of nationality. As I am still far from well I know you will excuse this crude scrawl. It is impossible to give you an address out here but should you care to reply my home address is 5, Saltburn Place, Bradford and a letter addressed there will be forwarded in time.

Yours sincerely, J. B. Priestley, 2nd Lieutenant, Devon Regiment.

Dear Mrs Farrar,
I am writing to tell you that I have met Gerald Finzi. He came to Leeds for the Leeds Philharmonic Society performance of his *Intimations of Immortality* with the Yorkshire Symphony Orchestra conducted by Sir Malcolm Sargent. I was able to meet Mr Finzi through the kindness of Mr and Mrs A. A. Evans of Otley Road, Leeds, with whom he stayed. I paid my visit last Wednesday morning and they put two deck-chairs on the lawn for us and we had a talk that lasted an hour and a half. What a charming fellow he is, and how I loved his music which I heard the same night. Naturally our talk turned on E. B. F. and in the course of it Gerald Finzi raised the question of doing something to secure that E. B. F's unpublished work is not allowed to be forgotten. I said that I would write to you asking for your thoughts on the following idea. If we wrote to the Oxford University Press and asked them how much it would cost to have the score of, say, *Lavengro* published would you be prepared to allow them to see the manuscript in order to reach an estimate? Then when we

knew the amount we would approach interested people inviting subscriptions to cover the amount, who could reply to this proposal either to Mr Finzi or to me, or to both. This seems to me an admirable way of at least beginning to let the nation have some more of the very fine music we know exists.

I saw Ethel Farrar at Christmas time but have not been over to Whitkirk since. Sorry to say my wife has been very ill with a duodenal ulcer. She has had weeks in bed but is now up and is making good progress. I do hope you are keeping well. Needless to say there is never a day passes but I have some thought of Hollins Road. A thousand things continually remind me of those happy days.

Yours sincerely, H. P. Dixon

My Dear Olive,
The enclosed speaks for itself. Could you possibly let me have by registered post the scores of the Variations [for Piano and Orchestra] on a British Sea Song or *Lavengro*? I don't know the *Elegy for Soldiers* [Heroic Elegy] but if you think that it would be a good choice too perhaps you could include it.

Forgive this hasty note, I am rather overwhelmed with things at the moment.

Love from us both, Yours affectionately, Gerald.

The Correspondence of Gerald Finzi and Ralph Vaughan Williams

Hugh Cobbe

On 17 November 1923, Vaughan Williams replied to a letter he had received from a young composer, Gerald Finzi, who had apparently asked him for permission to use a folk tune which Vaughan Williams had collected on an expedition to Herefordshire with Ella Mary Leather in 1912. Vaughan Williams's response was typically generous but at the same time punctilious in protecting the legitimate interests of others:

Dear Mr Finzi
As far as I am concerned, with pleasure. But please ask Mrs Leather as well . . . By the way perhaps I ought to tell you that I also have used the tune in a choral work published by Stainer and Bell.

Yours sincerely, R. Vaughan Williams

The tune which Vaughan Williams refers to is 'The truth sent from above' which he had collected at King's Pyon, Herefordshire, with Mrs Ella Leather in August 1909. He had used it as the opening tune in his *Fantasia on Christmas Carols* (1912), while Finzi used it as the basis for his Christmas carol setting 'The Brightness of the day' published by Stainer & Bell in 1925 (with permission granted by Vaughan Williams and Mrs Leather duly acknowledged).

From this seed, friendship developed steadily. By 1927 Gerald appears to have been coming to see Vaughan Williams regularly for advice about his compositions, and getting to know his wife Adeline: she writes in March to thank him for two photographs he had taken of the cat which the Vaughan Williamses were looking after for R. O. Morris and his wife, Adeline's sister Emmeline (always known as Jane). In late 1927 Finzi consulted Vaughan Williams about his Violin Concerto, which had been first performed in May. In November, Vaughan Williams asked to have another look at it, and on 2 December, having agreed that if it was revised he would give it a second performance at a Bach Choir concert the following February, wrote 'We've fixed up the Concerto now. It only remains for you to write it.' Finzi replaced one movement and altered much else for this second performance.

Just after this, the Vaughan Williamses moved to the country, first briefly to Holmbury St Mary, while they looked around for a permanent house. Finzi became a regular visitor: in August 1928 he received the following instructions how to reach them:

(1) 23rd will suit me very well.
(2) Come as early in the morning as you like.
(3) Take a bus at Dorking to Holmbury St Mary & enquire for the foot path up.
(4) But if you want a longer walk you can take a bus to Wotton Manor Farm or Crossways & walk here via Abinger Common.
(5) You have been here before.
(6) Certainly bring some stuff with you.

After the move to The White Gates in Dorking, Finzi became a regular 'house-sitter' when the Vaughan Williamses spent time in London. Though letters are still addressed to 'Mr Finzi', the development of their friendship is marked by the fact that Finzi was invited to the Vaughan Williams's box for the second performance by the Camargo Society of the ballet *Job* on 6 July 1931 at Sadlers Wells and, significantly, to the run-through of Vaughan Williams's Piano Concerto by Nora Day, Vally Lasker and Helen Bidder on two pianos at St Paul's Girls School later that month. The following January he was summoned to a further performance by Lasker and Bidder, the first outing of the Fourth Symphony:

> We are trying through the sketch of my new symph (2 pfts) at St Pauls G. S. next Wednesday (Jan 6th) at 2.0 p.m. Do come if you can—go to the side entrance (48 Rowan Road) & ask for Gustav or me—& be on time if possible as Gustav does not want to keep the headmistress's bell ringing all afternoon.

In 1933 there was great excitement over Finzi's engagement to Joyce Black. Adeline wrote: 'Ought we to know? Anyhow we do & the more I think of it the more glad I am for your sake & for hers & for ours.' The Vaughan Williamses were especially touched that Joy and Gerald determined that they would be married at Dorking Registry Office with them as sole witnesses (and it was from now that 'Dear Mr Finzi' becomes 'Dear Gerald'). On 7 July Vaughan Williams wrote a characteristic letter about the arrangements—Finzi was concerned that there might be steps at the door of the Registry Office which would be an obstacle to him, as he was lame at the time:

> Dear Gerald
> The following facts are true—
> (a) I fell into the brook.
> (b) I broke my ancle [sic]
> (c) I mayn't put my foot to the ground for a month.
> But—
> (a) I have no pain.
> (b) I am quite well.
> (c) I was not drunk at the time.
> Don't wait to examine those registry steps till my foot is well—but come over one day—both of you—and see us.
> [Later] I find that Ellen has reported about the steps as follows—there are none.
> Mayn't I play the harmonium?
> Yrs RVW

By the time of his marriage, therefore, Finzi had established a relationship with the Vaughan Williamses which must have done something to alleviate Ralph's loss of Gustav Holst in 1934. For from now on there is a steady stream of letters advising about Finzi's compositions and, eventually, asking for advice about his own work. In early 1934 Finzi sent Vaughan Williams 'Nightingales', one of the Seven Poems of Robert Bridges, to which Vaughan Williams replied:

> It's real you, I think, & v. good—the only place I am doubtful about is the tenor lead at b.7—which may sound a little dreary (you know what tenors can be when they try)—but we must hope for un-tenory tenors.

In April 1935, Vaughan Williams's Fourth Symphony received its first performance, and the first surviving letter from Finzi is dated four days later. (Vaughan Williams did not keep letters once they had been answered, so that inevitably—except where his correspondents kept copies of their own letters, which the Finzis did in a few cases—one side of the correspondence has for the most part to be reconstructed from what is said by the other.):

> Dear Uncle Ralph
> I was purposely not going to write to you about the sym. in spite of what I felt about it, because you always acknowledge letters & I can imagine how many you'll have to tackle. However, there's something else about which I have to write, but I must first say how tremendously I admired it. Even the slow mvt, which sounded like nothing on earth on two pianos, sounded wonderful on Wed: I expected the rest to sound something like it did, but didn't expect to be so completely bowled over. All congrats. Fergie [Howard Ferguson] wondered whether we shd have to wait for Jacques to retire from the Bach choir before a min. score comes out!
>
> About the other thing. I mentioned the possibility of doing an article on Gurney. Since then there seems to be a better scheme on foot . . . The idea is that at least 2 articles shd appear & Foxy [A. H. Fox-Strangways, editor of *Music & Letters*] likes this idea for his October issue. Walter de la Mare is going to be asked to do one on the verse: Wd you be willing to write something about his music? Please don't think that this is a case of shirking responsibility & shoving it on to your already rather laden shoulders! Honestly, its much more important for Gurney's reputation if the seal is set by you, rather than by an unknown person, or by the wrong person.
>
> Forgive me for troubling. Our love to all.
> Yrs Gerald Finzi

In his reply Vaughan Williams remarked that 'we must never again say that Adrian [Boult] is not a great conductor—it was he who found out how to do the slow movt.' He added that Finzi would be the person to write about Gurney. Thus started a crusade by both on behalf of Ivor Gurney—at this time in an asylum—and his music. In July 1937 Vaughan Williams was able to report that he was 'sending the Gurney songs to Foss [Hubert Foss at the OUP] tomorrow. I have been through them with Herbert [Howells] . . . You have done a great work in your copying & editing for which we are all very grateful.' In this letter he goes on to remark:

> Could you send me a complete list of all gramophone records, pfte duet or solo arrts of Sibelius symphonies.
> I want these
> (a) because, as you know, I can't read a full score
> (b) because, being no longer able to compose, and having by my mode of life unfitted myself for any useful occupation I think it is time I learnt something about music.

This is interesting, because Vaughan Williams started work on the Fifth Symphony about a year later, in mid-1938, and dedicated it to Sibelius 'without permission'.

At this time both Finzi and Vaughan Williams were each at work on what some have claimed to be their respective masterpieces—respectively *Dies natalis* and the Fifth Symphony. On 9 January 1939 Vaughan Williams wrote enthusiastically to Finzi:

> Dear Gerald
> We listened to your 2 songs yesterday. You have hit the nail on the head—it ought to be spread abroad that here is the exact equivalent of Hardy & to a certain extent of all English poetry of the post-classical period.
>
> When is 'Dies Natalis'—I am excited to know—especially as I have had a mysterious letter about it from Captain Gyde (Sophie Wyss' husband).
>
> I sent S. W. a sheaf of songs by various English composers which I thought she ought to know—especially as she only seemed to know the wrong-note variety. I included Y. M's [Young Man's] exhortation . . .
> Love to Joyce
> Yrs RVW

Later in September he advised Finzi about the size of the orchestra: 'Adrian Boult says he can get a better pp out of many strings than out of few—so, to my mind, when you get past the chamber orchestra stage the number of strings does not matter.' *Dies natalis* was clearly a work which Vaughan Williams regarded highly—in 1943 he heard a performance by Eric Greene and wrote:

> 'Dies' is lovely—we were all much moved last night—the nuisance was that it set me thinking of all my sins of omission. I still prefer the soprano—it gives a lightness of quality which the tenor cannot have.

In due course, Finzi was invited to hear Hubert Foss and Alan Richardson play through the sketch of the Fifth Symphony 'to see if I like it well enough to go on with it. Your criticism would be much valued, if you could come.' Gerald and Joy also attended the first orchestral play-through at the Maida Vale BBC studios in May 1943.

In 1942 Finzi dedicated *Let Us Garlands Bring* to Vaughan Williams to mark his seventieth birthday. Adeline took a protective interest in the wording of the dedication: 'I am not saying a word to Ralph. I know it will make him happy to have his name on a work of yours. But may I suggest that just this work should not remind him that he is 70. I know he can't escape being 70 but in print mayn't he? Could it not be "For"—or "On" his birthday October 12 1942? or would that seem wrong to you?' Gerald complied and tactfully inscribed the work 'For Ralph Vaughan Williams on his birthday Oct 12th 1942'.

Both composers took a strong line about each other's failures of confidence: When Finzi sent Vaughan Williams his *Farewell to Arms* apparently with some deprecating remark, Vaughan Williams sternly replied:

> Don't call it 'small beer' because it isn't & you know it isn't. If you did think so you ought not to have published it but I hope you take a proper pride in your own work—which is quite a different thing from the modesty which sees the vast difference between the final result & what we all feel of our work it might have been—so don't denigrate your own work.

Gerald's turn came later, when Vaughan Williams was having doubts about *Sons of Light*:

20 October [1952]

Dear Uncle Ralph,

There is no room in the world, as you say, for second rate work. But no work from a first rate mind is ever really second rate. Would you prune the Bach Gees: [the Bach-Gesellschaft complete edition] of all the inferior works written by J. S. B?

Surely it is the total projection of an individual creative mind that really counts. It's worth while knowing that Homer could nod. I don't think you ought to spend time on revising the work, and the idea that you are getting past writing first-rate music is not worth discussing. Strictly speaking you never wrote a bad work (once you got started) whilst you had to struggle to write, though wrote immature works. After 1920 or thereabouts, when your technique began to get working, you wrote quite a number of unmemorable works. *King Cole*, for instance, and *The Poisoned Kiss*, isn't really one of your best works; yet, these were works written amongst your major works.

Yet these are surrounded (in time) with your major works, and you would hardly have asked at the time 'shall I stop writing'.

Anyhow, it's a good job you didn't!

Although the core of the correspondence deals with the two men's compositions the subject matter ranged widely. After Gerald and Joy Finzi had founded Newbury String Players, Gerald often seeks Vaughan Williams's advice about programming, performers, obtaining music and the like. And in 1943 Vaughan Williams thanks Finzi for pointing out errors in the parts for the *Tallis Fantasia* and asks him to complain to Curwen as it would be more effective coming from the performer than from the composer. There was discussion of other composers—notably Robin Milford, Kenneth Leighton and Edmund Rubbra. On a more domestic front Adeline wrote to Joy throughout the whole period following the Finzis marriage about practical matters—arrangements for visits (*inter alia* for Joy to draw Vaughan Williams for his old college, Trinity, Cambridge), thanks for flowers (often cowslips) and honey—a special treat in wartime. Later on Ursula Wood enters the scene, asking Joy for advice about the cover of her new book of poetry.

The surviving correspondence between the Finzis and the Vaughan Williamses amounts to about 200 letters, and it is obviously impossible to give a full account of it in a short piece. However, perhaps the foregoing will give some idea of the nature of the friendship between the two composers. Ralph Vaughan Williams was a man for whom friendship was immensely important. His letters from his university days onwards demonstrate over and over again the loyalty that he felt for his friends—and they for him. As a composer, he continually sought the advice of musical and other friends without in any way depending upon it. While his closest confidant was undoubtedly Gustav Holst, whose death in 1934 was an irreplaceable loss for Vaughan Williams, it seems that his friendship with Gerald Finzi, as has been suggested, went some way to fill the gap. This is clear from the letters written by Ralph and Ursula when news of Gerald's death in September 1956 reached them on holiday in Majorca. These letters are transcribed in Joy's journal:

> Dearest Joyce
> You know how great a friend he was and what a staunch adviser—I always came to him for advice & help.
> I am thinking of those days which we have spent with you & him—they are bright spots in our memory framed in that lovely view of the downs.
> All love to you and the boys, from Ralph

> Dearest Joy
> . . . It seems to me that you have made something between you that has enriched many people. We were so happy with you, and so glad that we had those lovely few days, & that drive onto the downs—and that's only one, of many many times, for which we are glad. And Gerald—'all that I do is me, for this I came' could be most truly and wholly said of him . . .
> We were going out today—& we sat in a remote hermitage high on a mountain with the island & the sea below us in a pale blue haze, & Ralph dictated the letter he is sending to *The Times*. It all seems very fitting, & there were swallows—perhaps some of yours on their way south . . .
> Love to you all, Ursula

Hugh Cobbe is extremely grateful to both Christopher Finzi and Stephen Banfield for their ready co-operation in allowing him to make use of transcriptions of the correspondence between the Finzis and Vaughan Williamses prepared by Stephen Banfield in the course of his work for the Finzi Trust. He would also like to acknowledge much advice from Ursula Vaughan Williams, Howard Ferguson and Oliver Neighbour.

Thomas Hardy and music

Norman Page

From childhood onwards, music played a central role in Hardy's life. He grew up in an atmosphere of amateur music-making, and one of his most touching poems, 'The Self-unseeing' (set by Finzi), depicts him as a small boy dancing to a tune played on his father's fiddle. Early on he too learned to play the violin and soon joined his father in playing jigs, reels and other dance-tunes at country weddings and similar festivities. His novels, stories and poems are full of references to music and dancing, often in relation to love, romance and sexuality.

The other side of the coin is his deep attachment, also implanted in childhood, to church music, and one of his earliest novels, *Under the Greenwood Tree*, affectionately commemorates the church band to which his father belonged and wistfully records its demise as a victim of Victorian 'progress'. One of the paradoxes of Hardy is that, as one of the most celebrated non-believers of his day, he could also describe himself as 'churchy' and admit to a keen and abiding interest in the aesthetic appurtenances of Christian worship, including Anglican hymnody. One result of this is that when he writes a poem about his unbelief, like 'The Impercipient', it is liable to be somewhat ironically cast in a form familiar from *Hymns Ancient and Modern*.

Hence, although provincial life in the mid-nineteenth century provided few opportunities for hearing professional musicians—the visit of a touring company performing *Il Trovatore* was a rare exception to this rule—Hardy's early life was saturated with music. Making and listening to music, song and dance, were associated with the regular patterns of life such as Sunday church-going as well as with high days and holidays, and much of the power music retained for the rest of his life was owed to these early associations.

All of this makes it unsurprising that the kind of poetry he wrote should, in Walter Pater's phrase, aspire to the condition of music. Most of it is rhymed verse in a vast variety of stanza-forms, and much of it is strongly or subtly rhythmical. Small wonder, then, that in his own day and in ours his poems should have made a strong appeal to composers. Hardy once made the revealing comment that he sometimes began by conceiving a poem as a 'tune' before ever beginning to find words for it, and the inherent musicality of his verse must help to explain his appeal to those in search of words-for-music.

At the same time this predilection has surely been reinforced by the fact that the distinctive Englishness of his work, and its relationship to traditional and popular forms, have obvious affinities with the music of those consciously working within a native tradition. Of all English writers Hardy is one of those most closely associated with locality, landscape and the pre-industrial community, and this kind of representative, almost symbolic quality must have formed part of his attraction for a composer like Benjamin Britten, who was also drawn to another provincial poet, George Crabbe, for somewhat similar reasons.

It will not do to suggest, however, that what I have called the inherent musicality of Hardy's verse makes him an 'easy' poet to set, a soft option for composers. For there is often a subtlety, even an ambivalence of tone and feeling that constitute a problem and a challenge, and it is interesting when two composers set the same poem (Britten and Finzi, for example, setting 'Proud songsters') to find them responding to this challenge in different ways and producing two different interpretations of the same poem.

Later in his long life, Hardy numbered several composers among his acquaintance, and there were projects, not always realized, for collaboration. Gustav Holst, who early in his career had produced settings of three Hardy poems, visited Max Gate, the writer's Dorchester home, more than once and dedicated to him the tone-poem *Egdon Heath*, which was inspired partly by a walking tour in Dorset and partly by the opening chapter of *The Return of the Native*. (Hardy just missed hearing *Egdon Heath*, first performed a few weeks after his death in 1928.) Edward Elgar, whose career has some striking parallels with Hardy's, was at one stage interested in writing an opera based on one of his works; but although Hardy reciprocated his enthusiasm the idea came to nothing. There was a more successful outcome to another operatic project following a visit by Rutland Boughton to Max Gate. The two men of different generations got on well together (Hardy said later that he found Boughton's communist views interesting, though he could not share them), and Hardy attended a performance of *The Queen of Cornwall* at the Glastonbury Festival in 1924.

Hardy is on record as having told Boughton—perhaps not entirely tactfully—that he had not kept up with modern music. His musical tastes seem in fact to have been quite eclectic, though with a marked leaning towards the traditional and the middlebrow. *The Blue Danube* waltz and the *William Tell Overture* were, he confessed to Boughton, among his favourites, though he also wrote a poem about one of Mozart's symphonies.

Above all, however, he relished the folksongs, ballads, dance-tunes and hymns that were a link with his early years. It is the structures and rhythms of these that underlie so many of his poems—poems that, while making their own kind of music, also invite the composer to continue the work.

Edmund Blunden

Percy Young

Was there ever a more musical poet than Edmund Blunden? I think not. He was, perhaps, born to love the twinned arts in equal measure and to express his pleasure through words rather than notes. His early years gave him a knowledge of nature that came from the Kentish village where his father was schoolmaster, organist and choirmaster. He soon attuned his ear to the refinements of musical expression, as well as to the particular and peculiar musical virtues within the infinite patterning of words. Edmund was fortunate in one sense, for he lived in the last years of polite literacy, when letters (and musical scores) were written by hand in ink. We were then fortunate in the depth of information and the warmth of feeling that could be certified with a penny (or twopenny) stamp. As a correspondent Edmund had only one peer; the gentle Elia from whom we both learned.

The beginning of more than one friendship came from shared affection for a school. So it was that on 12 May 1943, in respect of his having read an essay of mine, he wrote to me. His letter ended:

> I missed you at C[hrist's] H[ospital] by ten years nearly but the smiling & harmonious presence of Robert Wilkinson joins our eras; I rose no higher musically than a place in the choir but rejoice that he sent forth some true musicians & wish you & the others all success and a restored Europe for its setting.

At the time my interest was centred in Handel, on whose biography I was working. The subject turned Edmund's musical enthusiasm towards Edmund Holmes, his *Ramble among the Musicians of Germany* and *Life of Mozart* (with a proposal that I should devote some time to an adequate appreciation of Holmes). To assist the Handel project he at once, characteristically, sent select items from Southey's *Commonplace Book* and Charles Dennis's *Select Fables*. Edmund knew where to find everything. On 4 August 1944, he ended another budget of information: 'This afternoon I hastily go over to Yalding, with its many memories for me of Handel's most popular music as I first heard it in our church or at home.' On 22 January 1947 he concluded a postcard with a sad remembrance:

> O what a loss you tell me of, dear R[obert] W[ilkinson] gone. I thought him immortal, and well understand your feelings, tho' I was only in the choir.

During that year Edmund was commissioned to write an Ode for St Cecilia's Day, for performance on 22 November, the music by Gerald Finzi. In verses worthy of a Cecilian Ode of an earlier age, Edmund called up the celestial imagery of the Platonists and lauded the noblest musicians of our land:

> Stand with us, Merbecke, and be Byrd close by;
> Dowland and Purcell, lift the theme on high;
> Handel is here, the friend and generous guest,
> With morning airs for her, and choral zest.[1]

Before the first performance of *For St Cecilia* took place Edmund—for the second time in his life—was on the way to Japan, where for his memorable teaching of English literature he was to become much honoured. A close association between Gerald and Edmund might have been preordained. The mute endorsement of their friendship lies in the sixty-three works of Edmund in the Finzi Book room in the University of Reading. After his return from Japan in 1950 Edmund was a frequent guest at Ashmansworth, content in books and garden, and subject for Joy's fine portraiture. In the summer of 1953 he wrote the text of the *Dede of Pittie*, a celebration of the Quartercentenary of Christ's Hospital (for which I was responsible for the music). Soon after this his poem 'White-flowering days' was set as a part song by Gerald for inclusion in *A Garland for the Queen*, a Coronation night offering. Later in the summer Edmund was put under friendly pressure at Ashmansworth to prepare an

[1] When first written, these lines read: 'Stand with us, Merbeck, and be Byrde close by, | And Arne, and Wesley, lift the theme on high, | Even let old Handel in the midst announce | Himself a Briton every inch and ounce!'. They appeared in this original form in Blunden: *A Hong Kong House: Poems 1951-1961* (Collins, London, 1962) p.88.

anthology of poems by Ivor Gurney, as yet virtually unknown whether as poet or musician.

From 1953 Edmund held a Chair of English Literature in the University of Hong Kong for ten years, with frequent intermittent periods of return to England. Throughout his time in Japan he was in various ways musically active. In 1949 he sent me *The Musical Miscellany: A Fragmentary Appreciation of some Selections*, a fascinating, deftly explored, appreciation of 'forgotten song collections of the eighteenth century'. In 1950 came the composition of the text of a College Song (carried by an eighteenth-century melody) for the Tokyo Women's Christian College. Six years later Edmund organised a performance of Milton's *Comus*, preceded by Dryden's *Secular Masque* of 1700.

In a letter dated 16 January 1955, Edmund wrote to me from Hong Kong, in respect of a subject then of particular interest:

> I should like to 'meditate' a little poetically on Elgar, especially as the Enigma Variations are for many years the music to my own boyish inward imaginings at Twyford on the Medway. The scene has been damnably degraded lately but even now the secret tune is with me.

Seven years later Edmund's *A Hong Kong House: Poems 1951–1961* was published. In 'A Variation'—emotion recollected in tranquillity—he continued the same theme:

When these sweet strains of Elgar die,
The sea shall overhang the sky;
When this enchantment powerless goes,
Brown nightingales shall sing like crows;
And when the music quits my mind,
My earthly life goes with the wind.

What is it in his tune we hear?
I speak; I loved a river clear,
I heard it summer day on day
Melodious at the tumbling-bay,
And yet this water-song was only
A murmur from something old and lonely.

The river-voice went still with me,
And I went far; and suddenly
The immense notes that it just began
Came in on me; nature taught by man;
Not tuneless sighed my evening weir
But Elgar made its music clear.

Thereafter when I hear the Past
And my poor river binds me fast,
This is our singing, scarce we know
It was not ever and always so;
Though he who gave this heavenly air
In our lost summertime had no share.

The following heart-felt elegy, in memory of Gerald Finzi, concludes with a complementary meditation.

For a Musician's Monument: G. F.

Twine buds and leaves with some full blooms, to dress
This marble copy of desire to bless,
This spirit ever confident of spring;
It may be thus to bring him happiness,
And let us while we give the garland sing
Some of that music which from him has been
Clear spirit to many in days that discord wound
With thorn and burr; well then his art unbound
Prometheus still, in town or village green.

And so, he rests; I knew him much unresting,
Never an omen of his resting now,
No fear to see so ended his bright questing
While every way he gained some golden bough.
And so—but shall we in our simplest thought
Open the deepest dream of life and find
This Gerald seeking all he lately sought
Where other buds and leaves and blooms are twined?

Nature herself delighted in him making
His harmony of garden and plantation,
For certain hours his music books forsaking,
And hastening here and there, the one salvation
Of kinds of tree and herb and flower and cane
Neglected: his small Kingdom so had grown
A little paradise; along his lane
He had but to walk, green life arose and shone.

Now these my verses close, and they shall wait
His judgement, when it happens as before;
For was he not of verse the delicate
But masterly good reader? from his score
And baton turning, with what love he met
The sister muse through all her mingled measure;
Each curious beauty choosing, may he yet
Show us, with his kind face of thankful pleasure.

In November 1966 I asked Edmund if he could write a new text for a beautiful song 'Life, be kind' by Daniel Purcell, which I thought merited fresh publication.[1] At the time he was not well, with his creative activity beginning to run down. Paraphrasing the original text of Henry Carey, he sent this departing reflection: '. . . here again I have been at least stirred by the old scene of the children coming out of school to the extent of writing some lines . . .'

Life, be kind to all these hastening
Homeward, swift and happy young;
Not that there will no chastening,
Loss or pain or deathbell rung.
But the mercy of content
Deep delight in love and truth
Go home with them as much unspent
In their bright age as in their youth.

[1] Song for solo or unison voices and piano: 1000 copies were printed by Chappell in June 1967.

X

The concentrated eye

A self-portrait

Joy Finzi

My first portrait was of Christopher asleep at the age of six. Gradually through the enthusiasm of Gerald, and drawing people in movement talking to him, I discovered the fascination of trying to catch a fleeting aspect and came to learn that everything is laid down in the face and often hidden in immobility.

Vaughan Williams had such a traumatic experience being drawn by William Rothenstein in middle age—having to keep absolutely still and silent for great lengths of time—that he had avoided any other attempt. But he felt that he could not refuse to be drawn for the Trinity College collection of Honorary Fellows by contemporary artists, and he asked me. Without Gerald's help I could not have achieved it. Vaughan Williams appeared with a tie on, and his hair brushed! We were both alarmed! But he was immensely relieved to be able to forget me in lively conversation with Gerald, and I tried to capture his outward public and often humorous aspect in a morning.

Later in the day when we sat around the fire after the evening meal—Aunt Adeline sitting opposite him—he slumped down in his armchair with broken springs and a naked electric light bulb overhead, dozing and waking as the evening talk went around, I drew a private aspect of him while he was completely unaware. This portrait I gave to Gerald, and afterwards to the National Portrait Gallery. After I had no longer the luxury of Gerald enlivening the sitters I had to develop my own way of keeping them alert and talking—a sort of split personality: the entertainer and the observer.

I never went to art school except for a term at the Central School of Art and Design when we married and lived in London. I studied under John Skeaping, the sculptor, who worked direct in his material, and I wanted to learn about tools and techniques that were necessary and preferred to make my own discoveries. Perhaps feeling shape beneath my hand had something to do with the way I draw portraits—they sort of emerge from a dappled paper into the light.

Tom Perkins—letter carver

Ann Warner-Casson

Ashmansworth: a sunny and warm day, June 1992. The Friends had gathered together for a music workshop and to listen to Ian Partridge sing. Close to the little church porch, Tom Perkins carved beautifully throughout the day. The elegant letters were formed carefully in the green slate of Gerald Finzi's headstone. He was adding the name Joy with the poignant inscription:

Joy
1907–1991
This root this stem
this flowering tree

Many of us stopped to watch and admire the work during the day, and I very much wanted to know more about the artist.

Tom Perkins, letter carver, was born in Plymouth in 1957. His birthplace has probably been an important influence in his artistic development, being historically significant as the last port of call of the Pilgrim Fathers before they set sail across the Atlantic and during Elizabethan times associated with such legendary figures as Drake and Raleigh. Contemporary Plymouth remains an important naval base and indeed the artist comes from a long line of shipwrights and skilled artisans, so craftsmanship is part of his heritage.

At primary school, Perkins showed an interest in letterforms from an early age, winning prizes for handwriting and later at secondary school, was fortunate in having an art teacher who was also interested in lettering. At thirteen he was introduced to Roman letters and his fascination with letter forms dates from that time. He learned letter carving in Richard Kindersley's workshop in London. Richard is the son of David Kindersley, who worked with Eric Gill in the 1930s. Gill's influence is very strong and is the inspiration for Tom Perkins' choice of stone as his material. He had done no letter carving before he joined the workshop, having just finished two years of calligraphy at Reigate School of Art and Design. He feels there was a great advantage in learning in a workshop environment, where there was the constant opportunity to watch a skilled practitioner at work. 'So much is learned in a way that would be difficult to verbalise.' There was also continuous discussion and demonstration of ways of carving letters.

There is a great variety of work. Tom Perkins has 'done everything' from large signs for buildings to small paperweights with carved initials. The main part of his commissioned work tends to be for headstones, as for Joy's, and wall mounted plaques to record an event or a person. When he has time, he enjoys doing pieces of a more personal nature for exhibition. He does not regard himself as a sculptor, although he is very interested in contemporary abstract work, such as that produced by Brancusi, Barbara Hepworth or Henry Moore.

Perkins works mainly in slate: blue/black from Wales and green from Cumbria, also Yorkstone, and Portland stone from Dorset. He has recently used granite for the first time and has also worked in marble. He finds slate a remarkably homogeneous, finely textured material that takes a precise and well-defined letter. The surface can be rubbed to a fine eggshell finish providing a marked contrast to the incision when a letter is cut into it. It has excellent weathering properties, retaining clear readable inscriptions for hundreds of years. Portland is a very pure limestone, a warm cream colour and of medium hardness (used in the construction of St Paul's Cathedral, London). Whilst not as finely textured as slate it will, with careful selection, take a good letter, provided it is not too small in scale.

Orthodox tools are used, tungsten carbide tipped chisels with a straight square edge for carving. These retain a good working edge for much longer than steel chisels. All parts of a letter are cut with the same square ended chisel, which is held in the left hand. A mallet, weighing some one and a half pounds is held in the right hand and this is used to drive the chisel into the stone. 'Working in stone, one gets a very real sense of fashioning an object and a direct interaction with the material.'

The feeling of much of his work tends to be one of visual simplicity. Perkins prefers a 'pared down quality, even austerity—things which are simple, direct and proportionate, rather like a Shaker chair.'

Tom Perkins is married to the calligrapher Gaynor Goffe, and they live near Ely where he has a workshop behind his house. They have two daughters, Laura and Ann, who spent that lovely summer's day at Ashmansworth, watching their father carve. His presence, and the privilege of watching the progress of that subtle, graceful work certainly enhanced in great measure the joy of the day for me.

Writing a book on Finzi

Stephen Banfield

There is nothing quite like the feeling of holding in one's hand, between two hard covers, the fruits of seven years' labour. I can only compare it with the pleasure of producing a child or seeing him or her graduate, which, for those who have done that, may help readers understand why every time I have produced a large book (this is now the fourth) I have vowed, 'Never again!' (I mean it this time.) For the pleasure is momentary, and the pain chronic, outlawing rest until the monstrous being has finally been brought to birth. Remission feels worst of all, merely a procrastination of the battle. There was a great deal of remission involved in this project: it lay completely fallow for three years, after a protracted start when it jostled for attention with the two previous books (itself an unsatisfactory situation) and prior to a dreadful race against time to get it finished within one calendar year, a period that was nevertheless as exciting for me, the author, as it was tense, because until the very last minute I really didn't know whether I could do it or not. I guess—though the comparison is immodest—that Finzi must have had something of the same feeling over *Intimations of Immortality*, and maybe over one or two of his smaller works too. I say somewhere in the book that Kiffer recalled his father writing the Amen to one of his choral pieces in the car on the way to the post or a rehearsal or something. Plus ça change: I seem to remember that my closing three or four paragraphs (Chapter 12) were frantically tapped into the computer on the kitchen table on a Monday lunchtime prior to taking the whole script for xeroxing and posting and subsequent to having spent the weekend desperately trying to cut the first four chapters, which were far too long (I got rid of 8,000 words—not bad going).

And then, as our Vice-Chancellor reminded the proud but long-suffering mums and dads at last summer's University of Birmingham graduation ceremonies, 'a graduate is for life, not just for Christmas'—never finally off their hands, it might appear. The feeling that immediately follows the euphoria is a sinking one, as all the mistakes that have somehow eluded five, six or seven pairs of eyes at first and second proof begin to show up. (So far I have found fifteen.)

It is often remarked, nowadays, that one can never really know another person. Possibly my author's misgivings about whether I have really learnt how to represent Gerald Finzi are familiar to the spouse of several decades who still wonders whether they have understood their partner aright; turns the evidence and the feelings this way and that; senses that all they can do is continue to trust their instincts whilst keeping a tight hold on their reason. I feel like that about Finzi, and just re-listening to a couple of pieces on the hi-fi, find myself reacting: 'Goodness! Does that work really sound like that? Have I actually conveyed anything at all about it in my pages of analysis, criticism, explanation of how it came into being and where it stands in his output?' Somehow its essence, grasped in a moment of listening, persists in evading capture in verbal argument, and you feel that everything is still to be said about it.

Yet the responsibility is there and can't be shirked, for music wouldn't exist if we didn't have a name for it, and we are stuck with verbal communication, even of art, whether we like it or not. All over the world music is not just performed or listened to but talked about. And I don't regret for a moment having talked about Gerald Finzi and his music at such length—about 200,000 words at the last count, twice the number I was commissioned to write—even if I do regret having had to draw a line under the research where I did. One could, of course, go on for ever, and in this case an unusual contract and financial arrangement, with the Finzi Trust rather than with the publisher, was probably a good thing all in all when it forced the line to be drawn sooner rather than later. Solicitors' letters concentrate the mind wonderfully, even if they don't actually help the agonising business of writing the next paragraph (which is why one of them remained unopened for two or three weeks, I can now confess). Nevertheless, there are always other questions to be asked, other stones to be turned.

Writing a biography, not just a critical study of an output, proved a more difficult and, especially, slow task than I had expected. For a start, I discovered that there is a maximum pace at which you can go to get the basic chronology right, not least when there are over 3,000 letters, some of them lengthy, to be typed onto the computer (for which I had a good deal of research assistance), read, assimilated and used to reconstruct dates, sequences of events, attitudes and reactions. Often the letters were undated, but in order to date them I needed to be able to tie them in with an event for which I was searching for a date anyway! Preventing such research from becoming circular is not always easy. (Incidentally, one of the biographer's most vital tools is a perpetual calendar, so that you can work out which day of the week a particular date was on in any year. There's a good one in *Whitaker's Almanack*.) All this can be painfully slow, and there is absolutely no short cut to developing gradual and overall familiarity with your material, however comprehensively you cross-reference it (and that's another story). It's like learning a score.

Be that as it may, I was acutely conscious that I had been trained to write about music, not about people. Checking and double-checking the 'facts' of a score against one's critical distillation or impression of it is a great deal easier than finding out, choosing, interpreting and checking the 'facts' (the inverted commas just as necessary) of a life. People are such messy creatures: they leave events and relationships and memories lying around all over the place, and you never know where to look for them next or when to stop looking. I keep thinking of the additional things I meant to ask Kiffer. Did GF lend his books to people? If so, to whom? Did he (Kiffer) by any chance have a little jingly roundabout-type toy as a small child? (Joy, in her 1939 journal, described the 'rapture' movement of *Dies natalis* as an 'angelic roundabout'. It would be wonderful to discover that the opening of that movement immortalised the domestic trivia of Beech Knoll. Small chance, but you have to ask. I didn't.) Whole areas of Gerald's life remain unilluminated. I didn't track down his medical records at the Radcliffe Infirmary, or indeed have time to pursue them beyond a first attempt. (One of the problems of research is knowing which leads to follow first or next or which to persevere with: there are always a dozen or so loose ends arising from the last letter you wrote or received back, from the last book you found, failed to find, or saw a reference to, from the last thought you had about influence and impulse. And all the while you have to be getting on with the narrative.) Do the Kingswood School pupil records survive? Probably not, but how can you be certain without pursuing your researches indefinitely? Where and what was Mount Arlington, Hindhead (another of Gerald's schools)? Is it still there? Could we discover why he was sent to those particular institutions? And then what about his wartime work? Who was the friend or relative who helped get him into the civil service or at least tipped him off about a job? Was it mere ironic coincidence that he worked, like his father, in shipping?

Often you are told two quite different things by different people. How do you decide which of them is right? Again, you use a combination of instinct and reason. Then again, you need above all critical distance, an expensive commodity, for it comes at the price of possible offence to those closest to the person you are writing about, whom you nonetheless must milk dry in order to get the facts and statements, even the prejudices, you need to make your point. These are not always, in fact almost never, taken simply at their own valuation, for that is only one of the bricks you are building with (which is why I have not been eager to show interviewees how I have incorporated their quotes: you need to see the entire context, perhaps even the whole book, to judge the tenor of representation).

For this reason, the book could not have been written, or at least could not have been published, while Joy Finzi was still alive. We saw Gerald so much through her eyes; wonderful eyes they were, but more than half his life was over before those eyes first saw him, and it is important to try to reclaim it, even where necessary from her possession. She would have rebutted so many of my conclusions, and all the while I would have had to stick to my guns.

Or would she? The biographer's task is like the portrait artist's; Joy was a supreme portrait artist. You can only show your subject in one light, which is your narrative or critical viewpoint; it must be consistent. Sometimes the sitter dislikes the portrait, or finds that it pinpoints weaknesses or underlying identities he or she was trying to hide. It may tell him something about himself he did not even know. Nor need it be a matter of metaphysical or psychological discovery. Quite practical matters, such as what a colleague said about someone in a letter that the person referred to naturally never read, can thicken the plot and tangle the biographer's web. It is not just Gerald who has had to be depicted warts and all (though I drew the line at his piles), but his friends and family. Clearly one tries to avoid gross offence, but what do you do when, say, a soloist or a conductor sang, played or directed a premiere indifferently and perhaps never knew, though it was the stuff of correspondence, reactions by all concerned, and even reviews? Their best friend may not have told them; the biographer must.

I've rather stressed the biographical side of the book here; but the music takes up as much space. I've tried to blend the two into one narrative, which proved more feasible than I had expected, even allowing for Finzi's infuriating habit of leaving works on one side for years on end and destroying the sketch evidence when he did finally complete them, so that you can never be quite sure which bit was written when (another problem that can lead to circularity of argument about his style).

There are, I think, some surprises in the book. I found myself elevating some works at the expense of others when I really began to think about them; facts emerged that had been forgotten, never noticed, or somewhat distorted in the frequent re-telling. Above all, a mythology of reception (the terms in which we view and hear Finzi) has gradually grown up over the years, which has needed unpicking in a great many places: look at any piece of writing on Finzi and you will see the same words, phrases, images being used again and again. I'm afraid we copy each other in our intercourse and pass these things on from one generation to the next. Think back to the very first time you heard Finzi's name mentioned: you will have heard or been told something, by a friend, a relative, a teacher, in a rehearsal, over the air, or in conversation when you tested your reaction to a piece against someone else's, that helped place him in your mind and fit him into your artistic theology. That process belongs to the history of reception, not necessarily to the music's genesis. And of course it can actually feed back to the composer himself, influencing him in his future labours. So I've tried to blow the dust off Finzi's musical and mental furniture as frequently as possible. I think you'll see this process at work where *Dies natalis* is concerned, for example. But I'm not going to say any more about particular instances here, for I want you to go out and buy the book. Do, and see what you think.

Richard Shirley Smith 'The Paintings and Collages'

Jeremy Dale Roberts

Richard Shirley Smith is one of that fair tribe of talented artists and musicians whom Gerald and Joy Finzi befriended and encouraged when young—one might even say fostered—several of whom went on to make successful careers for themselves from their respective vocations. 'Shush', as he came to be called, was taken under their wing when he was still a schoolboy: a refugee from London bombs, he was thrown together with Kiffer and Nigel, and thus had the good fortune to grow up in touch with a household in which 'making'—creative work—was taken for granted.

That, and the unusually liberal spirit which prevailed, and the cultivation of the most discriminating taste in all things, could only be propitious in the development of someone with his exceptional gifts. Another encouraging figure—a more avuncular presence, maybe—was Howard Ferguson, who lived just around the corner from his parents in Hampstead Garden Suburb.

And later there was David Jones; and of course his teachers at the Slade, people like Coldstream, John Aldridge; and no doubt others. What a lot we owe, and how comprehensively, to our guardians and mentors.

As would be clear from the most cursory glance at any one of the plates in the book under review,[1] Richard Shirley Smith is a 'virtuoso': not just in the modern sense of a consummate and versatile master of dazzling accomplishment; but also in the eighteenth-century meaning of the term. He is a collector of objects of virtu; or, rather, ideas, images, iconography, hoarded over years of travel—armchair travel as well as actual—the congruity and incongruity of which make up the texture of his sometimes bizarre imagination. Indeed, he might claim to have made a very fruitful 'Grand Tour' when he spent a couple of years shortly after his first marriage in a hillside village just outside Rome. Long shafts of memory still connect him with those days: that sunlight, those bits and pieces, shards. Later explorations in the Veneto and in the ruined cities of Asia Minor yielded even more; and like his forebears he is not above acquiring for himself, like some trophy or talisman, a lump of classical antiquity (actually a cast of the right foot taken from a Roman copy of the Greek statue of the Apollo Belvedere in the Vatican museum).

Much in Richard Shirley Smith's work is 'fantastic': for all the formality and pristine elegance in the technique and presentation, the archaisms, the subtle and muted range of the palette, there is a startling and highly idiosyncratic imagination at play here. His exuberance and sense of theatre, the slightly foxy air of mischief, sheer fun—all betray a perennially youthful spirit: you have only to mark that keen eye in the photographs. He keeps you on your toes. He is a master of the capriccio: those curious extravaganzas confected by Piranesi, Tiepolo and others in the eighteenth century: bouquets of sometimes weirdly disparate items tossed together with a flourish. A short step from there to the alarming confrontations of surrealism: and here he is happy to place himself in the

[1] *Richard Shirley Smith: the Paintings and Collages*, (Richard Shirley Smith/John Murray, Marlborough, 2002).

tradition of de Chirico and Max Ernst. Indeed the latter's attraction to dismemberment, and the use of montage/'cut and paste', connect him closely with Shirley Smith's employment of collage, which is vigorous and witty, but also searching and poignant. 'These fragments I have shored against my ruins'.

A Winter Night from *A Point of Departure*, wood engraving, 1961.

Nothing is ever simple. Some of the faces that stare out from the pictures impose a disquieting ambiguity upon the carnavalesque or monumental backdrop: portraits of women, quite still; at variance with the operatically gestural postures of the other figures or the grotesque attitudes of the Pulcinelli; looking askance, poker-faced; discountenancing the viewer.

He is an artist who has made a brilliantly successful career—on his own terms. Disinclined to immure himself in an ivory tower, his industry and technical facility, sureness of aim—quite apart from the individual character of the work—have brought immense distinction to the genres of book illustration and mural decoration. Here again he stands, quite contentedly, in a tradition. And if occasionally there may be just a trace of affectation or decorative whimsy, perhaps inherited from Rex Whistler, surely we can relish that as part of the enjoyment?

His place in the tradition of woodcut engraving is another matter: I know of no other British artist who has so consistently invested and contained his deepest insights in this most modest medium. The range of idea, the malleability of technique, the understanding of the material, the concentration of focus: I don't believe I am alone in considering that his finest work is found here. And there's a kind of truth as well: in his little pictures of cats, grasses, crockery, babies, he shows a candour akin to Watteau's drawings.

And what about the book, you might ask! Well, it more than illustrates everything I have found pleasurable in Richard Shirley Smith's work, although its reference to the woodcuts is inevitably minimal. Beautifully produced, and lavish in the number and quality of the plates, it includes a number of penetrating essays, reviews and biographical material which place him convincingly in a context. Roy Strong's Preface is especially useful: it doesn't surprise me that he is a champion.

A personal note: almost half a century ago, when we were both students—he at the Slade, I at the Royal Academy of Music—we shared a tiny flat in the basement of Catherine Powell's house in Holland Park. (I had inherited my share from Nigel Finzi, who'd gone off to study with Rostal in Bern.) It has been extraordinary for me, appraising this life's work, this catalogue raisonné, to recall those beginnings: the day Shush brought in the huge press for printing lithographs—I can't think where he got it: intractable, cumbersome beast like a dolmen; the endless fiddling and re-assembling of scraps for the collages; the infernal treachery of ink; and the gentle way he tested woodblocks for their suitability, weighing them in his hands, scrutinizing the grain: almost as though it were a live thing. It makes a marvellous sound, boxwood. What an education for a composer!

Inspired by English Song

Exhibitions of work by highly acclaimed artists Graham and Ann Arnold have been held at the Silk Top Hat Gallery in Ludlow to coincide with each English Song Weekend to date. In 2001 they answered questions posed by Ann Warner-Casson.

AWC: What are you most moved by, what is the inspiration behind your work?

GA: My paintings are motivated by particular feelings that I have for certain landscapes, or people I know well, or certain poets, writers and composers. This sounds like a wide spectrum, but in reality is not so as I return frequently to the same inspiration. I love things which contain the past in ghost form, and many paintings use this as a starting point. At a simpler level I paint objects which as a small boy of eight or so my father would arrange for me to study. He did this in order to instruct me in drawing, perspective and the use of oil paint. I still have these objects and they frequently appear in my painting. Almost all my interests can be traced back to those early years, except for my love of music. My father introduced me to a love for painting, for poetry and a love of nature and natural history.

Until the age of eight I lived in Sydenham near London, then in 1940 I was evacuated to Hay-on-Wye; this sudden change from the built-up world of London to the wildness of Wales and the mountains was perhaps the greatest visual shock I have ever experienced. In 1942 when we returned to London, Wales became a land of dreams, of lost content, always lingering at the back of my mind. It was not until 1986 when we moved to the Borders that I felt I had returned home.

I would say that my two great passions in life are painting and music. Much of my painting is inspired by music. The mind does have the ability to translate one sense into another; think only of the music of Debussy or Vaughan Williams and Elgar. Are not the paintings of Giorgione or Gainsborough musical? So in my case Subject is all-important, I can only paint a person or a landscape when I feel strongly about them. The painting is an attempt to clarify these feelings. Why we paint the way we do is so complex that we hardly ever try to analyse the process.

AA: I am most moved by sudden glimpses of 'Paradise' or when for longer periods my vision of the world, and by that I mean those things that I actually apprehend with my senses, deepen and intensify, producing a feeling of intense joy. Thomas Traherne expresses this feeling with immense clarity, and Finzi's music, of course, in *Dies natalis*, increases the emotion yet again, so that one is 'almost mad with ecstasy'.

AWC: You were both founder members of the Brotherhood of Ruralists. What philosophy do you share?

GA: Originally in 1975 there were seven of us that formed a group called the Brotherhood of Ruralists.[1] We shared some ideas but never had a Manifesto or a Philosophy. We all believed that painting should spring from feelings and emotions and that our aim was to communicate, as clearly as we could, these emotions to others (to express emotion and not betray emotion) in the form of a painting in a frame that could be hung on a wall. Seven of us could produce enough paintings to have our own exhibitions which we could arrange ourselves, free of the constrictions of the London Art World. For this reason it was important for us to move out of London and go and live in deep country. Two of us went to Cornwall, two to Somerset and three to Wiltshire and from 1975 until 1984 we were having four exhibitions a year jointly. Most of us had solo exhibitions as well. All of us were moved by landscape and it was important that we lived and painted within it. The landscape was English landscape, one of great trees, of bird-song, of wildflowers, of streams; an ever changing world of mist and rain; the humid heat of August afternoons, a landscape so rich and varied that one can never exhaust the limitless possibilities. It is a countryside of immense age, tended by countless generations all of whom have left a little of themselves within its soil. For us, living in Wiltshire, near Avebury, the rolling hills and ancient remains were a source of inspiration.

AA: It's hard to say that as Ruralists we actually share a philosophy. We perhaps share and delight in the natural world: an imaginative involvement rather than an analytical appraisal. This world includes Humanity as an integral part rather than nature's adversary: 'Man versus

[1] Ann and Graham Arnold, Peter Blake, Jann Haworth, David Inshaw, Annie and Graham Ovenden.

Nature' jars considerably. A figure in a landscape could have a symbolic or poetic connotation or be a beloved person. It is seldom merely a portrait.

AWC: Can you say what it is about Finzi's music and English song that you love?

GA: It is impossible to say when I first became aware of Finzi's music. It was probably in the 60s. We both knew Traherne and it is likely that we discovered Finzi, like so many, by his setting of Traherne in *Dies natalis*. His music to me is like the opening line of Wordsworth's autobiographical poem *The Prelude*: 'Oh there is blessing in this gentle breeze | That blows from the green fields and from the clouds | And from the sky . . .'

Just as gentle breathing sustains life, so the breeze 'the lovely lively air', as Traherne writes, pervades landscape. Finzi's music expresses this quality that no other composer quite does. Butterworth explores similar feelings but Finzi is natural, open and unaffectedly original. The essence of Finzi is for me his sixty or so songs; they contain music of such profound lyricism and many give form to the same feelings I have for the true countryside I wrote of earlier. I hear behind much of his music the lost echoes of far away folk song where the music inhabits the same world as the late etchings of Samuel Palmer. In these great songs, verse and music blend into a vision of 'radiance rare and fathomless', to quote a line from Hardy's poem 'When I set out for Lyonnesse'.

AA: I have always wanted to do a series of watercolours directly inspired by Finzi's and Traherne's *Dies natalis* and am so thrilled to be offered such an opportunity by this exhibition.

AWC: Has music directly inspired you to produce specific pieces of work?

GA: Yes, music has inspired many works. Mozart's Symphony No 40 became the inspiration for a memorial to my mother in 1969. The Ruralists exhibited over forty works inspired by the music of Elgar; the exhibition toured the country ending at the Piccadilly Gallery in London. My works included one expressing Elgar's time at Fittleworth in Sussex, where the late chamber works and the Cello Concerto were written. A period for Elgar of autumnal melancholy. Most of my work is inspired by music; in some paintings I have attempted to combine a number of sections, like the movement of a symphony or sonata, that are related to each other by various 'motto' themes. In other paintings it is rather the mood of a particular piece of music—one that comes to mind is *Ein Heldenleben* by Richard Strauss. Then there are paintings called 'Homages' which are made for certain composers.

AA: Usually I do not paint in response to a particular piece, although music is very important to me. I don't use it directly but it is part of one's diet and who knows what is being fed and nourished by it.

At this juncture it is important to say that imagery is the tool of our trade: colour, form, texture etc. Whatever the verbal intention, one has moved into another form of expression and these things dictate their own ends.

AWC: Hardy is particularly important to you as he was to Finzi. Can you elaborate on your love for Hardy?

GA: My love for Hardy began when as a sixteen-year-old I read his description of Egdon Heath 'untamed and untameable wild' at the beginning of *The Return of the Native*. Hardy was one of four writers introduced to me by my father; Richard Jefferies, Wordsworth and Gilbert White were the others. These four have remained central to my imagination ever since, they are also a constant inspiration to my painting. I should make it clear that these four are never subjected to any form of criticism or analysis. I have always loved them as old friends and I return constantly to their work as if it were for the first time. All four lived in a particular stretch of country and their creative life was, to a large extent formed by its uniqueness. Hardy in 'Wessex', Jefferies in Wiltshire, Wordsworth in the Lakes and Gilbert White in Selbourne. Perhaps it is the intensity of their looking and noticing the world around them that makes them so special. Hardy and Wordsworth were also supreme story-tellers in the sense of taking one on an emotional journey. The sonatas of Schubert engender the same feeling of a journey. Holst's *Egdon Heath* is the heath seen through the lens of Hardy. His description touches on so many layers of feelings from the living 'now' to geological time and even beyond to a cosmic eternity. So Holst's *Egdon Heath* is altogether different from an impressionistic sound painting of the Heath.

AA: I was introduced to Hardy by a dear friend and teacher at Art School at seventeen years of age. It was the novels at this time that engaged me. The idea was revealed of a narrative unfolding against and in, a particular countryside, so that the landscape interwove and subliminally emphasised the story. It was later that I read the poems of Hardy. Graham and I spent our honeymoon in Cornwall and he shared the poems with me. Being there, I was very aware of the links with Hardy and his remembered early love for his wife. We even lost a cup in a small stream's waterfall like the incident related in the poem 'The waterfall'. Hardy evokes the feeling that 'now' is merely the latest manifestation, the tip of the branch, other twigs will grow to replace them. So one's awareness of time and place and eternity; of now and here, are caught and held. All these things I would like in my paintings. There is little topographical reference to Hardy's places because their particularity is replaced by my own.

AWC: How do you intend to approach the Ludlow exhibition as part of the 'Weekend of English Song'?

GA: I will be celebrating Finzi in a large painting, and possibly Hardy. The writing of Hardy and in particular the poems used by Finzi in his song cycle *Earth and Air and Rain* will also be the starting points for several works. Traherne lived near Hereford during the middle years of the seventeenth century and the landscape is little changed to this day. This stretch of the valley of the Wye is renowned for its glorious light and subtle colour and more than any other quality I would like my work to express the intensity I feel for this landscape.

XI

Making music

Newbury Junior Orchestra

Michael Shiner

As I write this short article, I have in front of me a picture of the Newbury Junior Orchestra, given to me upon my handing over the conductorship to Miss Gillian Lovett towards the end of 1951; and also a letter, from Gerald Finzi, thanking me for singing with the Newbury String Players, and for my help in founding the NJO. Without both these lovely reminders one might find one's memory fading, but that is not so—it seems only yesterday! Gerald Finzi was, as usual, the inspiration behind the NJO, and in a characteristic way: 'Look', he said to me one afternoon as I sat in with the NSP, 'at all the dear greying heads in this room; what's to become of the String Players when they are too old to play any more?'

I have no idea what he expected me to say, but mercifully he forestalled any reply by going on to add, 'You must start a junior orchestra, so as to have a resource to replace those who feel that the time has come to give up playing; we'll discuss this together, but get on with it straight away and contact all the school and local teachers and ask them which of their pupils they would like to see in an orchestra.'

I went home totally bemused, because I had so little idea of how to play any instrument other than a piano; I was not then any sort of conductor, and I was a very junior schoolmaster in Newbury, singing as a hobby with the Newbury Choral Society under John Russell.

Then followed what one could only call the experience of a lifetime.

Gerald arranged for me to have a 'crash course' with one of the teachers for each instrument that would be played in the proposed orchestra, so that I might have some basic idea as to how it was played—and what were its difficulties and capabilities. I also sent myself to Downe House Summer School, and did the conductor's course under Sir Adrian Boult. John Russell capitalised on that by having me take his choral society rehearsals for *The Dream of Gerontius* whilst he had flu.

Gerald, meanwhile, asked me to sing *Let Us Garlands Bring* with the String Players in preparation for their forthcoming performance in a concert; then, allowing me to conduct them once or twice, I was 'loaned' the NSP for an afternoon to give a concert in the school where I was teaching. Meanwhile, I went off at every spare moment to learn how to play the various instruments. There was also the leader of the orchestra to be chosen: Gwynneth Reed was an inspiration to us all, and a true friend to a young conductor doing what seems commonplace now that we have, in nearly every county, a county youth orchestra—but all this was long before that day.

Gradually there came into being a string section of the orchestra; then the wind and finally the brass. Various wonderfully devoted teachers also gave their services for a while, to act as leaders of each section so that bowing and breathing mysteries were in the hands of experts. On looking back, I wonder that I had the nerve to start such a venture, but behind it all and at every step, there was Gerald's inspiration, and as I encountered various problems, he would quietly mutter '. . . of course you can!'

How much else he did, neither I nor anyone else will ever know, but it was natural that he became our President and never will I forget his enthusiasm after our first, very immature, concert. His encouragement of young people to enjoy and make music was very contagious and we went from strength to strength.

There came inevitably the time when I had to hand over the reins to another, because I moved house, and so Gillian Lovett became the conductor. She is now a professional musician, and remembering that, one wonders how many another member of the NJO eventually found happiness in music as a profession or as an absorbing hobby? Gerald's influence, as so many of us know, does not grow less with the passing years; it is lovely to hear, again and again, people saying that they were moved and inspired as they listened to such-and-such a piece by Gerald Finzi, of whom they had never heard before. To go beyond that inspiration, and to be allowed to work with him and for him musically was a privilege of pure joy.

To end this reminiscence it would seem only right that one should quote from the letter to which I referred in the opening paragraph, for it says all in one brief sentence:

> I can't help feeling that you'll look back to your work with the Newbury Junior Orchestra as one of the best things you have ever done . . .
> Yours ever, Gerald Finzi.

Recording 'Earth and Air and Rain'

Stephen Varcoe

I was first introduced to the music of Gerald Finzi through the singing of Wilfred Brown, on his famous recording of *Dies natalis*. Here seemed to be the most perfect marriage of words and music that I had ever heard, interpreted by a man who understood and felt it all so deeply. Ever since then, I cherished the ambition of one day recording some of his songs, and even went so far as to suggest as much to two record companies, but without success. The very day after the second of these negative replies, Joy Finzi's letter arrived saying that the Finzi Trust intended recording the Thomas Hardy settings; did I know them? And would I be interested in taking part? My reply was in the post before the ink was dry! After the initial disbelief and euphoria (which never entirely disappeared), came the work involved in preparation for the event. Between us, Martyn Hill and I had forty-three songs, and of course Clifford Benson was involved in every one. That meant a good deal of concentration when spread over only three and a half days' recording. For those of you not familiar with the making of records, a song must be performed twice at least, in order that the producer may have a choice and/or a back-up for any unnoticed defect or mechanical problem. Then the performers are bound to be dissatisfied with certain aspects of what they have done, and so may want to re-take all or part of a song several times. Soon, therefore, that number forty-three has increased to 100 or even 200. Think of the difficult task facing the producer, the long-suffering Mark Brown, making the final decisions about what goes on to the record and what should be discarded.

There are many things which stand out in the memory about those days of recording. First of all, the great pleasure of meeting Joy Finzi for the first time. She was present at all the sessions, and though she made few comments about the work as it went along, I know that her prescence was a help to us all. Then there was meeting Clifford Benson and working with him—a marvellous experience for which I'm very grateful to the Trust. Another bonus for me was hearing Martyn Hill sing the tenor songs, very few of which I was familiar with. How lovely it would be to sing some of them transposed down a little, though perhaps Finzi's wishes were that the original keys should remain unaltered. Anyway, what a wonderful opportunity we had to be involved in such exquisite works of art, and to share them all with a wider public.

Recording the Finzi Cello Concerto

Raphael Wallfisch

When I first discovered Finzi's Cello Concerto, I was absolutely bowled over by its strength and majesty, and completely captivated by its sheer melodic beauty. Here, I felt, was a work absolutely on a par with the Elgar and Dvorak concerti—but why do we seldom hear it?

I was also intrigued that the first performances were given by the cellist Christopher Bunting, an artist I greatly admire, and whom I have known since I was a small child, since he used to have a duo with my father. He told me of the frequent visits he made to Gerald Finzi's house to discuss the composition, and I feel that at least some of the exhilarating virtuosity of the solo part reflects Christopher Bunting's supreme mastery. My first opportunity to play the concerto was also an unusual coincidence. On a visit to Liverpool, Andrew Burn asked if I happened to know the Finzi concerto—we also discussed another of my favourite composers, Kenneth Leighton. Several months later, Andrew invited me to participate in the Oxford English Music Weekend to play both the Finzi concerto and Leighton's *Veris gratia*. From that occurrence grew the project to record both works, and what a fantastic musical experience that was for me! Between the Oxford performances and the recording came two performances with the BBC Philharmonic, which gave me a chance to grow even more into the piece. I was deeply grateful for Joy Finzi's constructive comments on those performances; and then another year's work prepared me for the Liverpool performances. At this point I must say that Vernon Handley's incredibly deep perception of the score, and truly sympathetic and encouraging support was a deep inspiration, and I felt that every moment of the recording sessions was charged with re-creation and very much alive music-making. How lucky I felt to have been given the chance to experience this great work surrounded by people who feel as passionately as I do about the music. Now, I look forward to any chance to play it again, and only hope that on hearing the strength and beauty of this great English concerto, concert promoters will be encouraged to programme it as frequently as the more familiar works.

Recording 'Seven Poems of Robert Bridges'

Paul Spicer

The Finzi Singers' first recording for Chandos came out at the beginning of June [1991] consisting of the complete shorter choral works by Gerald Finzi. At seventy-nine minutes and fifteen seconds, it was a close shave, since the maximum amount of music that it is currently possible to fit onto a CD is eighty minutes. I wanted to take the opportunity to write a short appreciation of the Bridges Part Songs which form the central part of the recording. I have to say that I went into preparing these pieces with a gloomy heart. I thought I knew them (or at least some of them) and that they were rather typical of their period, being somewhat indulgent Edwardian settings in a slightly superficial, madrigalian style. How wrong I was!

The beauty of these touching settings is the variety which Finzi achieves by careful choice of contrasting poems. Herein also lies the secret of a successful approach to their interpretation in performance. Additionally, it is crucially important to think oneself into the world of the touchingly naïve words. The simple text, if taken seriously, can regain its almost childlike innocence which can sound so old fashioned—even silly—in this sophisticated, street-wise age. This is certainly the secret of success in the first song, 'I praise the tender flower'. On the surface, this is a sentimental little poem about maidens and flowers. However, it carries within it a feeling which many have experienced, but few have actually expressed so eloquently. Finzi seizes on the mood with characteristic insight to produce a wonderfully tender and lyrical piece which goes right to the heart of Bridges' poem.

'I have loved flowers that fade' is set for soprano, alto and tenor only. The poem was tailor-made for Finzi, for whom the transitory nature of human life was a recurring theme. This is what the poem is all about and

Finzi's music reflects the pathos and the beautiful poetic imagery.

'My spirit sang all day' is pure exuberance and a celebration of Joy, his beloved wife. The first line continues 'O my joy!', and the word comes back again and again. How wonderful to have a wife with such a name who could be celebrated in such high spirits. This part song is by far the best-known of the set, and it is easy to see why. Quick to make its point, yet subtle and effective in its means, it is a tour-de-force of choral writing which leaves the singers, and the audience, buzzing with excitement.

'Clear and gentle stream', by contrast, is one of the longest of the set, and also the most lyrically memorable. Finzi's music raises the slightly sentimental poem to something of real beauty. There is a sense of time standing still which makes you stop to think that there really was a time before our hectic age when people might sit by a stream and reflect as the poet does here. Perhaps having a stream in my own garden in Herefordshire (where I lived at the time of writing) makes me sensitive to this point, as I know how powerful flowing water can be to the imagination!

'Nightingales', the fifth song, is a five-part piece with double sopranos. It is different from anything that has gone before partly because of the much more complex poem which is mirrored brilliantly by Finzi's setting. It is the most difficult of the set to sing, and has some awkward, but highly effective harmonic shifts, which need perfect tuning to be effective. 'Nightingales' is a piece full of opportunities for vocal colour. There are a number of wonderful images in the poem: 'barren are those mountains and spent the streams', and 'Alone, aloud, in the raptured ear of men we pour our dark nocturnal secret' and so on, are gifts for the choral conductor. The final section which finishes: 'As night is withdrawn from these sweet-springing meads and bursting boughs of May, dream, while the innumerable choir of day welcome the dawn' makes a wonderfully dramatic ending.

'Haste on my joys' is another Joy poem. The breathless nature of the setting once again mirrors Finzi's 'panting heart'. It begins with a vigorous allegro vivace, which later on settles down without losing any of its urgency. Much of the poem is, once again, about the transitory nature of youth, and the impossibility of a return to that halcyon state. It has a magical last page.

The final song 'Wherefore tonight so full of care' is a moving piece of choral writing where Finzi is in his element describing all the pitfalls of life, whilst ending on a note of great optimism, praising his days for all the wonderful things they bring.

Finzi's choral music is consistently effective and of considerable quality. 'Lo, the full, final sacrifice', now such an iconic piece of twentieth-century religious music, the Magnificat, the Drummond Elegies, and 'Welcome sweet and sacred feast' together with these Bridges Part Songs are amongst the best of the period. Finzi has left us with a rich legacy which is all the greater for the intensity of feeling and insight into the poetry, for which he was almost unrivalled in his generation. The music is also beautifully written for voices. It is music which, whether sad or joyful in mood, lifts the spirits to perform, and that is rare.

Thoughts on 'Intimations of Immortality'

Philip Langridge

I first came across *Intimations of Immortality* many years ago in Kidderminster. The Choral Society there mounted a performance of it, with one rehearsal for me, with the conductor and a pianist, during the afternoon of the performance day itself. You can imagine my surprise when I heard the glorious orchestral textures that evening! From then on I was 'hooked' on the piece. Later there was a BBC recording of the work, which fell a few days after a tragic air disaster in Paris, and which of course again made a big impression on us all.

When I was approached by the Royal Liverpool Philharmonic Orchestra to perform the work in their concert hall—followed by a recording—I jumped at the chance. Richard Hickox was the conductor, and the performance was again an unforgettable experience. The words alone, of course, are very compelling, but coupled with Gerald Finzi's marvellous setting, I find this work has the power to inspire.

I very much hope the recording is able to bring out that special quality, and that this great work may be brought to an even wider audience.

Gerald Finzi at the Three Choirs Festival

Anthony Boden

Talk given in Worcester, Three Choirs Festival, 8 August 2005.

A glance at the Annals of Three Choirs will show that the music of Gerald Finzi has been included regularly in Festival programmes since a performance of *Dies natalis* was given at Hereford in 1946. But for over a quarter of a century before that, before ever a note of his music was heard at the Festival, Finzi had been familiar with Three Choirs country. In fact, he had been visiting this part of England since 1920, the year in which, at age nineteen, he had come with his mother from their home in Yorkshire for a three-week summer holiday to Churchdown in Gloucestershire. Effectively, this was an excursion from one health-giving spa town—Harrogate—to a village close to another spa—Cheltenham. In Churchdown, Mrs Finzi and her son stayed in the lee of Chosen Hill, a delightful outlier of the Cotswolds, and perhaps their choice of destination was no coincidence.

From Christmas 1917, Finzi had been a pupil in Yorkshire of that great teacher, organist, composer and conductor Edward Bairstow, the organist of York Minster; a man whose considerable abilities were widely admired but whose reputation as a teacher was that of a severe and inflexible pedagogue. Another of his pupils, the soprano Elsie Suddaby, had experienced something of the fearsome side of Bairstow's nature, recalling vividly what happened when she arrived for her first lesson with him. She was a few minutes early, and had to wait, overhearing another young soprano in mid-lesson in Bairstow's teaching room. Suddenly, the door flew open, out dashed the young pupil in tears, with Dr Bairstow behind her uttering uncomplimentary comments about the poor girl's musical talents. Then, a few seconds later, thrown at high velocity, out followed the pupil's music!

Suddaby herself had no such problems; possessed of a beautiful voice, good diction, an attractive appearance and the ability to communicate with an audience, she became one of this country's leading singers. She appeared regularly at Three Choirs and other major festivals; her career flourished from the 1920s to the 1950s, paralleling that of Gerald Finzi, and she was to become an important interpreter of his music.

Serendipity is a marvellous and mysterious thing, and it certainly seems to have exerted its sometimes life-changing influence on Gerald Finzi. One day in York in 1920, that same year in which Finzi and his mother were to take that first holiday in Gloucestershire, Gerald had visited Bairstow just in time to hear him accompanying Elsie Suddaby in a voice lesson. She was singing Ivor Gurney's setting of John Fletcher's 'Sleep', and Finzi knew immediately that this was one of the great songs, written with such intensity of feeling that, as he put it, 'it was not being wise after the event to say that one can feel the incandescence in Gurney's songs that tells of something burning too brightly to last, such as you see in the filament of an electric light bulb before it burns out'. This was the epiphany that set Finzi on a quest to investigate Gurney's work and bring it to public attention.

Surely, though, it could not have been serendipity that brought Gerald and his mother to take a holiday in Three Choirs country in the summer of that very same year. Could it, by any possibility, have been a coincidence that Mrs Finzi settled on a spot within easy walking distance of Chosen Hill, a place of inspiration for Ivor Gurney, Herbert Howells and their poet friends Will Harvey, Jack Haines and Pat Kerr? Is it not more likely that Finzi had asked specifically to visit that very special place? If so, the little hill at Chosen worked its magic upon him, and he and Mrs Finzi returned in March 1921 to spend several months at Chosen Hill Farm on the slopes of the hill itself, before moving in 1922 to set up home at King's Mill House in the beautiful Gloucestershire village of Painswick. 1922 just happened to be a Three Choirs Festival year at nearby Gloucester—and what a year it was!

At Elgar's prompting, the Gloucester organist, Sir Herbert Brewer, had commissioned no less than three substantial new works, one each from Herbert Howells (*Sine Nomine*), Eugene Goossens (*Silence*) and Arthur Bliss (the *Colour Symphony*). Finzi attended the Festival, getting close enough to Elgar to notice that the great man was wearing stays. Eugene Goossens left a partial account of the Festival in his book *Overture and Beginners*. He describes how, whilst waiting his turn to conduct *Silence*, he sat by Elgar's side in the choir stalls, where, hidden from sight, they discussed the proceedings. The concert began with a performance of Scriabin's erotic *Poem of Ecstasy*. 'To think that Gloucester Cathedral should ever echo to such music,' sighed Elgar. 'It's a wonder the gargoyles don't fall off the tower. Heaven forgive Brewer!'

The *Poem of Ecstasy* drew to a noisy, disorderly close, and the groined vaultings of the cathedral turned the blare of trumpets into a shattering infamy. Goossens started to leave for the choir-loft. 'Write a festival Mass, Eugene, and atone for this outrage', said Elgar. 'All right, Sir Edward', Goossens replied, 'but Mother Church won't approve of my modernisms.' 'Never mind', said Elgar, 'I'll be in Heaven by then; I'll make it all right for you! Don't forget, plenty of percussion in the Sanctus!' But Elgar admired Bliss's *Colour Symphony* immensely. He was, wrote Goossens, an amazing, loveable man.

Finzi also admired Bliss's 'vivid symphony', and must have said so in a report on the Festival that he included in a letter to Bairstow, who seems not to have expected anything very interesting of Three Choirs. 'Many thanks for your account of the Festival', he replied, 'it was all pretty much what I imagined—except Bliss'. But in addition to the innovative music, that 1922 Festival was also remembered for the unveiling by Viscount Gladstone of a memorial tablet to Sir Hubert Parry, a composer whose influence on Finzi was immense.

Finzi's attachment to this region was affirmed in the composition of *A Severn Rhapsody* in 1923, the year in which he attended the Worcester Festival and Elsie Suddaby made her very successful Three Choirs debut. He missed Hereford in 1924, but was back at Gloucester in the following year. By this time, Finzi had befriended Herbert Howells and would move from Gloucestershire to London to study with R. O. Morris. Even so, his correspondence with Edward Bairstow continued, revealing an unexpected vein of warmth and wit in his former teacher. In August 1924, Bairstow, smarting from a refusal by Novello to publish his Morning Service in D, wrote to Finzi—opening his letter in Edward Lear-like verse:

> You talk about Publishers! What of Novello?
> They've treated me scurvily. I'm sure no fellow
> Could ever have got from a firm of such status,
> (and one which from profits of cheap things should fête us)
> A letter so cheeky as I got. (O hell O!)
> From stingy, material, un-seeing Novello.

At about this time, Finzi began working on *Intimations of Immortality*, a setting of Wordsworth's great Ode, one of the unquestionable glories of English literature—and an enormous challenge for any composer. 'Child of Joy', the phrase chosen by Ivor Gurney to best describe his innermost joy in nature and life. But, of course, the phrase is not of his invention; it was coined by Wordsworth in his Intimations Ode, where the poet writes:

> Land and sea
> Give themselves up to jollity,
> And with the heart of May
> Doth every beast keep holiday;—
> Thou Child of Joy,
> Shout round me, let me hear thy shouts, thou happy
> Shepherd-boy!

So once again we see the power of a creative cross-fertilisation in music and verse. Finzi was inspired by Gurney, and both Finzi and Gurney were moved profoundly by the genius of Wordsworth, whose theme in Intimations, a theme so very close to Finzi's heart, is the rapturous joy of childhood innocence, untainted by worldly care and human weakness. When childhood has passed, just as when the rainbow has passed, 'there hath past away a glory from the earth'.

Finzi embarked on his long struggle to be worthy of a text which he felt compelled to set. As he told Howard Ferguson many years later, 'I don't think everyone realises the difference between choosing a text and being chosen by one'.

In London, Finzi's circle of friends expanded to include Ralph Vaughan Williams, Robin Milford, Arthur Bliss, Edmund Rubbra, Herbert Sumsion (always known to his friends as John) and, of course, Howard Ferguson. But in September 1926, R. O. Morris sailed away to take up a teaching post at the Curtis Institute in Philadelphia, taking with him Sumsion as his assistant. When they returned in 1928, Sumsion had married his beautiful American wife, Alice, and was destined to succeed Herbert Brewer as organist and choirmaster of Gloucester Cathedral. Sumsion and Finzi became lifelong friends. And when Finzi married his beloved Joy in 1933, she and Alice Sumsion soon became the closest of friends too. Joy was a wonderful, talented woman; an artist, and a perfect partner and muse for Gerald. With happiness came creativity, and by 1937 he had embarked upon the composition of a masterpiece that would soon establish his reputation. *Dies natalis* is a perfect setting of texts by the then little-known seventeenth-century clergyman Thomas Traherne, and it also marked a return to the theme of transcendental innocence that Finzi had first discovered in Wordsworth's Ode.

The first performance of *Dies natalis* was planned for the 1939 Three Choirs Festival at Hereford, the year in which Gerald and Joy moved into their newly built home at Ashmansworth. Thanks to prodding by Robin Milford, Finzi had written to Percy Hull, the organist and chorus master at Hereford Cathedral, offering the piece for performance at the Festival, and to Finzi's surprise, had received an almost immediate acceptance. A premiere at Hereford would, of course, have been entirely appropriate: Traherne was the son of a Hereford shoemaker. However, Hitler put a stop to that; the Festival was suspended throughout the Second World War, and Finzi set to work at the Ministry of War Transport in London, feeling 'like an exile in the city', as Ursula Vaughan Williams puts it in her autobiography. The delayed first performance of *Dies natalis* was eventually given by Elsie Suddaby and the New London String Ensemble at a Wigmore Hall lunchtime concert in January 1940.

A return to peace ushered in both a revival of the Festival at Hereford in 1946 and a strong bond between Finzi and Three Choirs. It would be useless to pretend that the standards of music making in that first post-war Festival were uniformly excellent. In a letter sent to Robin Milford, Finzi wrote that 'some of the performances (Atkins's B minor for instance) were shatteringly bad, but John Sumsion did a very good *Gerontius* and oddly enough, Dyson's Vaughan Williams *Pastoral Symphony* was lovely'.

Dies natalis was at last given its first Three Choirs performance in 1946, conducted by Finzi and sung by Elsie Suddaby. It was at once clear that Three Choirs had returned with a work of lasting worth in its hand—'inexpressibly rare and delightful and beautiful'. But in his letter to Milford, Finzi reported modestly that '*Dies* went all right'. Perhaps he had been disappointed by Elsie Suddaby's interpretation; she had, after all, been before the public for over a quarter of a century by this time, and one can imagine that her voice no longer radiated the tonal purity so essential to a successful performance of *Dies natalis*.

Every year from 1946 until his death, Gerald, Joy and their two sons, Christopher and Nigel, came to the Festival and were frequently to be seen among the many familiar Festival faces, often in company with the magisterial figure of Vaughan Williams. Three Choirs gave the Finzis a rare and delightful opportunity to meet up with friends, to join with Alice Sumsion in organising entire house parties, and to enjoy themselves thoroughly. Typically, when *Dies natalis* was repeated at the Gloucester Festival in 1947, the soloist was their friend, the tenor Eric Greene. As a relaxing preparation for the performance, he joined the whole Finzi family in a game of rounders on the Gloucester King's School paddock—a typical example of Three Choirs off-stage informality and fun.

Also at the 1947 Festival, Finzi, uncomfortable in morning dress, conducted the first performance with orchestra of 'Lo, the full, final sacrifice'. I tend to agree with Stephen Banfield that it is a work that hardly seems to gain from orchestration. In his biography of Finzi, Banfield writes that, 'All in all, "Lo, the full, final sacrifice" is a magnificent incarnation of the metaphysical experience', and in his opinion, 'its opening page is the best thing that Finzi ever wrote'. It is difficult to disagree, but unfortunately, in 1947 Finzi had no experience of conducting a large choir in a professional setting; the Festival chorus failed to come up to scratch—and went flat. More successful was a performance of Finzi's orchestration of four of the *Five Elizabethan Songs* by Ivor Gurney: 'Under the Greenwood Tree', 'Sleep', 'Spring' and

'Orpheus with his Lute'—every one a perfect delight. In 1947 they were sung by Elsie Suddaby accompanied by the Jacques String Orchestra.

'Lo, the full, final sacrifice' was repeated in 1948 at Worcester, but this time the baton was in Sumsion's experienced hand. Again, Finzi wrote to Milford, telling him that 'Sumsion got a really good performance' of his piece. 'The choirs never sagged and it was lovely to be able to sit and listen (in plain clothes!) and at the end be able to feel that it couldn't have been better done'. He went on, 'I went for a few days' walk after the Festival. The Ridgeway, Wansdyke, Marlborough Downs, etc.'

The 1949 Hereford Festival saw the first performance of the magical Clarinet Concerto, with Frederick Thurston as the distinguished soloist. Again, Finzi was pleased, telling Milford that 'we had a pleasant time at Hereford (though too expensive!) and the Clarinet work went off well. Thurston took a lot of trouble and I was lucky enough to have been given an extra rehearsal, so I think we got a good performance'.

The Gloucester Festival of 1950 will be remembered for the first performances of both Gerald Finzi's *Intimations of Immortality*, which had been a quarter of a century in the making, and Herbert Howells's *Hymnus Paradisi*. It was also the year in which Herbert Sumsion was joined by two newly appointed young colleagues at Hereford and Worcester: Meredith Davies and David Willcocks. Sumsion conducted the first performance of *Intimations*, Finzi's most ambitious work, dedicated to Adeline Vaughan Williams who died in the following year. The excellent first tenor soloist was, inevitably, Eric Greene, and *The Times* reported that 'One could not help thinking in this cathedral how Parry would have been pleased at this choice and setting of noble words. Finzi's melodic idiom has been nourished on English madrigals, folk-song, Bach and Parry, but it is his own and his harmony has a modern richness not to be found in the tradition from which this noble cantata derives.'

Fittingly, Finzi's string arrangement of Parry's *Chorale Fantasia on an Old English Tune* for organ was also performed at Gloucester in 1950. *Intimations* was repeated in the cathedral at Worcester in 1951, the year of the Festival of Britain, and Finzi conducted *Farewell to Arms* in a Worcester cinema. Although no Finzi works were included in the Hereford Festival of 1952 or at Worcester in 1954, Gerald and the family still attended.

Intimations was heard for a third time at Gloucester in 1953, when it was conducted by David Willcocks, and Finzi conducted the second performance of his Clarinet Concerto with Gervase de Peyer as soloist. Sadly, Frederick Thurston died in 1953 at the early age of fifty-two.

As greatly as the Finzi family enjoyed their annual visits to the Three Choirs, Gerald often worried about the great expense of the Festival week. Robin Milford, responding to a letter from Finzi about the 1954 Festival, wrote: 'I'm sorry to hear of all your expense at Gloster, ours is a great and glorious but also an idiotic profession, isn't it? I mean to say, the ordinary businessman (not engaged upon producing an *Intimations*) gets first-class meals, any amount of drinks, car fares, telephones, hotel bills, etc, all gaily put into his "expenses" sheet. Why not you? As I say, it is absurd!'

Even so, the family was back at Hereford in 1955 for *Dies natalis*—which brings us to Gloucester 1956, the last Three Choirs that both Gerald Finzi and Ralph Vaughan Williams were to attend.

'It was', wrote Joy Finzi in her journal, 'one of the happiest . . . we have ever had'. Gerald conducted the first performance of the full orchestral version of *In terra pax*, conducted by Herbert Sumsion, with Elsie Morrison and Bruce Boyce as soloists. Eric Greene was the soloist in the first performance of Howard Ferguson's *Amore Langueo*, dedicated to Gerald and Joy. Frederick Grinke was the soloist in *The Lark Ascending*, and Vaughan Williams himself took up the baton to conduct; he was one month from his eighty-fourth birthday. As the great man took his place on the rostrum both audience and choir rose to their feet in tribute. They stood again at the end. Ursula Vaughan Williams has described that memorable Festival in her biography of RVW:

> The best week of all that summer was that of the Gloucester Festival. A large party stayed at the King's School House, just behind the cathedral; the whole Finzi family were there, the organist of Worcester, David Willcocks, and of Hereford, Meredith Davies. Howard Ferguson, and Harold Browne, the Treasurer of the South Western Arts Association. It was like an end of term week at a glorified educational school, Ralph said. We had a wonderful Sunday when the Finzis drove us out to Chosen Hill and Gerald described how he had been there as a young man on Christmas Eve at a party in the tiny house where the sexton lived and how they had all come out into the frosty midnight and heard bells ringing across Gloucestershire from beside the Severn to the hill villages of the Cotswolds. Gerald's Festival work, *In terra pax*, was a setting of a poem by Robert Bridges about such an experience. For us it was still summer, with roses in the tangled churchyard grass where the sexton's children were playing; blackberries in the hedges and the gold September light over the country we all knew and loved . . . One night we came out of the concert to find rainy clouds carrying shadows of the floodlit

cathedral, four towers standing mighty and mysterious in the sky above the real tower.

There is, of course, a sad postscript to attach to the account of that visit to Chosen Hill. One of the sexton's children was suffering from chickenpox, and Finzi, already weakened by Hodgkin's Disease, contracted the virus. On returning home to Ashmansworth after the Festival, he became ill and the doctor sent him to hospital in Reading. He took a number of manuscripts with him but was unable to work and quickly became unconscious.

Gerald Finzi died on 27 October 1956 at the age of fifty-five. Writing to Robin Milford in 1946, Finzi had commented on a fitting memorial for a creative artist. With typical modesty he wrote: 'I was always attracted to the Parry memorial in Gloucester, which says:

Hubert Parry
Musician

what more could one want?'

Wilfred Brown

Stephen Varcoe

In 1969 Wilfred Brown started coming to Cambridge each Monday of term time to teach singing to the choral scholars of King's College. That was how I met one of the most important influences of my life. He was not by any means a flamboyant or charismatic character like some of my subsequent teachers, but a quiet man, thoughtful and persuasive. He would suggest ways of thinking about a text or a phrase of music so that it might become one's own. His modern languages degree meant he was ideally suited to interpreting the German and French repertoire, and his feeling for poetry, whether in a foreign language or in English, coupled with his extraordinarily clear diction, enabled him to communicate his understanding to a remarkable extent. During this time that I knew him, Wilfred was suffering from the effects of a brain tumour that had resulted in a partial loss of movement down one side, and from the drastic medical treatment he had received. All this was borne with great dignity, and, for the time I studied with him, it never impaired the clarity of his mind. He died in March 1971 at the age of forty-nine.

I first heard the recording of Finzi's *Dies natalis* with Wilfred Brown singing and Christopher Finzi conducting as a student at Cambridge, and it was quite simply a revelation to me: a text of such sublime innocence and purity, music that touched something deep within, and a singer who radiated something I can best describe as spiritual health. Indeed, that quality in Wilfred's singing was an inherent part of the man himself and of his convictions as a Quaker. I do not mean to imply that only a Quaker can possess this kind of spiritual integrity, but that a musician who has certain qualities can create a healing aura in his or her performance. The burning question here is: what are these qualities? And if we as performers know what they are, can we learn to gain them ourselves and thereby become healers? I would answer by saying that I believe these qualities are reflections of the human spirit, and that they are latent in us all. Here's one of the stanzas from 'Wonder':

> A Native Health and Innocence
> Within my Bones did grow
> And while my God did all his glories show
> I felt a vigour in my Sense
> That was all SPIRIT: I within did flow
> With Seas of Life like Wine;
> I nothing in the World did know
> But 'twas Divine.

That's what we need to become healers, and Wilfred's work showed that it could be done. I'm not speaking here of Lourdes-like miracles with audience members leaping out of wheelchairs and the like, but of a less definable thing, a kind of healing of the soul. Whether Wilfred was conscious of his ability to reach out to people in this way, I cannot say: he would probably have been too modest to make any such claims. But even today through the medium of recordings he touches me, enriches my life, and I thank him for it.

Recording 'Dies natalis'

Christopher Finzi

So distant, and yet so vivid. My memory of the recording is patchy but so many things stand out clearly through the gap of over thirty years. The occasion was made easier for me because I knew almost the entire orchestra personally. I remember the immense certainty of Adrian Beers' bass playing and what strength it gave the whole orchestra. Manny Hurwitz, the leader, I knew well as a fine violinist, but was most impressed by how closely he had studied the score and words.

We had difficulty with the last movement ('The salutation'), and I struggled hard to get the opening viola melody to float without bulges. Cecil Aronowitz, the leader, was a wonderful player. After several tries that got us nowhere, I stopped and said that all that was missing was the innocence. This caused great mirth among the rest of the orchestra, but it did work.

Bill [Wilfred Brown] was a dream to work with, and again I knew him well, as he was my form master at Bedales. His authority was so great that he didn't really need to say much. He expressed so clearly through his singing exactly what he wanted and there was such an inevitability in his direction that it really wasn't a case of accompanying (one following the other) so much as taking what seemed to be an inevitable musical route.

We didn't do any small takes, but recorded each movement in its entirety, repeating them if we were not satisfied with the previous take. Bill's unassuming authority never interfered with the music, but let it speak through him without hindrance. Any success the resulting record has had is very largely due to his inspiring input.

Impressions of Wilfred Brown

John Carol Case

My impressions of 'Bill' Brown—we all called him Bill—are getting somewhat faint after all this time, but my lasting memory is of a truly good man: he was a practising Quaker, and this permeated all that he did.

He and Mollie adopted six children of different nationalities—I particularly remember an enchanting Japanese girl with the very English name: Emma. They all made a secure family unit.

He never spoke ill of anyone, nor would he be unkind in any criticism, although he would be honest in what he said. I have a delightful memory of us singing as soloists in a Bach B Minor Mass during the very early days of attempts at being 'authentic'. The orchestra was using modern instruments, but the conductor decided to have the same number of players as he had singers in the chorus: the singers were hopelessly overwhelmed and could hardly be heard. As we left the platform, Bill was obviously unhappy with the balance between singers and orchestra, but when the conductor asked him 'What did you think of my "authentic" performance?', with a charming smile Bill said 'Oh yes, it was different.' No-one was offended and Bill had replied in a way which would have done credit to the Delphic Oracle.

As he was a student of modern language, his singing in French and German was impeccable, and he was able to bring a truly meaningful understanding to the words, particularly in the *St Matthew* and *St John* evangelists, where, as Christus, I often had the pleasure of joining him. I remember the *Times* critic, William Somervell Mann, who had been with me at Cambridge, writing after a performance by Bill singing in German, that 'it was wonderful to hear Wilfred Brown savouring the words.' He had that understanding of the inner meaning of words, which makes his recording of *Dies natalis* so magical. Thank goodness this is still with us.

Two other memories: during rehearsals in order to keep his shoes in pristine condition he used to wear galoshes; once he forgot to take them off and went on the platform wearing them for the performance. Thereafter, he carried a large drawing of a pair of galoshes inside every copy of music, and those of us who knew him well would make sure he never again went on the platform wearing them; he had been so disturbed when this had happened earlier.

The other memory: we both made our Three Choirs Festival debut together during the 1954 Worcester Festival, singing the arias in the *St Matthew Passion*, and we often sang for the Festivals not only at Worcester, but also at Gloucester and Hereford. Bill became very popular, and had a retinue of female admirers. During one of the Three Choirs Festivals, as we came out of the Cathedral, he saw this lady approaching and whispered to me 'Don't leave me alone! Keep on talking to me—if you don't I'll never speak to you again. I'll do the same for you one day, if necessary!'—which it was, and he kept his word.

If I had to sum up my friendship with Bill, I would do so as I began: he was a truly good man.

'In Years Defaced'

Jeremy Dale Roberts

It all started at a Finzi Trust meeting. We were all 'brainstorming' madly—as one does—considering all sorts of notions of what we might try to put into the Finzi Centenary Year that would be a little out of the ordinary. Already, exciting projects were afoot, most notably the revival of Gerald's early Violin Concerto, in which publishers and recording companies were promptly showing an eager, not to say beady-eyed, interest. Naturally, we were looking to promote neglected work as well as old favourites. It was Robert Gower who mentioned Gerald's arrangement for small orchestra of 'When I set out for Lyonnesse'. This had originally been made at the behest of the tenor Steuart Wilson, who had sung it at a Lemare concert in 1936 (considerately transposed up to G minor). This was the programme that had launched the *Milton Sonnets* and *Farewell to Arms*, dark-hued and reflective respectively. It occurred to me that maybe the Hardy setting—quite bracing for Gerald—had been put in as an encore? Whatever the pretext, it was a one-off: easy to get overlooked.

Anyway, what to do with it now? If it were to be effectively revived, it would need companions; and so the idea of an orchestral set of Finzi songs came into being. As I recall, the concept was thrashed about—con brio—in the course of that one afternoon. We rejected quite brusquely the proposal of orchestrating *Earth and Air and Rain* in its entirety: too long, MUCH too long—we weren't in the business of rewriting *Das Lied van der Erde*! And the suggestion that one composer only should undertake the task was also quashed: too much responsibility. Much more interesting, surely, to invite a whole gang of composers to add their own individual mark to the music; and so we had a lot of fun considering whom we would want to join in.

Already two composers, Christian Alexander and myself, were 'on site' and available; we needed another three or four to make up a reasonable quorum. Michael Berkeley seemed an obvious choice: he was a Vice President of the Friends and obviously devoted to English music. Then there was Anthony Payne: anybody who could do such an inspired job on the Elgar Third Symphony was clearly worth pursuing. Judith Weir, out of the blue it appeared, had written an extraordinarily perceptive and enthusiastic review of Stephen Banfield's biography: I had never imagined that Finzi would be quite her bag. So in the light of that we approached her too (a bit gingerly). Finally, Colin Matthews—the spouse of Belinda, who had seen the Banfield book so smoothly through the corridors of Faber—seemed a biddable candidate: a remarkable composer with a proven mastery of the art of orchestration, as anybody who knows his work on Britten and Mahler Ten can testify.

We failed to entice Michael Berkeley—he was in the travails of another opera—but all the others responded with enthusiasm, especially when it appeared likely that the whole set might be recorded, as well as feature quite prominently in one of the centenary concerts! There still remained the problem of finding a suitable selection of songs from which to choose. Some songs of Gerald's cry out for orchestral treatment: when Howard Ferguson was sounded out about the project (yes, we'd thought of Howard, too), although he was curiously negative with regard to his own possible contribution, he was quick to single out 'Channel firing' as one that might be enhanced by the orchestra. But then that colossal Mussorgskian song would require a big orchestra and a baritone, and we were rather tied to a chamber orchestra (double wind, two horns, and strings) and a tenor. And the restriction to the tenor voice proved to be the most irksome, for most of Gerald's songs for voice and piano are for the lower voice. The early tenor cycle, *A Young Man's Exhortation*, yielded nothing: too pianistically contrapuntal to lend itself to orchestral expansion. We trawled backwards and forwards, not ruling out transposition, and in the end distributed around half a dozen songs which sort of held together, not only in mood but in tonality also.

I'd already put in a bid for the Flecker setting, 'To a poet', but I knew there were others that I could be quite comfortable with. Christian had brought off a scoop when he found a hitherto unpublished, and unique, setting of Edward Thomas's 'Tall nettles': an early fragment, written in open score, unmistakably suggesting orchestral colouring. Anthony Payne, who was already thoroughly familiar with the ground, blithely disdained the proffered list and volunteered 'Proud songsters' (transposed up a minor third), the concluding song of *Earth and Air and Rain*. This was obviously close to home for him: he is a confessed Hardy buff, and had himself made a setting of that poem. Judith and Colin were evidently less familiar and needed a bit of a nudge in the right direction: in Judith's case, the posthumously published 'At a lunar eclipse', and in Colin's, 'To a poet', which he quietly snatched from beneath my nose. That left me with 'In years defaced'—a gift!—which presented itself as an appropriate title for the set.

I'd decided to 'blow up' Gerald's original orchestra to allow for more weight as well as more variety of approach. A couple of trumpets were added as 'optional extras', together with timpani, percussion and harp. In the event, none of us was extravagant, preferring to fall in with the composer's own fastidiousness: the curious touches—Tony's use of the tambourine for the chattering finches, Christian's crotales glinting in the sunlight—all the more effective for their understatement.

The recording session could have been hairy: six items—none of them familiar to the City of London Sinfonia—had to be got into the can in six hours. But it could not have run more smoothly: Chandos's producer, Brian Couzens, presided, entirely benign; and Richard Hickox, committed, focussed, often ebullient, kept things on the boil, using every minute constructively. The singer, John Mark Ainsley, standing apart from the rest, seemed inexhaustible in stamina and good humour, constantly refreshing the inflexion of his interpretation. Everybody was in a good mood.

The music did the trick. It sounded so well: Gerald's voice unmistakable, of course, against a background which had been affirmed and elucidated and enriched with such remarkable insight and imagination by one and all. Judith brought an almost Holstian quality to the eclipse, with her luminous use of winds and harp and austere processional counterpoint. Then Colin's mastery of nuance, the subtle transmuting of instrumental colouring lends devastating poignancy to 'To a poet'. The shifting lights in the Edward Thomas setting, that owe so much to Vaughan Williams's *Pastoral Symphony*, are beautifully brought out in Christian's version. And Anthony Payne's 'Proud songsters', the inevitable envoi, rings with vitality, that tugging energy which is almost the most heartbreaking thing of all.

The whole occasion was oddly moving: Gerald was absent, but then, so were so many others. Of the little squad of living composers that had been assembled to 'shake him by the hand', only Tony, with his wife Jane Manning, and I were able to be present.

However there was a great sense of satisfaction at the end: these six orchestral songs make a rich bag. As Tony said, 'Why can't we do more?

XII

Composer's gallery

An appreciation of Howard Ferguson

Hugh Cobbe

'We generally met once a week at either his house or mine. We played through each other's compositions, discussed them, talked and made music endlessly.' So Howard described the early days of his friendship with Gerald Finzi. If, as I believe, Howard saw Harold Samuel as his musical father, Gerald was certainly his musical brother and, since Gerald's death, he has provided a living link with the musical world which they both inhabited and created. With Howard's death on 1 November [1999] that link was lost.

Howard was born in Belfast the youngest child of Frances and Stanley Ferguson, a banker. The story of how the pianist Harold Samuel spotted Howard's talent when adjudicating a piano competition in 1922, and thereupon urged his parents to send him to London to study with him, has often been told. Howard remained amazed to the end of his life that his parents had agreed so readily to the proposal and recorded his profound gratitude to them in his will: '. . . their help and sympathy enabled me to lead the life I wished to lead and to pursue the work that has meant so much to me.'

Howard's life thereafter fell into a series of phases, of which the first covering his student and early professional years culminated in the blow of Harold's early death in 1937. These years saw the completion of his studies under R. O. Morris and (briefly) Vaughan Williams at the RCM and privately at home with Harold (in whose house Howard and his adored nanny, May Cunningham, lived from 1925), the publication of his first Violin Sonata, the Octet and the Partita, and the establishment of the lifelong friendship with Gerald and Joy.

The next phase was one overshadowed by Harold's death and the war. In it Howard learnt to find his feet without Harold to guide him. His place was, in some ways, taken by his great friend Myra Hess, and after a spell spent, at Gerald and Joy's suggestion, in the gardener's cottage at Ashmansworth, Howard found a house near to hers in Hampstead Garden Suburb and he stayed there until 1973. He wrote only one major work at this period, the F minor Piano Sonata dedicated to Harold's memory, for his energies were diverted to what was perhaps his most notable public service: at the outbreak of war he had joined the RAF Central Band and at the same time he had agreed to help Myra with the concerts she was organising at the National Gallery. These were so successful and provided such a vital boost to public morale that he was soon released from the RAF to work with Myra full-time. It is felt that Howard's crucial role in the management and planning of these concerts has not been adequately recognised, although he himself, devoted to Myra, never sought such recognition.

The concerts, which ran without a break from 1939 to 1946, left Howard a legacy of close friends who influenced his working life after the war: Arnold van Wyck, the South African composer, inspired the Five Bagatelles, and Ursula Wood, later to marry Ralph Vaughan Williams, was close to them both. He formed duos with Yfrah Neaman, the violinist, for whom he wrote the second sonata, and Denis Matthews, the pianist, with whom he brought the piano duet repertoire to the concert audience; Kathleen Ferrier recorded the song cycle *Discovery*. Dorothy and Toty Navarro had encouraged an interest in medieval poetry which eventually led to his biggest pieces, the cantatas *Amore Langueo* and *The Dream of the Rood*, written for the Gloucester Three Choirs Festivals of 1956 and 1959. These two works brought Howard's composing career to an end for he found that he had said everything musically that he had to say. The decision was characteristic of his unflinching artistic integrity. One may also speculate (though there is no concrete evidence for it) that Gerald's death in 1956 may have contributed to Howard's decision to cease composition—Gerald was no longer there as a sounding board. Certainly Howard was profoundly conscious of the loss of his close friend.

Howard now found a different outlet for his need to produce music in the editing of keyboard music—this brought together in happy conjunction his instincts as a composer, his practical insights as a first class pianist and his aptitude for meticulous scholarship. The greatest achievement of this period was the complete edition of Schubert's piano sonatas published by the Associated Board; this has been praised as one of the most remarkable practical editions of classical keyboard music of recent times. With this corpus of pedagogical work Howard passed on to younger generations something of what he had himself learnt from Harold Samuel.

The last part of his life was spent quietly at Cambridge, where he moved in 1973. He continued to see his old friends and make new ones until the end of his life, for his genius for friendship never deserted him. New friendships never displaced longer standing ones: once offered and accepted, his friendship could only be shaken by an affront to his rock-like personal and artistic integrity.

Howard's friends will have vivid memories and a mental association with green ink to treasure. His more public monuments will be his music and his writings (musical, autobiographical and culinary), the last of which is an edition by him and Michael Hurd of his lifelong correspondence with Gerald, which was finally completed just days before his death. This conveys a more vivid picture of the two friends than anything written by others possibly could. With this final debt of friendship paid, the symphony that was Howard's life has come to a peaceful end.

Memories of Vaughan Williams and others

Joy Finzi

Several of the composers included in the Summer Weekend of English Music [Oxford 1984] crossed the paths of Gerald and I. We did not know either Elgar or Delius but Gerald was devoted to Holst whom he knew through RVW. Gerald took me to see him in a small nursing home in the west of London in the early 1930s. He was alone in an empty room in a hospital iron bedstead, I think recovering from a fall that he had in America. Malcolm Sargent was at the same time in a famous West End nursing home, his room filled with flowers. Holst asked me to sit on his bed and tell me what I was going to make Gerald do when I married him; I said that I thought it would be an advantage if he could be persuaded to sit down to eat his meals rather than walk around with a plate in his hand!

Vaughan Williams and Gerald enjoyed a long friendship, and 'Uncle Ralph' was a frequent visitor to our home at Ashmansworth. I drew him at his home in 1947 as we sat around the fire after supper.

Gerald met Rutland Boughton when he attended the Glastonbury Festival as a young man and helped where he could. In the 1950s I remember driving Vaughan Williams out to see Boughton in his home near Gloucester while we were at the Three Choirs Festival. He seemed serenely happy in the heart of his country, looked after by his wife and tending a smallholding.

When Gerald was studying with Bairstow he once heard a fellow student, Elsie Suddaby, singing Ivor Gurney's 'Sleep'. He felt it to be like an electric light bulb which burns to brightness before it explodes—the intensity of feeling was so great. This led him to discover more of Gurney's music, and after his death to order and publish his manuscripts. During the first years of our marriage, he and Howard Ferguson were both going through all the songs and marking them with * * *, * *, *, in order of their excellence. I started to type the lists of his songs and poems, and discovered over 100 poems in a little black notebook which Herbert Howells gave to me, which Gurney had carried round with him in the trenches. We both felt as if we knew Gurney although we never actually met him.

Gerald saw a good deal of Howells as a young man, when he and his mother came down from Harrogate to spend a while at Churchdown. He had an admiration for his early work and (after the death of his son), *Hymnus Paradisi*. We did not see much of him, except I remember visiting him in his London home when Micky was a young boy.

After Gerald left Painswick in the late 1920s he went to live in London. Among those he met there was Arthur Bliss, whose company and eager mind he enjoyed. Arthur and Trudy went down to visit him in the Midhurst Sanatorium where he was sent for a few months in 1928. Gerald took me to lunch with them in their high East Heath Road house when we were engaged, and our first home was just below them bordering the heath.

Gerald had very few composition pupils, although he encouraged many young talents. Among these were Anthony Scott and Kenneth Leighton. I remember going back home one evening in the 1930s, and telling Gerald that the only work of interest in a concert of contemporary local English music that the Newbury Amateur Orchestral Union were giving, was one by Anthony Scott. I was playing among the fiddles and met Anthony and asked him to come up and visit us in Aldbourne where we were then living. He came to have lessons with Gerald, which meant days talking and walking and he became a lifelong friend. When Kenneth Leighton was at Oxford, Bernard Rose asked Gerald if he would look at the manuscripts of Kenneth's work, for he felt unable to teach him anything; Gerald immediately responded by getting the String Symphony and *Veris gratia* copied and performed by Newbury String Players all over the place. Later Kenneth was illuminated by his period of study in Italy.

Gerald set Edmund Blunden's words in his *For St Cecilia* and in two songs in the collection *Oh Fair to See*. Blunden never wholly returned from wartime France. He was haunted all his remaining life with those years and the death of his comrades. In his last days he had terrible dreams. Something of this was revealed in my unfinished drawing of 1962.

Alan Ridout's portrait emerged during the long dark and grey winter months of 1983; he, close to the light from a little window absorbed in his composition at the piano and oblivious of me; I, in the gloom with board resting upon the end of the piano.

Recalling Howells

Paul Spicer

Since the age of eight as a chorister at New College, I have found something about the music of Herbert Howells to which I respond almost chemically. When I went to him as a composition student at the RCM years later, I wanted to find out why this was, and why there was an influence at work in this music, which was unlike any other in my experience.

The first thing I discovered was that Howells was a very short man. In fact he was really tiny, and like many small men, he made up for it by dressing well and keeping himself really trim. He was always regarded as being very good-looking, his well-styled and flowing grey hair helped this impression, and it obviously helped him in his persistent flirting with the pretty young female students!

When I first saw him, before I had met him, he was coming through one of the corridors at College walking with the aid of a stick. I discovered later that he had badly injured himself running to catch a bus, jumping to catch it and missing (this was in 1970 when he was seventy-eight years old!). He fell very heavily and broke his femur. The additionally awful thing about this was that he had been trying to catch the wrong bus. Incredibly, he got himself up and onto the correct bus which took him to the nearest hospital casualty ward. He recovered from this ordeal, but was never quite the same in his mobility again.

When I did meet him and begin my period of study with him, I found a man who was at once outgoing and reticent, like a favourite uncle and yet also detached. I discovered much later that he was an accomplished actor in presenting himself to the world (his daughter, Ursula, the famous actress certainly inherited this gene). He was often uneasy talking about his own music, and when sometimes I would try to press him on a particular point (like the rather thirsty lap-dog I must have been), he would deftly change the subject to more neutral ground, or return to my own offerings. It wasn't that he didn't want to discuss his music, or people who had influenced him or with whom he had been friends, but that certain points seemed to be 'beyond bounds' for him.

I distinctly remember my first lesson with him: I was keyed-up when I went in after lunch. I sat down, and we talked before he began to look at my work. After a while, his pencil began to slip over the page and his head dropped while I looked on in horror thinking that he had died! He woke up, however, and managed to pretend that he had just been considering my work thoughtfully! After this the 'graveyard shift' of the post-lunch lesson was something to which I rapidly grew accustomed. It was all part of the scene for me at this impressionable age.

Michael was still the focal point of much of his emotional energy. His son, who died in 1935 at the age of nine, caused Herbert lifelong grief that was only partially mitigated by the composition of *Hymnus Paradisi*. The 'Choral Class' (now the RCM Chorus) performed this work under Vernon Handley in 1982 (Howells's ninetieth birthday year). I remember walking out of the Concert Hall with him after one of the rehearsals. He gripped my arm as we walked up the steps and told me that he wished to God he had never had to write the work. That certainly wasn't an act. He really meant it.

In a way, I find remembering Herbert an odd collection of sometimes conflicting memories and feelings. With many people, one would recall laughter and jokes, or some great pearls of wisdom imparted. I remember him as a generally happy, genial and loveable man who was genuinely interested in me and appreciated my interest in him and my obvious love of his music. He also imparted a great deal of wisdom. He was extraordinarily well-read and a powerfully intelligent and intellectual man, who had an encyclopaedic knowledge of music. I can also attest to the many tales about his predilection for his pretty female students! But there is something deeper which has certainly grown in me as an impression as the years have passed, and it always goes back to the music. Howells always said that he wrote with two things in mind—people and places. To me, the best of Herbert's music grows out of the arches of a cathedral—Gloucester in particular. It has the same strength and flow, and the power to lift one above oneself and to look upward in wonder, as in that great Perpendicular Quire at Gloucester. It was here that he had all his early musical experiences, and it was Gloucester which remained his spiritual home throughout his life. But somehow, because of the timelessness of a great building and the sense of awe that it imparts, there is also a sense of sadness and mystery, of pathos and perhaps most importantly, a distancing (what Katherine Eggar called 'remoteness') which conjures up the spirit of a past age whilst using contemporary language. This is what he learned from Vaughan Williams way back in 1910 when Howells heard the first performance of the *Tallis Fantasia* in Gloucester Cathedral. All this is etched into the fabric of Howells's music. I feel very privileged to have known him, very glad to have been able to bring so much of his unknown music to the public's attention, and to feel that his has been one of the strongest influences of my life.

Recalling RVW

Michael Kennedy

I remember particularly his eyes, grey-blue. They could pierce you, or twinkle at you, or convey a world of understanding. I remember that clipped voice, the words sometimes tumbling over each other. I remember him ladling kirsch over my ice-cream at his home in Hanover Terrace. I remember waking very early in the morning and hearing bits of the already completed Ninth Symphony floating up from the piano in the study. He'd dreamt a new theme for it, he told me, but he couldn't remember it, so he supposed he'd have to leave it as it was. I remember him white with rage while rehearsing Bach's *St Matthew Passion* at Dorking and afterwards collecting kisses from his army of 'nieces', all pretty. I remember his conducting of the *Five Tudor Portraits* at Dorking, with the original mezzo soloist Astra Desmond. No-one else has ever got that piece quite right; he knew just how it should go, and even though people said he was technically a bad conductor, he could make people play and sing for him in exactly the way he wanted. That, of course, was those eyes again, and the power of that personality.

He was an old man when I knew him, but apart from his deafness and his walking showed no other sign of age. He could be naughtily witty and he loved gossip. He was also extremely kind and thoughtful and must have helped hundreds of people by his interest and encouragement and in more practical ways. Most of all, he was always interested in music. He cannot have liked a lot of what he heard, but he tried to come to terms with it and blamed himself if he couldn't. He knew I adored his *Sea Symphony*. 'Oh, that old thing', he said. But when he also said to me 'I've never got over Whitman, thank goodness', I felt sure he was pleased that 'that old thing' could still evoke love. Of all his works, it brings him most vividly back to life for me, noble, visionary, generous, and richly human.

Kenneth Leighton

Paul Spicer

Kenneth Leighton died in August [1988] aged 58. The normal thing with an obituary is to present the bald facts of someone's life. I hope friends will forgive me if I write a rather more personal and full note in memory of a man for whom I had the very greatest respect and, sadly too late, a growing friendship.

Leighton's name is one of those that impressed me at a very tender age when I was a chorister at New College, Oxford. David Lumsden, who started at New College at the same time as me, was a keen advocate of his work, and I remember being very excited by this wonderfully effective music. Leighton had been a chorister himself, at Wakefield Cathedral, before going on to be a student at Oxford. He studied with Bernard Rose (although he actually read classics to begin with), going on to complete both his B.Mus and then D.Mus degrees. It was Bernard Rose who introduced him to Gerald Finzi who was very struck with an early string symphony which Leighton had taken to show him. At that time Finzi was conducting the Newbury String Players, who performed it. Shortly afterwards, Leighton wrote the Suite for oboe, cello and strings, *Veris gratia*, which the Newbury players also performed. Sadly, Finzi died before the publication of the work and Leighton dedicated it to Finzi's memory.

After Oxford he went to Rome on a Mendelssohn scholarship to study with Petrassi—a proving ground for a number of English composers. In 1950 and 1951 he was awarded the Royal Philharmonic prize, and in 1956 the Busoni prize for his Symphony. In 1970 he became Professor of Music at Edinburgh University (the Reid Chair), where he remained until his death. His works include three symphonies (he had begun work on a fourth and very much wanted to leave four symphonies behind to match Brahms's four—he was a devotee of Brahms's music throughout his life), an opera (*Columba*), nine concertos, a highly distinguished corpus of piano music, chamber music, organ and choral music. He was, to all intents and purposes, the complete composer.

Leighton was a quiet, retiring man. He was short in stature, and whenever possible, puffed at the pipe which seemed to be almost an extension of his right hand. He was genial, good natured and with a quietly potent sense of humour. There was always a ready chuckle and a sparkle in the eyes. He was self-effacing, but in a modest way knew the value of what he was writing.

In November 1987 I was privileged to have him in the BBC studio at Pebble Mill to give the first performance of what turned out to be his last solo piano work—the Four Romantic Pieces. He was so pleased to be playing the piano again. He was always a fine pianist, but in recent years other pressures had prevented him from playing as much as he would have liked. It was therefore a very happy occasion. He was on marvellous (and humorous) form and the recording was a great success. The pieces are extremely demanding technically and emotionally, and his performance was magnificent. It seems so odd to me that a man can be apparently so well and at the height of his powers in November and be killed by a lightening-quick cancer by the following August.

What seems saddest of all to me is that he had much more to say. I feel that he had only recently reached a full maturity of style and that he was beginning to work this through his new music. In a sleeve note that Leighton asked me to write for a British Music Society recording of his music, which he also recorded last November, I propounded the theory that the title 'Romantic Pieces' was a clue to the latest developments in his music. It was as if things had come full circle. He began as a composer following in the shadows of the great English romantics, went to Petrassi to have his palate cleansed and his soul purged, spent the major part of his composing life putting what he learned into practice and ended by drawing on his whole experience, giving full rein to all his faculties, emotional and intellectual. The result, to my mind, is some of the most powerful, imaginative and purely beautiful music to come out of this country in recent years.

It is profoundly saddening how little we value some of our artists and composers. We so readily pigeonhole and label people on the sparsest evidence—and sometimes, even on hearsay. We live in an age of people that are 'in' or 'out'—perhaps that has always been so. But there does now seem to be a terrible snobbishness about current top composers. We are expected to approve wholeheartedly of Birtwistle, Maxwell Davies, Harvey, Benjamin, Finnissy etc, etc, and to be wholly suspicious of the composers who write music in the manner of Kenneth Leighton. There is a real injustice here, for both are saying something that needs to be said in the way which, for them, is the most powerful or natural. Ask the average Radio Three listener who Kenneth Leighton is and you would quite probably get a blank stare for an answer—or probably an awareness of some church music, the area in which he is generally best known.

As with many composers however, there are several artists who have taken Leighton's music to their hearts. Amongst these are Peter and Raphael Wallfisch, Hamish Milne, Neil Mackie, the Edinburgh String Quartet, the BBC Scottish Symphony Orchestra through the ministrations of the Head of Music in Scotland, Martin Dalby, and Eric Parkin.

Many aspects of the musical life of this country have been made the poorer by Kenneth Leighton's death. He was a scholar, teacher, performer and, first and foremost, a composer. He will be sadly missed.

Kenneth Leighton—a seventy-fifth anniversary tribute

Paul Spicer

What makes a composer worthy of the attention of posterity? Why does part of this tribute regret the far-too-widespread neglect of such a composer as Leighton? To my mind, a composer should have the technique to put his ideas across eloquently, have the ideas worthy of that technique, and an inner creative fire which communicates those ideas powerfully. The commentator Hugh Ottaway once said most tellingly, 'idioms come and go and history finds little to choose between them; the enduring factor is the quality of thought, which alone makes the idiom a living and vital thing.' At one stroke he demolishes the whole fashion bandwagon and puts the emphasis squarely where it belongs on the composer's creative integrity.

Leighton always had a very strong Romantic streak. His earliest works such as the beautiful *Veris gratia* for oboe, cello and strings show his indebtedness to Vaughan Williams. It is no surprise that Gerald Finzi at the end of his life championed his music, encouraging this shy, working class northern lad, giving him his first performances with the Newbury String Players and thus gaining Leighton's eternal gratitude. Wakefield Cathedral was the first point of musical inspiration, and here it was that Leighton discovered the great panoply of music for the church which he himself so greatly enriched in future years. Careful nurturing at Oxford by Bernard Rose, in particular, ensured that his extraordinary natural compositional talent would be developed and recognised. First success came in the form of a Mendelssohn scholarship to study with Petrassi in Rome in 1951–2. This experience gave him wings and allowed his natural lyricism to flow between the science of contemporary techniques (which he used but rarely allowed to dictate style) and the ebb and flow of timeless counterpoint of which he was a master.

Leighton's stated influences were many and varied and included Bach and Brahms. If his developing style seemed far removed from the sound world of these mentors, essential elements of their style and processes became his staple diet. One of the most significant statements of Leighton's process came when he said 'All my days are spent trying to find a good tune'. If this is an exaggeration, it underlines the most important quality of his music which he shares with Bach and Brahms, that of lyricism. He also gained another hugely powerful tool from them in his use of pathos. Brahms understood the power of pathos instinctively. One only has to look at the simplicity of that perfect piano Intermezzo op.117 no.1 or the Amen from the *Geistliches Lied* op.30 to know how deeply he understood the power of quiet, reflective simplicity to affect the senses. Leighton, too, understood this and the third of the Romantic Pieces for piano op.95 is a moving example. This piece, for me, sums up why I believe Leighton deserves that recognition from posterity which I questioned earlier. It is only one example of which there are many, but it demonstrates timeless qualities which I believe to be essential to the positive judgement of future generations including a deep sense of humanity, of quiet protest, of overriding sensitivity, of joy and sadness, of resignation, and in the end, quiet acceptance of the inevitable. It is a life's journey in microcosm. Leighton talked of 'wonder' in nature when referring to his solo cantata *Earth, Sweet Earth* op.94, and if one characteristic seems to communicate above all others in his music it is this searching for something other—for meaning in life and the order of the universe, God and Love which brings an added dimension to his creative genius. Perhaps, if I were to pare it down to its basic elements I would recognise the quality of ecstatic spirituality which is seen in both his life-enhancing scherzi as well as his reflective meditations.

Possibly Leighton's strongest card, however, is that all this emotional content is so finely balanced with the acuteness of his intellect and his ability as a pianist. Each of these elements fed the others. Thus there was always the practitioner's practical appraisal of what was possible in performance, and the intellectual's appraisal of the challenge of balancing the elements of heart and mind, style and content. Nowhere is this more clearly demonstrated than in the *Fantasia Contrappuntistica* op.24—a homage to Bach which won the Busoni Prize and was premiered by Maurizio Pollini in 1956.

Perhaps Leighton's misfortune was to be born at a time when musical experimentation was at its height. Thus, his rather conservative style made even his serial compositions a search for lyrical possibilities. He was also to some extent a formulaic composer whose mannerisms were often transposed from work to work, and detractors would find reliance on certain notational figures and rhythmic cells tiresome. But this very insistence on his developed style was part of what makes the unique experience of Leighton's music. Hugh Ottaway's assertion about idiom goes to the heart of the matter. Sixteen years after his untimely death we are in a better position to recognise Leighton's vibrant creativity, his deep sensitivity, his communicating spirituality, and the depth of his intellectual and technical prowess. We now need performers in all genres to take this music to their hearts and to allow it to work its magic on a new generation of audiences.

Composer memories from Howard Ferguson

Sir Edward Elgar

Though I heard Elgar conduct a number of his works at Three Choirs Festivals and in London, I met him only once. It was in October 1928, when he was seventy-one and I was eighteen. My beloved master Harold Samuel had taken me to stay for the weekend at the home of Mr and Mrs Edward Speyer, who knew all the musicians of the day and had invited Elgar to lunch on the Sunday. He was shown into the music room where

Harold and I were sitting. Everyone knew that by that time he claimed to be more interested in horse-racing than in music; so it came as a surprise when he sat down at the piano and began to thunder out the overture to Bellini's *Norma*. 'Splendid stuff!', he explained: 'do you know it, Harold?'

Later Speyer said to him, 'Edward, I have something here that might interest you.' From the large cupboard that housed his famous collection of composers' autographs he took out a manila folder and handed it over. Elgar opened it, took one look and said in astonishment, 'Good gracious! I'd forgotten all about that.' What it proved to be was the manuscript full score of the 'Dream Interlude' from his *Falstaff*, complete and self-contained, but in a different key from that in which it appears in the finished work. Elgar must have written it before the rest, then found that it needed to be transposed in order to fit into its surroundings. I've often wondered whether it was a gift from Elgar, or whether Speyer bought it; but that was not divulged.

Frank Bridge

Frank Bridge, Ethel Sinclair (the warm-hearted Australian violinist who later became his wife), and Harold Samuel were fellow students and friends at the RCM in the years before the First World War. Thus it was that when I came from Ireland in the mid-1920s to study and live with Harold, we occasionally had a meal with Frank and Ethel at their delightful house in Bedford Gardens on Campden Hill, or they would come down the hill to eat with us in Clarendon Road.

Though Frank was no longer the regular viola of the English String Quartet, he used to rejoin them for Mozart and Brahms quintets at the Sunday afternoon chamber concerts I was taken to in the nearby studio of their friend Marjorie Fass. From these performances it was obvious that Frank was an outstandingly fine player. He was also an experienced conductor, but one who got less than his fair share of work; for, as he used to say, concert promoters only engaged him when another conductor fell ill.

From the outset his music showed an innate understanding of every musical instrument and total technical mastery. His earlier works were immediately attractive, and remained widely popular even when traces of Scriabin began to appear. But with the Piano Sonata of 1921/04, dedicated to the memory of Ernest Farrar, Bridge entered a new phase in which the influence of the Second Viennese School (particularly Berg) can be felt; and English audiences became puzzled by what they felt to be alien and uncongenial. (Even Harold had so little liking for the Piano Sonata that he managed to avoid giving its first performance.)

There can be no doubt, however, that the works from the Piano Sonata onwards are the finest that Bridge wrote, and only now are they beginning to be appreciated. These include the Third String Quartet (1926), the Fourth Quartet (1937), the Second Piano Trio (1929), the Violin Sonata (1932), the orchestral *Enter Spring* (1927) and *There is a Willow Grows Aslant a Brook* (1928), the cello concerto *Oration* (1930), and *Phantasm* for piano and orchestra (1931).

It is well known that Bridge was the most important musical influence in the life of Britten. In the pictorial biography of the latter there are two unexpected snapshots taken in 1933: one of Frank, Ethel, Harold and myself standing outside their house at Friston, in the downs near Eastbourne; the other of Frank, Harold and myself wielding shrimping-nets in the sea (with trousers well rolled-up) during the same weekend.

Ralph Vaughan Williams

The first time I heard any of Vaughan Williams's music was in 1924, when, as a very young student at the Royal College of Music, I stole into the Parry Opera Theatre in the middle of a rehearsal for the original production of *Hugh the Drover*. From that moment I was hooked. During the next thirty-four years I heard the first performances of twenty-seven of his major works, including the remaining four operas and all the Symphonies from numbers Four to Nine. The final rehearsal was often included, and in later years the private run-through to which he used to invite a number of friends. As he said, 'Like Gustav Holst, I ask everyone's advice and take no-one's.'

During my last year at the college I was able to get to know Vaughan Williams, for he nobly agreed to take me for composition during the absence in America of my regular teacher, R. O. Morris. The first thing he asked me to do was to write a fugue with twin subjects in the style of a Handel chorus. Though I'm afraid the fugue never got finished, his advice on practical matters, such as which clarinet to use and how to set out orchestral parts clearly, was invaluable.

In the summer of 1928, when Harold Samuel and I were staying in a cottage at Capel in Surrey, he cycled over unannounced from Leith Hill one afternoon for tea. The sight of Vaughan Williams on a bicycle was remarkable; yet, rather to our surprise, he appeared to be in total control.

Two meetings in company with Gerald Finzi stand out. The first, when the pair of us went to Dorking to play through some thirty Gurney songs, to allow Vaughan Williams to choose the twenty that would make up the initial two volumes published in 1938. And the second, at one of the daily wartime National Gallery concerts, when the programme included two first performances: the revised version of Vaughan Williams's Double String Trio (later to become the Partita for string orchestra); and Gerald's set of five Shakespeare songs, *Let Us Garlands Bring*, with their dedication, 'For Ralph Vaughan Williams on his birthday, Oct. 12th, 1942'. It was, in fact, his seventieth; and the blissfully happy five years at Hanover Terrace, following his marriage to Ursula, were still to come.

Recipes by Howard Ferguson

Recipes by Howard Ferguson were a regular feature of the Finzi Friends Newsletter *during the late 80s and early 90s, and a small selection is added here for 'flavour'. Ferguson's book* Entertaining Solo: a cookbook for the single host *was produced in 1992 to much acclaim, and soon sold out.*

Glüwein

Glüwein is the hot, spiced red wine served in Austria to warm the toenails after skiing. It has the same effect in England, even when there is no snow on the ground.

1 bottle of dry red vin ordinaire (claret or anything else, but don't use a fine wine for it would be wasted)
The thin rind of ½ a lemon, cut with a potato-peeler.
1 tablespoon (7g) of white sugar (more if preferred)
6 cloves

Simmer all ingredients in a saucepan for ten minutes, but don't boil. Serve in glasses that are not likely to crack when heated.

I hope this brings some Christmas cheer—it's very good and quite inexpensive. It even disguised the awful Algerian plonk that was the first wine to appear here at the end of the war.

Cold Cucumber Soup

A delicious summer soup that can be made quickly and requires no cooking!

1 cucumber (unpeeled)
1 clove of garlic
3/4 of a pint (450ml) of milk
1/2 a pint (300ml) of single cream
1/2 a pint (300ml) of yoghurt
1 teaspoon salt
Freshly ground pepper

Roughly grate cucumber into a bowl. In a saucer mash the garlic and salt with a fork, add some of the milk, stir thoroughly, and strain the milk into the grated cucumber. Add the yoghurt, cream, pepper, and the rest of the milk. Stir well. Chill for a couple of hours in the fridge.

When serving, be careful to include a share of cucumber with each ladleful of the liquid.

Beetroot Soup

This is the famous Russian Borsch, of which there are many versions, both thick (hot) and clear (hot or cold). The following are mine, and can be eaten either hot in winter or cold in summer.

1 1/2 pints (900ml) beef or chicken stock (or a stock-cube dissolved in the same quantity of water)
4 medium-size beets, raw
1/2 a glass (140ml) of dry red wine
1 dessertspoon red wine vinegar
1 teaspoon sugar
4 tablespoons (60ml) of either whipping cream, sour cream or yoghurt
Salt and freshly ground black pepper.
Serves four

Coarsely grate the raw beets into a large bowl. (This is quite hard work, for they are surprisingly tough; but don't use the cooked beets sold by many greengrocers, as they have already lost much of their juice and flavour.) To avoid grating your knuckles at the same time, spear one end of the beet on a fork and grate downwards. Add all the remaining ingredients to the bowl except the cream. Bring the stock to the boil, pour it over the beet, and press vigorously with a potato masher to extract the juice. Set aside for one hour to infuse.

Hot version: strain the liquid into a saucepan, and throw away the beet. Reheat, but do not bring to the boil as this would turn it brown.

Cold version: strain the liquid into a bowl and refrigerate for a couple of hours. Throw away the beet.

Both versions: ladle the liquid into individual bowls or soup plates, and carefully slide into the centre of each a tablespoon of whipping cream, sour cream or yoghurt. Do not mix them together, as both dark red soup and white cream should be visible.

Atholl Browse

Of the many friends to whom I have given this sweet, only two have been able to guess its ingredients. In The Scottish National Dictionary it is defined as 'Honey or meal mixed with whisky, used in the Highlands as a cure for a cold'. The Dictionary adds 'There is a tradition that the Earl of Atholl in James III's time captured the rebellious Earl of Ross by filling with honey and whisky a small well in a rock on the Isle of Skye, from which Ross was in the habit of drinking'. The mixture has ever since been known as Atholl Browse (Browse is a broth or potage). Whether or not this is true, the following recipe is a speciality of Trinity College, Cambridge. Its proportions, 4/2/1, are easily remembered.

For four:

4 fl oz (100ml) whipping cream
2 fl oz (50ml) of clear honey
1 fl oz (25ml) of whisky

To get the proportions right, pour the cream into a glass measuring jug; add the honey and whisky, and beat with a rotary whisk until the mixture thickens to just-pourable consistency. Pour into four pot-au-crème pots, place in the fridge for an hour or so (if necessary, it can be made a couple of days in advance and kept in the fridge), and serve with shortbread or sweet biscuits. As it is very rich it is best eaten with a teaspoon.

A dour Scotswoman once said to me, 'It should be made with oatmeal, not cream.' Personally I prefer the above version. If you have no clear honey, the 'set' (cloudy) kind can be clarified by placing the jar in a saucepan of simmering water: but let the honey get quite cold before making the sweet.

My Grandmother's Christmas pudding

This recipe was given to my mother by her mother, so it must be at least 150 years old and makes the best plum pudding I have ever tasted: for besides being full of fruit it is light in texture. The mixture can be used the day after it has been made, but is better when stored in jam jars for some months (it will keep for years), as this allows the flavours to blend and mature.

1 lb (450g) stoneless raisins
1 lb (450g) currants
1 lb (450g) mixed candied peel
6 eggs (well beaten)
8 oz (225g) breadcrumbs (2 day-old bread)
8 oz (225g) shredded suet
½ oz (12g) butter
10 oz (275g) sugar
1 wineglass (280ml) and 2 tablespoons (30ml) of brandy (or whisky)

Wash the raisins and currants. Cut the candied peel into thin slices, if not already cut. Grate bread. In a large basin mix all these with the suet and sugar. Add the beaten eggs and brandy (or whisky), and mix very thoroughly.

At this point the mixture may be spooned into jam jars and covered with clingfilm, when it will keep for a year or longer.

To use: The day before serving, butter the inside of a pudding-basin, spoon in enough of the mixture to come within ½ an inch of the top, and press down well with the back of a spoon. Cover the top with a floured cloth (or kitchen foil) and tie down securely. Steam for eight hours, in or above simmering water, topping it up whenever necessary.

Next day, steam for a further four hours. Remove the basin from the steamer, take off the cover or lid, and run a knife round the inside. Place a warmed serving-dish upside down on the top of the basin, hold the two together and invert them; give them a slight shake, and the pudding will be released on to the dish. Abandon the basin. Warm two tablespoons of brandy (or whisky) in a small pan, set it alight and pour it over the pudding. Serve with brandy butter.

Appendices

Appendix 1

Sources and selected further reading

All sources listed below come from the *Finzi Friends Newsletter* unless otherwise stated. Note: the *Finzi Friends Newsletter* mistakenly had two consecutive years of Volume 11; when this error was realised, Volume 13 was skipped. Volume 23 consisted of a single larger edition.

Banfield, Stephen—'Writing a book on Finzi', vol. 15, no. 2 (1997)

Banfield, Stephen—'Finzi and Wordsworth', vol. 10, no. 2 (1992)

Banfield, Stephen—'Ashmansworth centenary lecture', vol. 19, no. 2, (2001)

Bliss, Gertrude—'Memories of Ashmansworth and Gloucester', vol. 7, no. 1 (1989) excerpt

Boden, Anthony—'Gerald Finzi at the Three Choirs Festival' vol. 23 (2005)

Carol Case, John—'Letter from John Carol Case, OBE', vol. 15, no. 1 (1997)

Carol Case, John—'English song—John Carol Case recalls the early days of his career', vol. 16, no. 2 (1998)

Cobbe, Hugh—'The correspondence of Gerald Finzi and Ralph Vaughan Williams', vol. 10, no. 1 (1992)

Cobbe, Hugh—'Howard Ferguson 21st October 1908–1st November 1999', vol. 17, no. 2 (1999)

Dale Roberts, Jeremy—In Years Defaced. Vol. 18, no. 2 (2000) revised 2005

Dale Roberts, Jeremy—*Richard Shirley Smith: The Paintings and Collages 1957-2000*, book review vol. 20, no. 1 (2002)
Dale Roberts, Jeremy—'A composer's view: second thoughts', first publication
Eaton, Sybil—'Letter to Joy Finzi from Sybil Eaton', vol. 4, no. 1 (1986)
Edgeley, Lucy—'Memories of Church Farm', first publication
Ferguson, Howard—'Finzi and Howard Ferguson'. Gerald Finzi Twenty-Fifth Anniversary Celebration programme, 1981, as originally printed (subsequently altered at various times)
Ferguson, Howard—Recipes. Taken from various editions of the *Finzi Friends Newsletter* (1987–94)
Ferguson, Howard—'Frank Bridge', Summer Weekend of English Music programme book (1987)
Ferguson, Howard—'A meeting with Elgar', Summer Festival of British Music programme book (1990)
Ferguson, Howard—'Meetings with Vaughan Williams', Summer Festival of British Music programme book (1990)
Finzi, Christopher and Rees, Henry (Editors)—Extracts from *Joy Finzi 1907–1991: tributes from her friends* (1992)
Finzi, Christopher—'Memories from Christopher Finzi', vol. 15, no. 1 (1997)
Finzi, Christopher—'Memories of my father' vol. 19, no. 1 (2001) revised 2005
Finzi, Gerald—Letters from Gerald Finzi to Kenneth Leighton, first publication (Leighton Collection, University of Edinburgh)
Finzi, Gerald—'Absalom's Place'. (Bodlean Library)
Finzi, Gerald—*Dies natalis*, Three Choirs Festival programme book (1947)
Finzi, Gerald—*Intimations of Immortality*, Three Choirs Festival programme book (1950)
Finzi, Gerald—Letter to Mollie Sands, first publication in this form—*see* vol. 11, no. 1 for excerpts and short article by Howard Ferguson (1994)
Finzi, Gerald—'As Guardian of Genius', first publication (Gurney Archive)
Finzi, Joy—'Exhibition of portrait drawings by Joy Finzi'. Gerald Finzi Twenty-Fifth Anniversary Celebration programme book (1981)
Finzi, Joy—'In that place'. Summer Weekend of English Music programme book (1984).
Finzi, Joy—poems from *A Point of Departure* (1967).
Finzi, Joy—poems from *Twelve Months of a Year* (1981).

Finzi, Joy—two New Year poems, first publication.

Kennedy, Michael—'Recalling RVW', Summer Weekend of English Music programme book (1987).

Lancaster, Philip—'"Lo, the full, final sacrifice": an introduction', vol. 20, no. 1 (2002) revised 2007.

Lancaster, Philip—'Reflections on the Rejection of Cecilia' vol. 21, no. 2 (2003) revised 2007.

Langridge, Philip—'Thoughts on *Intimations of Immortality*', vol. 7, no. 1 (1989) revised 2005.

Leighton, Kenneth—'Memories of Gerald Finzi', vol. 6, no. 1 (1988)

Lipkin, Malcolm—'Finzi and Malcolm Lipkin'. Gerald Finzi Twenty-Fifth Anniversary Celebration programme (1981) revised 2005.

McVeagh, Diana—'A farewell tribute to Joy Finzi', vol. 9, no. 2 (1991)

Officer, Adrian—'Harrogate and Ernest Farrar', vol. 14, no. 1 (1996) excerpt.

Page, Norman—'Thomas Hardy and music', A Weekend of English Song' programme book (2001)

Pakenham, Simona—'Simona Pakenham on Finzi', *Journal of the RVW Society* no. 35, Editor William Hedley (2006)

Popplewell, Clare—'Church Farm, Ashmansworth', vol. 12, no. 1 (1995)

Salmon, Michael A—'Starshine over distant fields', first publication

Scott, Anthony—'Gerald Finzi as tutor of composition', vol. 15, no. 2 (1997) with additional material drawn from *Joy Finzi 1907–1991: tributes from her friends* (1992)

Shiner, Michael—'The Newbury Junior Orchestra', vol. 4, no. 2 (1986)

Shuttleworth, Anna—'Memories of Anna Shuttleworth', vol. 16, no. 1 (1998) revised 2005

Spicer, Paul—'Recalling Howells', Summer Weekend of English Music programme book (1987) revised 2006

Spicer, Paul—'Kenneth Leighton', vol. 6, no. 2 (1988)

Spicer, Paul—'Gerald Finzi's Seven Poems of Robert Bridges', vol. 9, no. 2 (1991) revised 2007

Spicer, Paul—'Kenneth Leighton—a seventy-fifth Anniversary Tribute', first appeared in *The Full Score* (2004) and vol. 22, no.1 (2004)

Stunt, Christopher—'Thomas Hardy and Gerald Finzi: an improbable partnership', BA Special Hons dissertation, University of Bristol, 1996. Adaptations of chapters appeared in vol. 14, no. 2 ('The too short time') and vol. 15 no. 2 ('Who is this coming with pondering pace') revised 2006

Thomas, Philip—'*Requiem da camera*' vol. 8, no. 2 (1990)

Thomas, Philip—'An introduction to Finzi's Clarinet Concerto', vol. 15, no. 1 (1997) revised 2005
Varcoe, Stephen—'Recording *Earth and Air and Rain*', vol. 3, no. 2 (1985)
Varcoe, Stephen—'Wilfred Brown', vol. 15, no. 1 (1997)
Venn, Edward—'Finzi's Serenade', vol. 17, no. 1 (1999)
Wallfisch, Raphael—'Recording the Finzi Cello Concerto', vol. 4, no. 2 (1986)
Warner-Casson, Ann—'Tom Perkins—letter carver', vol. 11, no. 1 (1993)
Warner-Casson, Ann—'Work inspired by Finzi and English song', vol. 18, no. 2 (2000)
Webster, Donald—'Ernest Bristow Farrar 1885–1918', vol. 16, no. 1 (1998)
Young, Percy—'Poet and musician', vol. 12, no. 2 (1995)

Selected further reading:

GERALD FINZI:

Banfield, Stephen—*Gerald Finzi, an English Composer* Faber and Faber (1997)
Dressler, John C—*Gerald Finzi, a Bio-Bibliography* Greenwood Press (1997)
Ferguson, Howard and Hurd, Michael—*Letters of Gerald Finzi and Howard Ferguson* The Boydell Press (2001)
McVeagh, Diana—*Gerald Finzi: his life and music* The Boydell Press (2005)
www.geraldfinzi.com
www.geraldfinzi.org (Finzi Trust)

JOY FINZI:

Finzi, Joy—*In That Place, The Portrait Drawings of Joy Finzi* Libanus Press (1987) limited edition of 300
Finzi, Joyce and Shirley Smith, Richard—*A Point of Departure* The Golden Head Press (1967)
Finzi, Joy and Simon Brett—*Twelve Months of a Year* Libanus Press (1981) limited edition of 110
www.joyfinzi.com

Appendix 2

Finzi Friends committee

In October1981, Robert Gower, Michael Salmon and Paul Spicer met to discuss the formation of 'The Friends of the Finzi Charitable Trust', following on the success of the Ellesmere Finzi Celebration held that July to commemorate the twenty-fifth anniversary of Gerald Finzi's death. With a cross-section of Trust members and enthusiasts discovered at Ellesmere, the less cumbersomely named 'Finzi Trust Friends' was launched at the Three Choirs Festival (Hereford) the following year, on 23 August 1982. The Friends worked closely with the Trust—with many overlapping objectives—until a change of constitution was found necessary during the organisation of the first Weekend of English Song held in 2001. The Song Weekend, an emulation of the spirit of the triennial Summer Music series organised by the Trust throughout the 1980s, was a massive undertaking, requiring self-sufficient status. 'Finzi Trust Friends' became 'Finzi Friends' in 2001, and became a registered charity.

The following list of committee members reflects the Trust cross-pollination of the earlier years: many committee members did not have titles (note there was no Chairman until 2001) but were very active in both Trust and Friends—and remained with the Trust after 2001. Joy Finzi, of course, remained an active figurehead and hosted meetings until a few months before her death in 1991.

Presidents

Joy Finzi 1982–1991
Vernon Handley 1992–2005
Iain Burnside 2005—

Vice-presidents

Michael Berkeley 1982—
John Carol Case 1982—
Howard Ferguson 1982–1999
Vernon Handley 1982–92, 2005—
Richard Hickox 1982—
John Russell 1982–1990
Michael Kennedy 1985—
Philip Brunelle 1990—
Raphael Wallfisch 1990—
John Sanders 1994–2003
Percy Young 1995–2004

Committee

Juliette Bigley 2002–06 (Secretary 2003–06)
Andrew Burn 1982–93
Martin Bussey 2007—
Sophie Cleobury 2007—
Joy Finzi 1982–91
James Gorick 2002—
Robert Gower 1982–93
Chris and John Harris 1998–2001 (Joint Newsletter Editors)
Charles Janz 2002– (Publicity Officer)
Rolf Jordan 2001– (Membership Secretary 2005– 6, Newsletter Editor 2007—)
Philip Lancaster 2000— (Newsletter Editor 2001–7)
Martin Lee-Browne 2002—
Emma Lowery 2001— (Membership Secretary 2002–05, Treasurer 2004—)
Denny Lyster 1987–2005 (Membership Secretary 1987–89, Treasurer 1987–90)
Jennie McGregor-Smith 2002—

Diana McVeagh 1982–85 (Newsletter Editor 1982–84)
Mark Opstad 2000–01
Jim Page 1993— (Sales 1995—, Acting Secretary 2002–03, Vice-chairman 2003—)
Keith Parker 1987–96 (Sales 1991–95)
Elizabeth Pooley 1982–2002 (Membership Secretary 1984–87, Treasurer 1984–87, Secretary 1987–2002)
Clare Popplewell 1987–96
Henry Rees 1988-2002 (Membership Secretary 1989-2002, Treasurer 1990-2002)
Jane Rigby (Secretary 2006—)
Michael Salmon 1982–83 (Secretary)
Michael Shiner 1983–87 (Secretary)
David Soward 2002–04 (Treasurer)
Paul Spicer 1992— (Chairman 2000—)
Ann Warner-Casson (Sales 1985-93, Newsletter Editor 1984-98)

Appendix 3

Finzi Friends Newsletter vol. 1, no. 1

COMPLETE TEXT OF THE FIRST FINZI FRIENDS NEWSLETTER.

There are now over 130 Friends, and the number grows constantly. We shall meet to celebrate our first anniversary at Gloucester in August; before that, in June, there will be another Newsletter, and information is very welcome. (The time and the hall for concerts would be useful.)

Michael Shiner, who knew Finzi, is joining Michael Salmon to help as Secretary.

Finzi's Ode *For St Cecilia*, composed for the 1947 St Cecilia's Day concert, and dedicated to Howard Ferguson, took its proper place again on 23 November 1982, in the royal concert at the Barbican Hall, It was performed by David Rendall, the London Symphony Chorus and LSO under Richard Hickox, who also conducts it on the record ZRG 896.

The Collected Poems of Ivor Gurney chosen, edited and with an introduction by P. J. Kavanagh, is published by OUP at £12.00. It is the most substantial and representative collection of his poems to date, and includes over 100 which have never before appeared in print. It has been hailed as 'a necessary addition to the canon of twentieth-century English verse'. Kavanagh acknowledges: 'after Marion Scott, it is to Gerald Finzi and his wife Joy (neither of whom ever met Gurney) that we owe most'.

Over Christmas in the USA there were performances of *In terra pax* at Iowa State University and the University of Minnesota, also at Houston, and in Delaware, Louisiana, Pennsylvania, and South Carolina; and of *Dies natalis* in Colorado, Delaware, Los Angeles and New York City.

NEW RECORDS

Two records, sponsored by the Trust, are being made by Hyperion in February:

Finzi's Prelude and Fugue; Interlude
Michael Berkeley's Sting Quartet; String Trio; *Three Moods*
Keith Marshall, Oboe; Amphion String Quartet

These are all first recordings, except Finzi's Oboe Interlude, which was played by its dedicatee Leon Goosens on RCA RL 25142 (now deleted). Berkeley's Quartet was commissioned by the Ellesmere Finzi Celebration with funds from the West Midlands Arts Association, and first performed at the Ellesmere College Weekend in 1981.

Finzi's *Till Earth Outwears*; Howard Ferguson's *Discovery* song cycle; Moeran's Four English Lyrics, 'The bean flower', 'Impromptu in March'; and songs by Frank Bridge.
Anne Dawson, 1981 Finzi song Award and 1982 Ferrier Prize Winner.

FOR HERBERT SUMSION

We are also glad to announce that Hyperion are making this record with Donald Hunt, his Singers and the Worcester Cathedral Choir:

Side 1 Te Deum (1935); 'They that go down to the sea in ships' (1979); Chorale prelude on Down Ampney, for organ (1980)—by Herbert Sumsion. *The Scribe* and *Inheritance* by Herbert Howells.

Side 2 'In Exile' (1981); Introduction and Theme, for organ (1936) by Herbert Sumsion. 'Lo, the full, final sacrifice' (1946) by Finzi.

Herbert Sumsion, known to his friends as John, was born in Gloucester and was organist of the Cathedral for thirty-nine years. Both Herbert Howells and Gerald Finzi were his close friends. Anyone wishing to join in this gesture of reward for all that John has done for music during his life in Gloucester—so nobly supported by his wife Alice—may like to send a subscription to:

Finzi Trust Sumsion Record
Brian Frith [address]

It is planned to issue this record in time for this year's Three Choirs Festival. A signed copy of 'In Exile' will be given to subscribers, and their names listed in the record.

Recent Hyperion releases include *Songs by Finzi and his friends* on A66015, with Ian Partridge, Stephen Roberts and Clifford Benson in Finzi, Milford, Farrar, Gill and Gurney; and *Fishing by Moonlight*, music by Robin Milford.

1983 THREE CHOIRS FESTIVAL
20-27 August

Finzi Trust Friends
Annual Three Choirs Meeting
Friday at 7.30
Andrew Motion on Ivor Gurney's poetry
With wine and light supper

Finzi's Clarinet Concerto
Ferguson's *Amore Langueo*
Friday at 20.00

Diana McVeagh on Gerald Finzi
Monday at 14.30

Michael Hurd on Ivor Gurney
The Man and his Music

1984 FINZI COMPOSITION AWARD
in association with the New Macnachten Concerts

To commemorate Finzi's work in assisting his young fellow composers with Newbury String Players, the Finzi Trust is holding a competition open to all composers resident in the United Kingdom. The Trust is particularly delighted to be associated with the New Macnachten Concerts since Finzi's music was performed in the Macnacheten-Lemare concerts in the 30s.

The judges are:
Odaline de la Martinez (director of Lontano Ensemble)
Anthony Payne (composer and critic)
Jeremy Dale Roberts (composer and member of the Finzi Trust)

There is a prize of £500 and the winning work will be given its first performance in the 1984 New Macnachten Concerts.
Details from Andrew Burn [address]

Details of newly published and planned Finzi scores may be had from Mrs Pauline Gower [address]

COMING FINZI PERFORMANCES

February

5 Clarinet Concerto	Keble College Chapel, Oxford 8.00
5 *Let Us Garlands Bring*	Lodden Home Appeal Concert, Reading
5 Magnificat	St Bee's School, Cumbria
7 Prelude for strings	Taunton Sinfonietta, Taunton
12 Clarinet Concerto	Pitville Pump Room, Cheltenham

March

7 *For St Cecilia*	Cambridge University Music School, 7.30
9 *By Footpath and Stile*	Wigmore Hall, London, 7.30
12 *For St Cecilia*	Queen's University, Belfast
19 *In terra pax*	Leicester Chamber Orchestra
26 *Let Us Garlands Bring*	Bach Cantata Group, St Stephens, Lansdowne Road, Bath

May

5	Clarinet Concerto	Haberdasher's Aske's School, Elstree, Herts
6	Romance for strings	Tunbridge Wells, Kent
23	Shakespeare songs	Wigmore Hall, London, 7.30

June

7	Cello Concerto	Bromley Symphony Orchestra
7	'Lo, the full, final sacrifice'	Carshalton Choral Society, Surrey
21	*For St Cecilia*	Bury St Edmunds Bach Society

March 19

Inaugural meeting of the English Poetry and Song Society, Rachel Fowler Centre, Melksham, Wiltshire, 7.30, to include settings by Finzi

April 29

Elgar and Finzi—talk by Diana McVeagh, Elgar Society, East Anglian Branch, Assembly House, Norwich, 7.30

May 7

Anthony Scott's *Mass of the Dawn*, Civic Hall, Guildford, conducted by Vernon Handley. Anthony Scott was Finzi's pupil and friend.

Diana McVeagh [address]
January 1983

Appendix 4

Finzi Friends events

1982: 23 August Three Choirs Festival, Hereford. Inaugural reception and meeting.

1983: 26 August Three Choirs lunch, Gloucester. Guest speaker—Andrew Motion: 'Ivor Gurney's poetry'.

1984: 22 August Three Choirs lunch, Worcester. Recital introduced by Howard Ferguson—Westminster Piano Trio.

1985: 19 August Three Choirs lunch, Hereford. Guest speakers—Diana McVeagh and Howard Ferguson: 'Finzi's Hardy songs'

1986: 23 March Radley College, Abingdon. Workshop on Gerald Finzi's Thomas Hardy songs—Stephen Varcoe and Clifford Benson. Workshop on Finzi's Robert Bridges partsongs—Christopher Finzi.

21 August Three Choirs lunch, Gloucester. Masterclass on Finzi's Cello Concerto—Timothy Hugh.

2 November Radley College. Michael Kennedy unveils the George Butterworth panel by Laurence Whistler. Recital—Michael George and Antony Saunders. Choral concert—Edward Higginbottom with Choir of New College, Oxford.

1987: 27 AUGUST Three Choirs lunch, Worcester. Guest speaker—Michael Hurd: 'Ivor Gurney'.

1988: 30 APRIL Reading University, tour of the Finzi Book Room. Workshop on Howard Ferguson's *The Dream of Rood*—Christopher Finzi.
24 AUGUST Three Choirs lunch, Hereford. Guest speaker—Andrew Burn: 'The music of Howard Ferguson'.
22 OCTOBER Gloucester Cathedral. Masterclass on Finzi's Interlude and Howells's Oboe Sonata—Nicholas Daniel and Julius Drake. Talk—John Sanders: 'Herbert Sumsion'. Evensong with works by Sumsion.

1989: 23 AUGUST Three Choirs lunch, Gloucester. Guest speaker—Andrew Burn 'Bliss's *Colour Symphony*'.

1990: 23 AUGUST Three Choirs lunch, Worcester. Guest speaker—Anthony Boden: 'A personal view of Ivor Gurney'.

1991: 21 AUGUST Three Choirs lunch, Hereford. Guest speaker—Percy Young 'Gerald Finzi and the metaphysical idea.' Sponsored recital—Margaret Fingerhut.

1992: 13 JUNE Ashmansworth Friends' day. Choral workshop on Finzi and Howells anthems—Paul Spicer. Recital—Ian Partridge and Peter Gritton.
25 AUGUST Three Choirs lunch, Gloucester. Guest speaker—Stephen Banfield: 'Finzi and Wordsworth'.

1993: 12 JUNE Ashmansworth Friends' day. Choral workshop on Finzi and Howells—Paul Spicer. Recital—Michael Collins and Noriko Ogawa.
26 AUGUST Three Choirs lunch, Worcester. Guest speaker—Philip Thomas: 'Finzi and Parry'.

1994: 11 JUNE Ashmansworth Friends' day. Recital—Henry Hurford and Julius Drake. Choral workshop on *The Oxford Book of Romantic Partsongs*—John Rutter.
24 AUGUST Three Choirs lunch, Hereford. Guest speaker—Raphael Wallfisch: 'The Finzi Cello Concerto'.
10 DECEMBER Ashmansworth Friends' day. Choral workshop on *In terra pax*—Paul Spicer.

1995: 3 June Ashmansworth Friends' day. Recital—Paul Barritt and Catherine Edwards. Choral workshop on Elgar songs—John Sanders.
26 August Three Choirs lunch, Gloucester. Guest speaker—Andrew Millinger 'The choral music of Herbert Howells'.
9 December Ashmansworth Friends' day. Choral workshop of carols including Finzi and Vaughan Williams—Richard Butt. Reading by Gabriel Woolf. Recital—Simon Perry.

1996: 29 June Ashmansworth Friends' day. Talk—Christopher Finzi 'Memories of my father'. Recital—Piers Adams and Howard Beach.
3 August Harrogate Festival. Talk—Donald Webster 'Ernest Farrar'. Recital—Jeffrey Lloyd-Roberts.
23 August Three Choirs lunch, Worcester. Guest speaker—Philip Thomas: 'Finzi's Clarinet Concerto'.

1997: 14 June Ashmansworth Friends' day. Recital—Rufus Muller and Denny Lyster. Choral workshop on Finzi, Ireland and Ferguson.
21 August Three Choirs lunch, Hereford. Guest speaker—Stephen Banfield: 'Writing a book on Finzi'.

1998: 27 June Moreton, Dorset. Talk—Simon Whistler on 'Glass engraving'. Recital—Andrew Locke Nicholson and Amanda Cook.
19 August Three Choirs lunch, Gloucester. Guest speaker—Paul Spicer: 'Herbert Howells'.

1999: 24 August Three Choirs lunch, Worcester. Guest speaker—Geraint Lewis: 'That sweet borderland . . .'

2000: 23 August Three Choirs lunch, Hereford. Guest speaker—Giles Easterbrook 'Finzi and Leighton'.

2001: 1–3 June First Weekend of English Song, Ludlow.
14 July Lichfield Festival. Lunch and first AGM of Finzi Friends. Talk—Jeremy Dale Roberts in discussion with Nigel Finzi.
21 August Three Choirs lunch, Gloucester. Guest speaker—Diana McVeagh: 'Gerald Finzi'.

2002: 22 August Three Choirs lunch, Worcester. Sponsored talk—Jeremy Dibble: 'Sir Charles Villiers Stanford'.

2003: 28 JUNE Ashmansworth Friends' day. Choral workshop on Bridges partsongs—Paul Spicer. Recital—Floreat Sonus. Recital—Howard Wong.
20 AUGUST Three Choirs lunch, Hereford. Guest speaker—Lewis Foreman: 'The Robin Milford centenary'.

2004: 3–6 JUNE Second Weekend of English Song, Ludlow.
9 AUGUST Three Choirs lunch, Gloucester. Guest speaker—Lizzie Merry: 'Hardy and Finzi'.
18 SEPTEMBER Northampton choral day, St Matthew's Church. Talk—Peter Webster 'St Matthews and art'. Choral workshop on Finzi, Leighton and Howells—Paul Spicer.

2005: 9 AUGUST Three Choirs lunch. Guest speaker—Anthony Boden: 'Gerald Finzi at the Three Choirs'.

2006: 10 JUNE Ashmansworth Friends' day. Talk—Hugh Cobbe 'Howard Ferguson'. Recital—Raphael Wallfisch and John Yorke.
1 JULY Oxford, Holywell Music Room. Speaker Diana McVeagh. Recital—Emerald Ensemble. Choral Evensong at New College Chapel—Charles Janz and the Colmore Consort.
10 AUGUST Three Choirs lunch. Guest speaker—Nigel Finzi 'Memories of my father'.

2007 31 MAY–3 JUNE Third Weekend of English Song, Ludlow.
6 AUGUST Three Choirs lunch. Guest speaker—Jeremy Dale Roberts 'A composer's view'.
30 SEPTEMBER Tardebigge Church, Worcestershire. Joint event with the Ivor Gurney Society. Talk—Philip Lancaster and R. K. R. Thornton. Recital—Nathan Vale and Paul Plummer.

SIGNIFICANT RELATED EVENTS:

Gerald Finzi Twenty-Fifth Anniversary Celebration 17–19 July 1981, Ellesmere College, Shropshire.
Summer Weekend of English Music 20–22 July 1984, Oxford.
Summer Weekend of English Music 16–19 July 1987, Radley College, Abingdon.
Summer Festival of British Music 11–15 July 1990, Radley College, Abingdon.

General index

Main entries listed in **bold**.

Index of Finzi's works

Index of contributors

1.vii.07